Praise for *Reas*

"Tim Albury's Reason If You Will is an excellent guide for young Christians who are facing doubts about their faith or who are looking for the confidence to discuss their growing faith in intellectual circles. Liberty University's mission has always been to train the next generation of "Champions for Christ" to positively impact the world through every profession and in every walk of life. I believe this book authored by a Liberty graduate will help fulfill that mission by strengthening and reinforcing the faith of its readers!"

Jerry Falwell Jr.

"In a growing secular society, Christians need to know how to respond to the questions that arise regarding the validity of the Christian faith. Much of what has been written is so academic that the person without a theological education finds it difficult to comprehend. In, Reason if You Will, Tim Albury speaks in the language of the common man. The Christian religion requires faith, but not blind faith. Both history and reason lead us to believe and share the Christian faith. This book will help you do both."

Gary Chapman, Ph.D.
Author of God Speaks Your Love Language

"Tim addresses a number of questions - both scholarly and popular - seekers, skeptics, and thoughtful Christians ask about the faith. You can tell Tim has thought about, and wrestled with these things personally. The breadth of questions addressed is impressive. A great resource and very readable!"

J.D. Greear
Pastor, The Summit Church

Reason If You Will

Tim Albury

For my children and their children.

Contents

Contents

Contents

Foreword

Tim Albury is one of the most gifted Bible teachers that I have known in my 25 years of ministry. Tim was on the search committee that interviewed me when I was hired as Student Pastor at Providence Baptist Church in Raleigh, NC. Shortly after I began ministry at Providence, I began sitting in a high school class that Tim and his wife led. I knew instantly that what Tim was doing was completely unlike anything I had ever seen and that he needed to reproduce it in some format.

Throughout my ministry years, I have been trained by some of the most gifted, brilliant, humble men of God. From these men I have learned hermeneutics, homiletics, systematic theology, ecclesiology, the intricacies of the Imago Dei, pastoral ministry, and much more. I have been afforded the great opportunity over the last four years of my life to work on my PhD at Southern Seminary, and through this experience I have sat under the teaching of some of the greatest Christian thinkers of the 21st century. I mention this to say that I have at least had great theological exposure throughout my years in ministry.

Tim Albury is simply a Christian man that helps people know what they believe about God and why they believe it. Tim is really good at asking questions that allow people to think and then he provides amazing biblical answers. Tim doesn't mind wrestling through the most difficult and controversial debates of our day through a biblical lens of Christian apologetics.

It seems that many churches are either afraid or unwilling to deal with many of the toughest issues or controversies of our day. Tim has discussed the toughest issues with college and high school students for almost two decades. Few people in the world have the experience and discipline as a practitioner as Tim Albury from his daily dialogue and weekly classroom preparations.

Tim has given the church a tremendous resource in *Reason If You Will*. I could not recommend an author or a book more enthusiastically than the one you hold in your hands.

Dr. Steve Wright
Pastor of Discipleship, First Baptist Church of West Palm Beach

Acknowledgements

Receiving my primary college education at Liberty University was a tremendous blessing in my life. LU's vision from Dr. Jerry Falwell, Sr. until now has always been to train "young champions for Christ." This vision was realized in my life, and my Bible-centered education is foundational to everything God has taught me over the years.

Shortly after graduation, I had the honor of meeting my good friend, Jonathan Scott. I am forever indebted to Jonathan, whom God used to call me into student ministry at University Baptist Church (Miami, FL) 23 years ago. He shared God's vision for me teaching the Bible to teenagers. God used his obedience in spite of my resistance to launch me on a path of ministry and growth. Jonathan loved me, was the first to recognize my spiritual giftedness, and gracefully pointed me into a ministry I would have never predicted, a ministry that fit me like a glove.

After my employer transferred my family and me to Raleigh, NC, we joined Providence Baptist Church. Providence played an integral role in the clarification of my calling to apologetics in student ministry. My journey as a Christian apologist began in earnest approximately 20 years ago in a Sunday school class at Providence. My wife and I attended a two-year class on apologetics based on study materials provided by Ravi Zacharias

International Ministries. Ravi Zacharias became my hero and apologetics mentor even though I never had met him.

Through Providence Baptist Church, God also led me into various phases of youth ministry, including high school, college, camp counseling, publishing small group teaching material, and leading several youth foreign mission trips. Providence is the church where I have spent the largest portion of my life with Christ. I will be forever thankful for her staff and ministry.

While at Providence, I served on a youth pastor search committee, which is when I met Steve Wright. Shortly after he assumed the Youth Pastor role, Steve shared with me another frightening vision that God gave him for my ministry. He challenged me to assume responsibility for the 12th grade class. He asked me to write my own one-year curriculum centered on apologetics for the sole purpose of preparing high school seniors for the onslaught of attacks they would face in college. That curriculum would become the foundation for this book. Over the course of my nine years serving in this capacity, I had the honor of writing similar materials for Christian camps, speaking at several churches in several states, and seeing God grow His kingdom as I had never dreamed possible through my life. Steve served as probably the greatest catalyst toward the writing of this book.

Due to a job change, we moved to Wilmington, NC, in 2009. Our new pastor, Tim Blevins, and others in the congregation of Life Community Church encouraged me to step further into God's vision. It was at Life CC where my realization of God's grace and the current, pervasive, and miraculous ministry of the Holy Spirit was expanded. It was this ministry that guided the spiritual tone of the final manuscript.

Most of my gratitude, however, is reserved for my wife, Charleen. After moving to Wilmington, God impressed upon her to challenge me with the vision of finally converting my curriculum into book form. Charleen has served faithfully as my classroom director, primary editor, and primary encourager. She has been my greatest inspiration in this work, second only to God.

My children, Cynthia, Catherine and Timothy, were a constant encouragement to finish this task in spite of how incapable I felt. It has been an immeasurable blessing to experience God speaking to me through my children.

My parents and brothers were also constant cheerleaders in this effort on even a weekly basis. In fact, all of the people I have acknowledged herein have prayed constantly over my life and ministry. It is through God's answers to these prayers that God has fulfilled His vision in this work.

Last but not least, as a reader, I thank you for being a part of fulfilling God's vision, not just in my life and ministry, but, most importantly, in expanding God's glorious kingdom through beautiful proclamation and defense of the gospel of Jesus Christ.

Introduction

Do you know what you believe about God and why? Where did we come from? Who are we? Why are we here? What is our destiny? This book is meant to equip Christians to defend the faith by examining the Scriptures to see why and how we are called to defend it. We will also examine evidence from outside of the Bible that supports our faith.

First, allow me to share a little information about myself. I am a disciple of Jesus Christ, happily married to my wife and college sweetheart since 1988, and a father to three wonderful, adult children. I have served my local church as a Bible teacher and spiritual mentor to youth for almost my entire adult life. I am a CPA and an executive in the pharmaceutical industry. I have learned, however, that very little of this background truly defines who I am. That is true because much of this background will not last beyond my burial. What will last for eternity is the fact I am created in the very image of God, and God chose to offer me undeserved forgiveness and salvation from all of my failures through the shed blood of His one and only Son, Jesus Christ. This grace gift alone defines my worth.

God did not stop there, however. Because of the grace of forgiveness and salvation, God has adopted me as his very own son. That would have been enough, but God also gave me an eternal inheritance of royal position in His kingdom. Because of all that He has done, I love Him with everything that I am and will devote my entire life to following Him, sharing in His presence, and joining Him in His work. I am His. If you are a follower of Jesus Christ, so too are you. A forgiven, adopted, joint heir with Jesus is who you are. That is your identity. Identity is where the struggle of defending the faith begins. After all, who we are determines what we believe. This book is written primarily to encourage Christians. But it should bless all who read it.

Many who profess faith in Jesus Christ ultimately abandon that profession sometime later in their lives. The primary cause for that abandonment is that they find themselves unable to defend their faith against the mounting intellectual challenges to Christianity the world presents. This book is written to demonstrate the evidence that supports our faith in terms and language that are easily understood, and to equip you to present that evidence in the respectful manner that Jesus modeled for us in Scripture.

This book is not written as a reference book or encyclopedia. Rather, it is a series of specific lessons summarized into chapters that present an argument for the faith that cannot be denied. It is titled *Reason If You Will* because it welcomes you to reason and challenges and prepares you to welcome others to reason.

Reason If You Will also teaches a technique that involves answering questions with questions, the most diplomatic method of reasoning. When done well, it is quite winsome. Each chapter includes discussion questions in bold. You can use these questions to assist you in reasoning with others as you defend the faith or present the gospel. While this is not a typical reference book, it can serve as a reference for many important philosophical questions because they are at the center of this book's intent. For that reason, the book makes it easy for the reader to find these questions and source them by topic.

I pray that you enjoy this book. My goal is not only to expand your knowledge base, but to equip you to use that knowledge to advance the kingdom of God in Christ. As you read these pages, therefore, it is also my prayer that you are encouraged to keep the faith, to know what you believe and why you believe it, to defend the gospel at all costs, and to pass the faith on to others. Keep the faith!

Section 1

Why, What, When, and How to Defend the Faith

W hy should we defend the faith? What does that even mean? When should we defend the faith? When should we *not* defend it? How should we conduct ourselves when defending the faith? And finally, how should we *not* conduct ourselves? If you do not have clear and confident answers to any of these questions, this section is for you

When attempting to defend the faith, many Christians often take the wrong approach because they lack a basic understanding of conversational apologetics. They might be willing to engage but can't see clearly more than one step ahead in their conversation. At the same time, there are many Christians who are paralyzed by fear and choose to do nothing. They have chosen fear over faith. In other words, they have agreed that unseen fears will come true rather than the unseen promises of a faithful God. We, who believe that the Holy Spirit is inside of us with all of the power that comes with God's presence, should not be afraid of anything or anyone. Many fears that Christians have with regard to defending the faith stem from a lack of training and discipleship on the subject. As a result,

Christians often seek to defend the wrong things with the wrong reasons in the wrong situations in the wrong manner.

This section will equip you with the knowledge you need to know why, what, when, and how you should defend the Christian faith. You will also learn powerful and proper techniques to use when defending the faith that are based on the Scriptures. After you have established this foundation, the other sections in the book will build upon this base in order to arm you with more techniques and evidence to equip you to become a seasoned defender and keeper of the faith.

Chapter 1

How Not to Defend God

Y ou are sitting in a college freshman English class when the teacher—out of nowhere—launches into a diatribe attacking the Bible and the very existence of God as described in the Bible. Aside from your initial bewilderment as to why you are being subjected to religious onslaught in an English class, you find yourself offended by diatribe. You have been taught your whole life that you are supposed to take a stand for your faith. Every fiber of your flesh wants to raise your hand and refute your teacher's claims, but a nagging question in the back of your mind gives you pause, "Is that really what I am supposed to do?" Have you had a similar experience? Do you know what you are called to do in this situation? Do you know what to say?

Let me take the pressure off. In this situation, unless called upon to share your opinion on the subject, you are expected to do . . . nothing. That's right, do nothing. Okay, don't stop reading until I have been given a chance to explain. In later chapters, we will examine more the commands in the Bible that give us specific guidance about how and when we should stand in defense of the faith. Yes, we are called to defend. But the question of the moment is *what* are we called to defend? Moreover, *when* are we called to defend it? This may surprise you, but the type of scenario described in the English class is not the right time or place for you to defend the Christian faith. First, the Scriptures do not command us to defend God. God does not need a defender. Even if He did, He certainly does not need *us* to do it for Him. Further, when *god* is mocked in a classroom setting like this, it is actually not *God* being mocked at all (notice the little "*g*" in the first "*god*"). You might be thinking that it sure seemed like the teacher was mocking God, but she was not. She was actually mocking something that she had created in her mind that is much smaller than the real God. In fact, the god she is mocking is so small that he can be subjected to mockery by his supposed creation.

The god she has invented in her mind is not God. God is proverbially bulletproof—it is impossible to mock Him. The moment you try, you have already started to invent in your mind a being that is *less than* God. The real God has eluded your thinking. Therefore, we know that this misguided English teacher, aside from being a very poor philosopher, is wasting her breath and your time in English class. It is too bad her actions do not warrant a refund.

Second, if it were possible to mock God, He still has not commanded us to defend Him. God did not hear this teacher, wring His hands, and cry out for help in defending Himself. He needs no defense. In his letter to the Philippians, the Apostle Paul illustrated this truth by sharing exactly why he was put in prison: "I am put here for the defense of the gospel" (1:16b). He was not put in prison for defending God, but for defending the gospel. It is the gospel of Jesus Christ that we are called to defend, not God Himself. The Holy Spirit sheds further light on our call to defend the gospel in 1 Peter 3:15: "But in your hearts honor Christ the Lord as holy, always being prepared to make a defense to anyone who asks you for a reason for the hope that is in you; yet do it with gentleness and respect."

We are called to defend the hope we have that springs from the gospel of Jesus Christ. The gospel is what we are called to defend with our very lives. God can take care of Himself.

Now that the question of "What are we called to defend?" has been answered, we can turn to the second question: "When are we called to defend it?" When I was a young child, my grandfather taught me two cardinal rules of advice: 1) Don't give advice if you are not asked for it and 2) Don't give advice if the person is not listening. This advice was based on the teachings of the book of Proverbs. Sadly, Christians often violate these two important rules when attempting to defend the gospel by answering questions they were never asked.

Disregarding these rules often harms the very cause we are trying to help. Notice again that in 1 Peter 3:15 we are called to give a defense to anyone who "asks." In other words, we have to be asked first. The English teacher in our earlier example was not seeking the truth; therefore, we are not to give it to her because she is not interested in listening. In Jesus' famous Sermon on the Mount, he said, "Do not give dogs what is holy, and do not throw your pearls before pigs, lest they trample them underfoot and turn to attack you" (Matthew 7:6).

Jesus even provided a few examples of such self-control in His earthly life. When Jesus stood before Pilate under trial, He answered some of Pilate's questions. But, there was one ironic question that Jesus did not answer. In John 18:38, Pilate asked Him, "What is truth?" Could this question have been more plain and direct than that? The Truth was standing right in front of him (John 14:6). Jesus gave no answer because Pilate was not really seeking the truth. In Luke 23, Jesus stood on trial before Herod. When Herod mocked Him, Jesus refused to even speak. Doesn't that situation sound familiar to the one with the English teacher?

In circumstances like the one with the offensive English teacher, we should respond as Jesus did to Pilate and Herod. The point is simple: reason with those who are reasonable.

Chapter 2

How to Defend Hope

I lived for almost two decades in Raleigh, North Carolina, which is an energetic and booming college town. One of my favorite colleges is N.C. State University because I identify with the spirit of the school over all others in the region. At N.C. State, there is a man referred to as the Brickyard Preacher. I think most colleges have one or more of these soapbox preachers. At the university, the Brickyard Preacher stands in the middle of a park in the commons area screaming condemning insults at passersby in the name of Jesus. He tells everyone that they are going to hell (even Christians who engage him). People like him, apart from needing to repent themselves, give us a clear example of what *not* to do when defending the Christian faith. Their behavior is destructive and a tool of God's opponents, not God. For all I know, this man may be my brother in Christ, but he is sadly deluded by his own pride as displayed by his hypocritical condemnation. He actually is being *counterproductive* at winning people over.

So, how *should* we defend the faith? It all begins with . . . hope! Hope is so important to us that when we lose it, we begin to die. Viktor Frankl, the father of logotherapy, was a survivor of imprisonment for years in multiple Nazi concentration camps. He witnessed how those who lost all hope of ever getting out eventually died. Those who kept their hope and planned on what they would do when they got out lived. **So what are you hoping for? What is the reason for that hope?** Again 1 Peter 3:15 says, "But in your hearts honor Christ the Lord as holy, always being prepared to make a defense to anyone who asks you for a reason for the *hope* that is in you; yet do it with gentleness and respect" (emphasis added). We clearly see that our call is to defend the gospel by giving the reason why we have hope.

Before you can fulfill your God-given calling to defend the gospel, you must first have hope. For what should the Christian hope? Our list includes things like forgiveness, eternal life, the eternal presence of God, spiritual success, advancing and inheriting God's kingdom, and the return of Christ. If you do not have daily active hope in these things and the other numerous promises of God to His children, then you have lost sight of grace and your adoption as God's child. Before you can begin to learn how to defend the faith, you must fully embrace the reality of Jesus taking our thorny sinners' crown while choosing to place His own crown on us.

If you do not have hope springing from your soul, how will others ever notice it or be so taken aback by it that they are motivated to ask you for the reason that you have such hope? After all, the process of defending the gospel begins with someone *asking* about the hope that springs from within you. When that question comes, the answers should flow naturally. Without hope, any attempt to answer questions about God will seem more forced or rehearsed. (By the way, the bulk of this book's content will center on these "reasons" so that you will know how to respond if the answers do not flow as easily as I suggest. And for some of us, answering questions is not as easy as for others.)

Having this matchless hope when the questions come and knowing the reasons why you have this hope are the foundational elements for an appropriate response. The next question is *how should you defend your hope in Christ?* The Holy Spirit answers that question in 1 Peter 3:15, "do it with gentleness and respect." Here is where the aforementioned Brickyard Preacher loses his effectiveness. He is far from gentle and respectful. Remember, *how* you say something is as important as *what* you say. Peter later teaches us to live in a way that we have "a good conscience, so that, when you are slandered, those who revile your *good behavior* in Christ may be put to shame" (1 Peter 3:16, emphasis added). Gentleness and respect are important aspects of a cogent defense of the gospel.

If you have trouble with this type of delivery, consider applying what Ravi Zacharias calls the 3 S's of apologetics:

1. Be a *Servant*. Remember, like Christ, you are called to serve those with whom you are reasoning. "Have this mind among yourselves, which is yours in Christ Jesus, who, though he was in the form of God, did not count equality with God a thing to be grasped, but emptied himself, by taking the form of a servant, being born in the likeness of men. And being found in human form, he humbled himself by becoming obedient to the point of death, even death on a cross" (Philippians 2:5-8). Jesus modeled this servant approach to ministry as he washed the feet of His disciples to reach their hearts. Your words and actions should have the same effect on those you are trying to reach. You must be their servant. Your knees should be down and your towels ready.

2. Be a *Student*. Remember that you don't know it all; therefore, don't act like you do. Don't be afraid to say, "I don't know," especially when you don't. I have learned so much from my atheist and agnostic friends. No, they

will never convert me, but I do learn from them. And, if you are like me, you have much to learn. Listen and process before speaking and answering. Nobody likes a know-it-all.

3. Be *Sympathetic*. Remember that without Christ, this person will die to face eternal punishment and separation from God. Demonstrate compassion. Avoid a condemnatory spirit like the Brickyard Preacher. Nobody wants what he preaches, but people do want the compassion that Jesus freely offers. Someone who doesn't understand the gospel is spiritually blind. You wouldn't punish a person born blind for not understanding the color red, would you?

Jesus came to serve, study, sympathize, and give His life for the very people God has placed in your life. He asks you to do the same as you share why hope so flows from you.

Chapter 3

Fighting Without Fighting

I n a scene from the movie "Enter the Dragon," Bruce Lee, a famous martial arts icon, is confronted by an irritating fighter, who is also a martial arts contender. In one scene, the two are riding on a large boat to a tournament with other fighters and children on board. The irritating man, after bullying the children on board, asks Bruce about his fighting style. Bruce responds, "My fighting style is the art of fighting without fighting." Curious, the fighter asks Bruce to show him this style. Bruce challenges him to join him in a rescue boat so that they can row to a nearby island and fight. The other fighter steps off the main boat into the rescue boat, and Bruce proceeds to shove the rescue boat off without getting in. With a rope tied to the rescue boat, Bruce and the children taunt the other fighter, making him look foolish. Bruce did in fact show him the art of fighting *without* fighting.

Have you ever been engaged in a conversation with someone regarding the Christian faith, only to find yourself argued into a proverbial corner? Have you ever felt so riddled with questions that it felt like you were drowning in your attempts to come up with answers? It is easy to be overwhelmed in the moment because you are being asked critical questions about God that you do not feel qualified to answer. We have all been there. In this chapter, we will study the fighting techniques of the greatest defender of the faith ever born. Here's a hint; it is *not* the Apostle Paul.

Do you ever think of Jesus as a *fighter*? Many people have this mental picture of Jesus as a mild-mannered pacifist. Nothing could be further from the truth.

Some people like to refer to the God of the Old Testament as *wrathful* and the God of the New Testament as *peaceful*. Jesus' earthly life was not always characterized by peace, however. His treatment of the moneychangers in the temple was not a very cuddly and cozy picture (Matthew 21; Mark 11; John 2). Jesus often aggressively contended for the truth during his ministry. He was a fighter. He *is* a fighter! We should be thankful that he is, because in a very real way, he fights and contends for you and me.

To learn a great approach to apologetics, one should examine the approach of Jesus as he defends the faith and the truth in the book of Matthew. Matthew 21:23-27 provides a wonderful opportunity to learn from the Master. It begins with the chief priests and elders of the people approaching Jesus to ask him, "By what authority are you doing these things, and who gave you this authority?"

Stop right there. Their questions were clear examples of willful attacks on the ministry of Jesus? Could anyone be more brazen than to look at God in the face and ask where He got His authority? Jesus' response in this passage provides an ideal example for how we should react to those who care more about attacking us than pursuing the truth (a.k.a. secular college professors).

Jesus answered their question with a question. "I also will ask you one question, and if you tell me the answer, then I also will tell you by what authority I do these things. The baptism of John, from where did it come? From heaven or from man?"

In his response, Jesus was asking if John's baptism came from heaven or man. This response by Jesus was brilliant! He answered their question with . . . a question.

Now his attackers were trapped. They huddled among themselves and plotted their response. If they denied John's baptism was from heaven, the people would be very angry since they rightly held John the Baptist as a great prophet of God. If they admitted John's baptism *was* from heaven, Jesus had a checkmate. He could then simply question why they did not trust John's baptism. As a result of Jesus' question, they were revealed to be cowards, saying, "We don't know." To this Jesus responded, "Neither will I tell you by what authority I do these things," providing yet another example of Jesus *not* answering the questions of a *non-seeking* attacker (Pilate and Herod were examples from Chapter 1). Like our annoying fighter in the *Enter the Dragon* movie, the attacker loses the ground from which to fight.

Why did Jesus answer a question with a question? The world calls this approach the Socratic Method. But since Jesus created Socrates, I call it the Jesus Method. If you can remember one thing from this chapter, remember this statement: **If you are going to answer an attack, answer the attack with a question.**

Why does this technique work? It works because volunteering answers to questions of attackers will almost always put you on your heels. But if you respond with a respectful question, you will usually and diplomatically put the attackers on their heels.

Employing the Jesus Method is the art of fighting without fighting. Jesus fought such battles here on earth with this method, and we are also commanded to fight "with gentleness and respect" (1 Peter 3:15). Answering attacks with questions will allow you to obey that verse and follow the example of Jesus. We are to master the art of fighting for the gospel without fighting. You can master this technique with practice.

In order to help you learn to employ the Jesus Method, sample questions on each topic are provided in each chapter (in bold) to aid you in practicing with others.

Today, try responding to genuine questions with questions. Be amazed how you move from the backseat to the driver's seat. After all, that is the seat Jesus called us to occupy.

Chapter 4

No Arguing Allowed

Have you ever argued with someone who opposes the concept of God and won the argument? That was a trick question. If you were arguing with them, you had already lost. Remember 1 Peter 3:15. How can you argue with gentleness and respect?

If you have read the previous chapters, you might think that I just contradicted my prior teaching of responding to questioners with questions instead of answers. But God never called us to *argue* about the gospel—He called us to *defend* it. Consider a sports analogy. Regardless of how intimidating the defensive team may look and act, is the defense the attacking squad? No, the offense is the one who attacks. Defense defends the goal, the end zone, or the basket. Defense is rarely, if ever, on the attack. It is the offense that is always attacking, always advancing, always being . . . offensive. Does an argument look more like offense or defense? It looks like offense, which is why it is so offensive. Remember, we are called to play defense when defending the gospel, but to do so with gentleness and respect.

In case you are wondering, keeping with the sports analogy, we also have a strategy for "offense." Our "offense" is known as evangelism, which is different from defending the gospel. Evangelism is the practice of actively sharing the gospel and leading others to a relationship with God. Evangelism can *involve* answering genuine questions about the gospel, but evangelism and apologetics call for different approaches.

Regarding arguing, in Paul's second letter to Timothy, he gives this advice: "Have nothing to do with foolish, ignorant controversies; you know that they breed quarrels. And *the Lord's servant must not be quarrelsome but kind to everyone, able to teach, patiently enduring evil, correcting his opponents with gentleness.* God may perhaps grant them repentance leading to a knowledge of the truth, and they may come to their senses and escape from the snare of the devil, after being captured by him to do his will" (2 Timothy 2:23-26, emphasis added).

In this passage, Paul advocated an approach characterized by kindness, patience, and gentleness instead of quarreling.

Some might argue that Paul seems to contradict himself in 2 Corinthians 10:5 when he said, "We destroy arguments and every lofty opinion raised against the knowledge of God, and take every thought captive to obey Christ." While this verse seems to advocate arguing with others in a conquering manner, that would be a misapplication of the verse. In the previous verses of 2 Corinthians 10, Paul explained that we do not war according to the flesh. We also know from Ephesians 6 that we do not wrestle with flesh and blood. Therefore, in 2 Corinthians 10:5, it is not possible that Paul is discussing "arguments" with other people (flesh). So, you might ask, "What kinds of 'arguments' is Paul referring to then?"

In addition to opening this chapter with a trick question, I will also admit to including a trick title with this chapter. You see there is one person that you *are* allowed to argue with at any time. That person is you. You are perfectly and morally free to argue with yourself anytime. And further, your mind (referred to as "thought" in 2 Corinthians 10:5) is where the true battle of defending the gospel is often fought. This book is not meant to teach you how to argue with others about God. If this book is preparing you to argue with anyone about God, it is only preparing you to argue with yourself. With others, we are supposed to *reason* with them about God. When you reread the verses included earlier with this theme in mind, Paul's intent becomes clear, we are to bring our thoughts in subjection to our King, Jesus Christ.

Remember how 1 Peter 3:15 begins, "But in your hearts honor Christ the Lord as holy." We should never allow a single thought to enter our heads unless it is made to bow to our King and stay bowed before Him until we escort it out of our heads. If Jesus is King over our life, no thought should ever be allowed by us to rise above Him. Making your thoughts subject to Christ is the only way to heed the admonition of Colossians 2:8 (NASB), "See to it that no one takes you captive through philosophy and empty deception, according to the tradition of men, according to the elementary principles of the world, rather than according to Christ."

If we are not to argue with others about God, what are we doing as we answer questions with questions according to the Jesus Method? This approach is called *reasoning*. In Isaiah 1:8, even God tells Isaiah, "Come now, let us reason together." If God chooses to reason with us, it is not beneath us to choose to reason with our fellow man. Arguing is very different than reasoning. For example, when you hear the word "argument," what picture comes to your mind? I bet you see two people facing each other, raising their voices with animated faces and hand gestures. What does reasoning look like? Reasoning looks like two people walking side-by-side down a sidewalk with both of them talking, listening, and shaking hands at the end as they look forward to their next meeting. That picture of two people engaged in a *conversation* about God and the gospel is the inspiration for the title and message of this book.

These principles will serve you wherever and whenever you find yourself in a tight place. I was teaching these lessons to a group of high school seniors. One of my students had a fitting experience in his public school's biology class practicing these principles. The teacher was "preaching" the glories of her religion, Neo-Darwinian evolution, as the origin of all species from a single-cell organism that was created by nothing. My student apparently had a noticeably confused look on his face. The teacher called on him to ask what his question was. He asked, **"I'm curious. How does that *not* conflict with the First and Second Laws of Thermodynamics?"** (By the way, these two Laws will be more fully discussed in Chapters 33 and 45). The teacher was stunned. She stumbled to mumble through an answer only to give up and sigh, "That is a good question. I'll have to get back to you." My student had her in the corner. He could have pounced at this moment of her weakness. Instead, he just said, "That's okay. I was just curious," and stopped short of an attack. The other students in the class turned their heads and looked at him as if he were a genius to be reckoned with. After class, the teacher thanked him for his participation, and a line of students waited outside the class with questions for him.

Now, that's how you do it.

Section 2

A Few Thoughts on Who God Is

It is impossible for man to describe God adequately. Only God can do that. Even if it were possible, all the paper in the world coupled with all of the electronic storage devices would not be enough space required to fully describe Him. That is why I named this section "A Few Thoughts on Who God Is." These next few chapters will discuss a few mind-challenging characteristics about God.

The characteristics addressed in this section are important because they are usually distorted into weapons against the Christian faith. Too many times people are fooled by arguments that attempt to define the Christian God but only end up describing a false god that does not exist. Those using these false arguments then proceed to attack the false god as the God of Christianity. Since you will likely one day be reasoning with those who have fallen prey to such arguments, it is important to help them reprogram their definition of the Christian God. In other words, it is critical that Christians recognize God as the person that He has revealed Himself to be. And that revelation is in the Bible and the Bible alone.

As a result of being fooled by false arguments, some Christians adopt portrayals of a god that does not actually exist. In doing so, they have adopted idols that falsely give them comfort. These idols must be diplomatically torn down in order for these Christians to truly understand the Christian faith.

The reason why the "what to defend" content of this book begins here is because all things have their origin in God. He is the Creator and inventor of all things. The gospel starts with God. "In the beginning, God..."

Chapter 5

Why We Put Sweaters on Dogs

Isn't it funny that we put sweaters on our dogs? Do you ever wonder why we sometimes dress up our dogs this way, even when it is not cold outside? The answer is pretty simple. It is the same reason why we talk to our dogs as if they were . . . humans. It is our human nature to approach things that are not human by pretending they have human traits so that we can relate to them more easily.

The word that describes this comical treatment of pets is anthropomorphism. Let's examine this term by breaking the word down from its Greek sources. "Anthropos" refers to human, while "morphe" refers to form or change. Anthropomorphism is when we falsely change things that are not human by pretending that they are or describing them with human terms. This is what we do to dogs and most things we can't fully understand, even things like cars and computers. In other words, we *humanize* them. This is generally harmless until we also attempt to treat God this way. If we pretend God is just another human then we fool ourselves into thinking we can fully relate to Him. We cannot. We have all been guilty of this erred thinking—Christians and non-Christians alike. Here are a few examples of how we have attempted to judge God as if He were human:

"God is a genocidal maniac!" This verdict refers to God's destruction of Sodom and Gomorrah and His conquest of Canaan for Israel, and other apparent atrocities.

"God is self-centered!" This verdict refers to everything He does being focused on solely His own glory above everyone else.

When you read those statements, do they disturb you in any way? If so, you are suffering from anthropomorphism. Each of these statements refers to God as if He were a man. He is not. "God is Spirit" (John 4:24).

The chief adjective that best describes God is "holy." This adjective is used in more than 600 verses in the Bible, which is more than any other adjective. The Hebrew word for "holy" means set apart and sacred. He is God, and there is no other. When you see a rabbit in your yard, you might say, "There is a rabbit," recognizing that the animal is one of many rabbits and not the only rabbit. But there is only *one* God. We often get confused because He took on flesh as Jesus (John 1:14), but this was not Jesus changing God from nonhuman to human. Instead, this act was God taking on human form as the second member of the Trinity so that He (God) could take the punishment for our sin as a man. While one of His names is Immanuel (meaning "God with us"), this does not mean that we can reduce God to just another one of us (Matthew 1:23). He still is who He always was and always will be (Malachi 3:6a).

With that backdrop, let's re-examine the human verdicts commonly lobbed on God that were listed earlier. Did God ever commit genocide? Yes. Does He forbid us from committing genocide? Yes. The difference is that God—the one who created all life from nothing—has every right to take it away however and whenever He pleases. In fact, we chose this as a premeditated consequence of our rebellion. Therefore, all human life will be taken eventually. What this criticism fails to appreciate is that God resurrects life in eternity. Additionally, God is always just in taking human life. The wages for sin is death.

Is God self-centered? Yes. But He is not selfish. In order for Him to be selfish, there would have to be another God that He is taking attention away from. And there is no other god. Only the creation can be selfish. **Can God really have a God complex?** That sounds like an absurd question, doesn't it?

Another way anthropomorphism thrives in our rationalizing of God is in the "man-made" definitions with which we attempt to bind Him. Other words we may think of to describe God may include omniscient, omnipotent, and omnipresent. Where are those words found in the Bible? Technically, these words are not in the Bible. Similar concepts are found in the Scriptures, but these exact words are not. This begs this question: **"Who gets the right to define who God is?"** Only God has that right. To illustrate, let's examine these three words more closely and see where God's Word disagrees with man.

Omniscient. The dictionary defines this word as "having complete and unlimited knowledge." Sounds right, but is it biblical? **Does God know everything?** God's Word describes how God blots out our sins, forgets them, and keeps no record of them (see Hebrews 8:12, 10:17; Isaiah 43:25; Psalm 130:3). Praise God! The dictionary got it wrong. The biblical definition of omniscient is that God knows everything that He chooses to know.

Omnipotent. The dictionary defines this word as "having unlimited and infinite power." How does this definition line up with the Scriptures? Hebrews 6:18 says that God cannot lie. And the list of things God cannot do does not stop there. You have probably heard the silly question, "Can God make a rock so big that He can't lift it?" The answer is simple. No, He can't. First of all, the question is ridiculous. Another way of asking this question to expose its flaws is as follows: "Can God do something that He can't do?" Secondly, it is not within

God's nature, or anyone's nature, to do what they can't. God is limited to His own nature. Therefore, God can only do that which is in His nature. And God's nature is good! He cannot stop being who He is.

Omnipresent. The dictionary defines this word as being "present everywhere at the same time." How does the Bible define omnipresent? In 2 Thessalonians 1:9, Paul says that God is *not* in hell. The dictionary is wrong again. The biblical definition of omnipresent means that God is everywhere that He *chooses* to be at the same time. Time is another one of those creations that God is not bound by. Therefore, biblical omnipresence also means that God is at all points in time at the same time, which is why in Exodus 3:14 and John 8:58 God refers to Himself as the great "I AM." He often speaks in the present tense even when referring to the past or the future. Wrap your head around that if you can. God's awesome nature surpasses the boundaries of our imaginations.

As we begin to reason with others about God, we must see through attempts to turn Him into a human being. We must allow God to define himself, which requires submission to his self-revelation in Scripture. He alone has already defined Himself. Remember who you are and who He is, never forgetting all of the awesome differences between us.

Chapter 6

Would A Loving God Do That?

❝ If God is all-powerful, He could defeat evil. If God is all-loving, He would defeat evil. Evil is not defeated. Therefore, no such God exists."

This argument sounds pretty convincing, doesn't it? How should we respond to it? As you try, be careful. There is a deeper problem in the logic *before* you get wrapped up with question of the timing of when He defeats evil. The main problem here is similar to why we put sweaters on dogs because the opening criticism is another example of anthropomorphism. We are forcing human qualities upon something that is not human (God) so that we can better relate. Or more precisely, this criticism is attempting to measure God (nonhuman) with human measures. God does not fit the measurement because He is not human. And by the way, this works both ways because we do not fit God's measurement since we are not God.

The opening semi-logical argument is wrong in at least two ways, which I will illustrate in the form of two questions: **"Who is man to judge God?"** and **"What kind of 'love' are we using as a measure?"**

Who is man to judge God? I feel very sheepish explaining this because the question needs no explanation. We were created in God's image, and our subconscious knows this truth. We see the power and the will that we are capable of wielding and confuse the *image* (man) with the *object* (God). When you look in a mirror, you see your image. That image looks exactly like you at first glance. **But can that image think like you? Is it capable of judging you? Can it understand you?** The answers to these questions are obviously no. Likewise, the Bible teaches, "No one understands God" (Rom 3:11). It is impossible for the image to fully understand the object.

In our case, the image (man) attempts to judge the object (God) as an image (man). But images are so much shallower than the objects, especially in this case. When you boil down the opening criticism, the critic is *actually* saying: "If I were God, I would . . ." That is both foolish and arrogant. We are not God. We are more unlike God than we are like Him. We are fools to compare ourselves to Him (Psalm 40:5).

What kind of "love" are we using as a measure? Most people who attempt to criticize God are undisciplined in this criticism. Sometimes, they even attempt to argue against God by using bad human measures (human "love" in this case). I had a student whose freshman English class was assigned the task of writing an essay pondering this question: "If God is so loving, why did He put the 'tree' in the Garden of Eden?" Given the anti-God bias of the teacher and the school, the implied accusation in the question was obvious. The student came to me for advice, and I advised her to ask the following questions in response: **How is love shown without giving a choice? Is eliminating the choice to love you an expression of love? If God had not given man a choice, is man free to love?** God knew that it was best to give man a choice and, therefore, for man to have limitations. So, God gave man *one* limitation. He did not give 497 limitations in the garden. He gave just one. **If you have children, do you love your children? If so, do you give them limitations and negative consequences outside of those limitations?** All responsible parents would answer, "Of course." **Does that imply that you *don't* love your children?** Of course not - we love our children and that is why we give them limitations and negative consequences if they transgress. The teacher's question and what it implied were using faulty reasoning that we would not even apply to ourselves.

Let's recall the opening criticism that was included in the beginning of this chapter: "If God is all-powerful, He could defeat evil. If God is all-loving, He would defeat evil. Evil is not defeated. Therefore, no such God exists." This criticism also measures God against a lesser measure of love which is yet another form of human love. To illustrate one aspect of how lacking such human love is, consider this example: I *love* my wife, and I *love* doughnuts. Do you see the problem? There are different definitions of human love. The Greek language (New Testament) has several words for love, including *eros*, *phileo*, and *agape*. Erotic love in the English language is from the Greek word *eros*. Family or friendly love is from *phileo*. For example, Philadelphia is nicknamed the "City of Brotherly Love" because its name has its root in *phileo*. *Eros* and *phileo* comprise most of the spectrum of human love.

God's definition of love, however, is *agape*, an unconditional, sacrificial, and totally selfless kind of love (1 Corinthians 13). *Agape* is a decision love, not an emotional love. Agape says, "No matter what you do, I love you." While *eros* is a "take" love and *phileo* is a "give and take" love, *agape* is strictly a "give" love. In perfect form, this is the highest form of love, which is much higher than man's love. One should not try to define God's love using the limited expressions of human love. **Without perfect *agape* love, what does man really know about love?** Our history proves that our human measure of love is utterly bankrupt. It is true—God does not fit that measure. But human love is the wrong measure with which to define God's character.

To illustrate human love, let's say you love your spouse. Imagine one day you pull into the mall parking lot and find the one you love in a car with your best friend "making out" and otherwise pretending to be married with each other. Now do you still love this person? Or are you about to "fall out of love"? **Is *this* the kind of love by which we want to measure God?**

God does not just love. He is love. He is *agape*. He is both the noun and the verb. He defines the word. In fact, He defines all words. Love begins and ends with Him. First John 4:7-21 is a passage of Scripture that clearly outlines how "God is love." When God loves, He is just being Himself. It is what He does. When we love, we are attempting to reflect God's love, to reflect God himself. That is what images do. When compared with God's love, all other reflections or forms of love fall terribly short. Using a flawed measure in an attempt to judge the real thing is a fruitless exercise. God judges our love; we do not judge his.

In contrast to the human illustration, God came to earth and found us "in love" with His enemy. He found us following Lucifer instead of Him. He found us worshiping that which Lucifer desires. He found us selling our souls to our destroyer rather than following and worshipping our Creator. And what was God's response? He stretched out His arms that we nailed to a cross and He cried out, "I love you!" God loved us so much that He took our guilt and died to pay the price for our cheating on Him. That is love! All other loves fail in comparison. In fact, God's love is the only measure of love worth using to measure anything because His love is indescribably beautiful and unconditional. Even when we fail and cheat on Him *again*, He continues to forgive and love us freely.

So how do we respond to the opening criticism? A loving God did defeat evil. And He did it in a way that forgives as many people as possible, even more people than we can imagine. Yes, that God does exist. Praise Him!

I don't want a god that loves like humans. I want a God that loves like Jesus!

Chapter 7

Think Outside the Box

I am a dog person. I have always loved dogs and dogs have always loved me. One time we were leaving the beach with our dog when I heard her yelp in pain. She had stepped on a bed of very large prickles. Her paw was covered with them even between her toes. She could hardly walk. We removed what we could see before we drove home. Once home, we removed the rest with scissors, tweezers, and knives. It was so painful for her that we had to hold her down during the procedure. Between her painful yelps, she periodically tried to violently attack us in an attempt to stop the removal of the thorns. She did not understand what we understood and how we were actually helping her.

In a similar fashion, sometimes we attempt to think like God but without His help. In the area of intellect, dogs are much closer to humans than we are to God. Yes, dogs are nowhere near as smart as humans. But in comparison, humans are even further removed from God's level of intellect than we are from a dog's level of intellect. This reality does not seem to stop some of us from claiming we can think like God or even better than God.

When I used to teach classes on the subject of God's intellect versus man's intellect, I placed several plaques on the wall of sayings that helped filter my teachings. One of these plaques was titled "Think outside the box." On it, there was a square. Inside the square were the words "Man's Intellect." Outside the square were the words "God's Intellect." We must remember that man's intellect is limited while God's is not. God's intellect is outside the box, not inside. Man's intellect is inside the box, not outside. We too often fail to think outside the box and try to put God inside the box.

If we are going to attempt to think like God, we must get outside of man's intellect. We cannot evaluate God's intellect from the view of an inferior intellect, like my dog evaluated me. My dog attacked me because she could not understand my actions. I knew that she would be better off when I was finished helping her, even if she could not see this truth. It is only when my dog follows my demands of her that she is more content. If you could speak "dog" and ask her what she thought I was doing when I was removing the prickles, she would have said very harsh things about me. But today, her tone would turn very positive. In fact, she has since come to me to remove prickles when they were stuck in her fur. She trusts me now. What a vivid picture of how we should relate to God.

We are flesh, but God is Spirit (1 Corinthians 2). Jesus also taught this truth with his words to the woman at the well (John 4:24). While we are made in His image, we naturally think with fleshly thoughts. Our flesh is the box. It is only by God's Spirit taking over our lives that we begin to think spiritually, like God does. This is why 1 Corinthians 2 concludes with the words, "'For who has understood the mind of the Lord so as to instruct him?' But we have the mind of Christ." When God gives us His mind and His Spirit, we begin the never-ending journey toward thinking more like Him. Our challenge until we reach eternity is to think outside the box as much as we can along the way.

It is our fallen human nature to arrogantly glorify the human intellect, even in the church. For example, man constantly claims to be able to determine what is good and what is evil. God, however, is the one who determines what is good and evil—not man. After the Fall of Man, man's intellect was broken and blinded from being able to perfectly judge good from evil. In fact, man is not qualified to be the judge of man, much less God. "There is only one lawgiver and judge, he who is able to save and to destroy. But who are you to judge your neighbor" (James 4:12)? That "lawgiver" is God—not man. A good example of man's distorted judgments is how the choice to kill innocent unborn human life is valued over human life itself.

On that note, here is another example. It always amuses me when someone claims that God did something evil or committed a sin, like killing for example. The person hurling this claim is thinking inside the box. As you daily absorb His Word and transform your thinking, you realize that sin is narrowly defined as "disobeying God"—nothing more and nothing less. It is impossible for God to disobey Himself. The commandment to not murder was a command from God to man. God's Law does not apply to God (his actions, however, are always consistent with it). When God takes a life, it is not murder. He created that life. He has a right to take that life. He is always just when He takes a life.

God created the Law. He is not subject to it. There is no law higher than himself. He can never be wrong. God is righteous because He is always right. When He takes a human life, He is right. When we personally take a human life, we are generally wrong. God is not human; He is the Creator of His Law and the giver and taker of life. His execution therefore of his Law is logical and reasonable.

The other common area where we fail to think outside the box is when we selectively apply His Word to our lives. Matthew 5:17-20 is a small but powerful portion of Jesus' Sermon on the

Mount. In verses 18-19, Jesus described the importance and eternality of the Law: "For truly, I say to you, until heaven and earth pass away, not an iota, not a dot, will pass from the Law until all is accomplished. Therefore whoever relaxes one of the least of these commandments and teaches others to do the same will be called least in the kingdom of heaven, but whoever does them and teaches them will be called great in the kingdom of heaven."

According to Jesus, every stroke of every letter of the Bible is important enough to be appropriately followed until the end of time. Therefore, one either takes the Bible in its entirety or not at all. God did not give us a license to parse it, pull it out of context, abuse it, manipulate it, or claim that some parts have no relevance. If you do such things to His Word, you are saying God is wrong and you are right. You need to think outside the box.

I have had friends over the years attempt to show me how their bad behavior is acceptable since they found an obscure Bible verse that gives them license to do so (ignoring all the obvious verses that oppose their conclusions). My response to this type of abuse of Scripture is simple. If you are searching the Bible for a flesh-pleasing loophole like you would search for a loophole in the tax code, you might find it. Your fleshly (non-spiritual) motives, however, have made it impossible for you to find the spiritual truth. Yes, there are gray areas in our minds. But these areas are gray because we are inside the box where our intellect is limited.

Romans 14:23 speaks about gray areas when it says, "But whoever has doubts is condemned if he eats, because the eating is not from faith. For whatever does not proceed from faith is sin." A gray area means we have doubts. To us, it is not yet black or white. This verse, however, clearly teaches us to treat such gray areas as if they are black, which would implore us to abstain. It is another way of saying, "When in doubt, don't." That attitude should underscore our application of Scripture to the gray areas of our lives. We should treat the Bible as the mind of Christ, always attempting to substitute the word of God for our fleshly thinking. That is how you think *outside* the box.

By the way, God does have perfect moral knowledge. He has an opinion on everything—black and white. With God, there are no gray areas. If we are to think outside the box, we must continually migrate to God's way of thinking and away from ours.

Section 3

A Brief Defense of the Faith

A tremendous amount of evidence exists that supports the Bible, Jesus, and His claims. This book is not meant to chronicle all of that evidence as an encyclopedia or a similar reference book would. There is a tremendous amount of evidence that supports the reliability of the Bible. Learning this evidence will serve you as you seek to defend the faith.

This section provides a brief summary defense that can be easily remembered. Once you have mastered this summary, you will be ready to move on to the more in-depth discussions that begin in section five. The summary defense include discussion of the following topics.

Resurrection of Jesus is a certain fact of history.

Archaeology proves the Bible is the most reliable book of history.

Miracles of Jesus are confirmed evidence of His deity.

Prophecies and fulfillment support Jesus' deity and the Bible's godly authorship.

Hopefully, you can remember R.A.M.P. for short. This section will equip you with a memorable defense that will bolster your faith and encourage you as you answer the call to defend the faith with eagerness.

Chapter 8

Is Jesus Guilty of Resurrection?

I n 2007, the Discovery Channel aired a documentary titled "The Lost Tomb of Jesus." It was produced by James Cameron, the director of *Titanic* and *Avatar*. The film claimed to have found the real tomb of Jesus with his bones intact, allegedly proving that he did not rise from the dead. If these bones do belong to Jesus, what does this do to the Christian faith?

This documentary was later discredited totally by most if not all non-Christian critics, including the head of archaeology for the nation of Israel. Cameron's work was discredited for lack of factual basis, gross internal inconsistencies, and undisciplined methods and claims. His agenda was clear: use every means possible to discredit the Christian faith by proving Jesus did not rise from the dead, an agenda that failed miserably.

Cameron and other critics know well that the resurrection of Jesus is what the Christian faith rests upon. If Jesus is still buried, He is not God and the Bible is full of lies. Christians would have zero hope. Like Cameron, Josh McDowell also knew this truth. McDowell was an agnostic who set out to examine the actual evidence of the resurrection of Jesus in order to disprove it. He was not prepared for what he found—the evidence instead supported the resurrection of Jesus. McDowell became a famous Christian apologist and author of many books supporting the resurrection of Jesus, including *Evidence That Demands a Verdict*. In this book, McDowell approached the evidence as in a court case, very unlike the undisciplined Cameron. He examined the evidence judicially as a lawyer, judge, and jury would. He arrived at the "verdict" in a disciplined manner. And for that reason, unlike Cameron's work, McDowell's work has not been discredited.

Continuing McDowell's judicial approach, let's briefly examine the evidence as in our own mock court proceeding to see if we find Jesus guilty of resurrection. In cases like this, there are three levels of evidence. While there are three levels, you can be convicted on just one level. And if you have a strong and consistent case on all three, a conviction is sure. The three levels of evidence include 1) eyewitness testimony, 2) physical evidence, and 3) circumstantial evidence.

Eyewitness Testimony. The earliest known record of eyewitnesses to Jesus' resurrection is 1 Corinthians 15:3-8 (A.D. 53-54, roughly 20 years after the event), "For I delivered to you as of first importance what I also received: that Christ died for our sins in accordance with the Scriptures, that he was buried, that he was raised on the third day in accordance with the Scriptures, and that he appeared to Cephas, then to the twelve. Then he appeared to *more than five hundred* brothers at one time, *most of whom are still alive*, though some have fallen asleep. Then he appeared to James, then to all the apostles. Last of all, as to one untimely born, he appeared also to me" (emphasis added).

In these verses, the Apostle Paul documented the post-resurrection appearances of Jesus, including his ascension, which was witnessed by more than 500 people. Many of the 500 Paul knew personally. They were still alive when this letter was circulated to the churches throughout the region. The proximity to the event allowed Paul's record to be confirmed by these eyewitnesses. Some of these eyewitnesses were founders of the churches that formed across the region in the years after the resurrection. These church founders also wrote their own letters and memos that were also circulated (some were included in the Bible and others were not). All of these eyewitnesses confirmed Paul's account of the post-resurrection appearance of Jesus from 1 Corinthians without exception. In fact, there are no eyewitness accounts that contradict Paul's account. There are no opposing eyewitnesses to call upon in this case.

There were also non-Christian contemporary historians that confirmed Paul's account of these eyewitnesses. For example, Rome commissioned a Jewish historian, Flavius Josephus, to record the history of Israel. Josephus was not a Christian and not a biblical author. In A.D. 94, he wrote *Antiquities of the Jews*, in which he recorded, "He [*Jesus*] was the Christ . . . He appeared to them alive on the third day, as the divine prophets had foretold these and ten thousand other things concerning him." This is one of many non-biblical endorsements of the eyewitnesses of the resurrected Jesus.

Let's further test the credibility of these eyewitnesses. Included in these eyewitnesses were eleven of the twelve disciples (Judas, the betrayer, committed suicide before the crucifixion). Of these eleven disciples, ten were brutally martyred for their devotion to the resurrection of Jesus (John was exiled to Patmos). **Would these 10 disciples allow themselves to be brutally killed for something they knew was a *lie*? If you were the last disciple to be martyred, would you still die for this lie?**

Aside from the 1 Corinthians reference to eyewitnesses, there is another aspect of other eyewitness accounts that lends them even more credibility. For example, the first eyewitness of Jesus' resurrection was Mary Magdalene (John 20). In Israel during the first century, a woman's testimony was unfairly considered worthless—even in her own rape trial. Therefore, if you were promoting a false religion during this time period, the last thing you would do in their culture is to use a woman for your first eyewitness. The only reason the gospel writers would record Mary as the first eyewitness is because it was... *true.*

And what about Paul? Before Paul met the resurrected Jesus, he jailed and even killed Christians. **What happened to Paul for him to completely reverse positions and become willing to die for the very thing he was trying to exterminate? Why would he now choose to travel over multiple continents and plant churches in the name of Jesus? Why would he devote the rest of his life to a cause that he knew would force him to suffer many unbearable hardships including imprisonment, chains, floggings, stonings, and martyrdom?** His life's radical transformation is consistent with the fact that he met a resurrected Jesus (Acts 9). His eyewitness testimony almost single-handedly convicts Jesus of resurrection.

We don't know exactly how many witnesses there were except that they exceeded 500. In a modern criminal case, imagine calling more than 500 eyewitnesses to the stand to confess to witnessing and identifying someone committing a crime. Only a conviction would follow. **On the basis of eyewitness testimony, Jesus is guilty of resurrection.**

Physical Evidence. The tomb was empty. The body of Jesus was laid in a well-known tomb belonging to Joseph of Arimathea. Joseph was so wealthy he could even afford a cave that was carved by workers in the garden located on his estate. It was a tomb reserved for his family, possibly known and marveled over by all in the region. Not only is a cave tomb uncommon today, it was even uncommon during the time of Jesus as well. The common form of burial at the time was ground burial in unmarked graves. The common man could not afford a cave, much less one that was hand carved by hired workers. As a result, almost everyone knew the location of this garden and cave in which Jesus was buried. By the way, in Isaiah 53:9, the prophet foretold that the Christ would be buried in a rich man's tomb—more than seven centuries *before* the event took place.

The tomb was also "sealed" by order of the Roman command with Roman guards posted by request of Jesus' enemies, the religious leaders. In fact, these same enemies claimed then what some critics claim today, that the disciples of Jesus stole His body (Matthew 28:11-15). **But if the religious leaders claimed the disciples stole the body, what did His fiercest enemies admit?** The fiercest enemies of Jesus are witnesses who have testified that Jesus died and that His tomb is empty. Now, if the chief contemporary enemies of Jesus admitted that Jesus died and His tomb is empty, we can be certain that Jesus died and His tomb is empty.

The tomb was empty. But, would the disciples have tried to steal the body? One thing we learned from the disciples' own written testimonies is that most of them confessed to being complete and utter cowards. In fact, in John 20 and Luke 24, we have record of them locked in a room together and hiding for fear of suffering a fate similar to Jesus. **Does confessing to being cowards sound like the confession of people making up a lie in order to prop themselves up as leaders of a new religion?** No! Their confession that Jesus rose from the grave rings true!

They were such hopeless cowards, so consumed by the belief that they would be crucified next, that they locked themselves in a room and hid for days with other witnesses. If they hid as cowards, **where would they have found the courage to break the Roman seal on the tomb? Would they have had the bravery to break through the armed Roman guards who brutally crucified Jesus?** Probably not.

By the way, the Roman guards provide testimony that opposes the resurrection. Their testimony was that the disciples stole the body while they were sleeping. While we understand that the religious leaders probably coached this testimony, it still begs a number of questions that under cross-examination would find the Roman guards guilty of perjury. **Since the punishment for Roman guards falling asleep on duty was death, what is the likelihood that all of them fell asleep on the job? If they all fell asleep, why were they not punished by death? How did the disciples move the great stone covering the tomb without waking the Roman guards? And if they were all asleep, how did they know it was His disciples who stole the body?** As witnesses go, the Roman guards fail miserably. **On the basis of the physical evidence, Jesus is guilty of resurrection.**

Circumstantial Evidence. The Christian church rapidly grew in Jerusalem first—the very city in which Jesus was publicly crucified and buried in a famous tomb. The proclamation of the early church from its very beginning was unapologetically the physical resurrection of Jesus. According to Josh McDowell, "The message of a risen man, could not have been maintained a moment in Jerusalem if the grave was still occupied." If Jesus had not risen from the dead in Jerusalem, this would have been the *last* place such a lie would have been successful. If there were no eyewitnesses and/or no empty tomb, this church would have died quickly. But the eyewitnesses, coupled with the empty tomb and all of the other evidence available at the time, spurred the church to flourish rapidly in the very place where it would have failed if the resurrection did not happen.

Luke, in his writings, recorded that 3,000 people believed the first post-resurrection sermon preached at a location just a few minutes from the tomb (Acts 2:41). Luke also recorded that the church was growing daily (Acts 2:47). By Acts 4:4, he recorded that the Jerusalem church had grown to 5,000 people. By Acts 6:7, Luke apparently lost count and just recorded that the number of disciples "continued to increase, and . . . multiplied greatly in Jerusalem." By the time of Constantine (306 A.D.), the church was estimated to have grown to approximately 30 million people. **On the basis of circumstantial evidence, Jesus is guilty of resurrection.**

If these three levels of evidence were properly presented together in courtroom fashion, before any assembly of reasonable jurors, the verdict would be that Jesus rose from the grave.

The physical resurrection of Jesus Christ is a *certain fact* of history. Be encouraged in your faith.

Chapter 9

Is the Bible Just Another Book?

We often hear critics claiming that the Bible is just another book. Most, if not all Christians, would immediately refute this claim without thinking twice. However, this raises an important question. As a Christian, do you live like the Bible is just another book? With too many Christians, there exists a disconnect between what they say they believe about the Bible and what their actions say they believe about the Bible.

When I taught this subject to teenagers, I would ask them to raise their hands if they had read the entire Bible cover-to-cover. In my 16 years of teaching hundreds of students in different churches, I can count on one hand the number of students who raised their hands. What does this suggest? It may seem like an unfair question, but by the age of 18, the average student has read numerous textbooks, novels, and even some books for fun.

And how different would the results be if we polled this same question among adults? If the Bible is the Word of God and the most important book ever put on paper, wouldn't we read the entire Bible over and over again? Have you read the whole Bible cover-to-cover? Is the Bible just another book in your life?

That said, let's address the question as if it is coming from the critic. The 66 books of the Bible were written by approximately 40 authors from varied walks of life over a span of 1,500 years covering over 4,000 years of history. These facts alone put the Bible in a category by itself. We can stop there and be supported in saying that the Bible is *not* just another book. **Is there another book that you can name that rivals those characteristics?** There is none.

The Bible was also written in different locations (wildernesses, dungeons, hillsides, palaces, jails, etc.) and on three different continents (Asia, Africa, and Europe). Its authors wrote during varied conflicting social eras (war, sacrifice, peace, prosperity, exile, etc.) and in varied conflicting moods (joy, sorrow, despair, certainty, conviction, confusion, doubt, etc.). The authors employed three languages (Hebrew, Greek, and Aramaic) and numerous literary styles (poetry, historical narrative, song, romance, didactic treatise, personal letters, memoirs, satire, biography, autobiography, law, prophecy, parable, allegory, etc.).

Out of all of these extremely disparate influences, one magnificently consistent historical account about God emerges from "In the beginning" to the closing "Amen." No other book known to man can even claim to belong on the same shelf as the Bible. Certainly no other religious book even comes close to it. The Bible is truly in a class by itself in every significant way.

The facts that are listed above are not disputed. These facts are even largely confirmed by atheistic scholars. What is disputed can be summed up in this question: "Is it true?" Most atheists do not dispute the unparalleled uniqueness of the Bible. What they do criticize is the validity of the facts, events, and people the Bible describes. As one examines the confident criticism of the opponents the Bible, it would be easy to conclude that evidence supporting the Bible's veracity must be sorely lacking. Such is not the case, however. There is no other book of historical antiquity that has been subjected to and passed more factual and historical scrutiny than the Bible.

I am a Washington Redskins fan. One of the most historic Super Bowls in sports history was Super Bowl VII, when the Miami Dolphins defeated the Redskins 14-7. What was historic about this game was the fact that the Dolphins completed the only perfect season in NFL history. They finished 17-0. How do you think the Redskins felt walking onto that field at the beginning of the game, realizing they were playing the only perfect team in NFL history? If you had been on the Redskins' team, what would have been running through your mind? Now imagine if you were on a team and your opponent had a record of 25,000 and 0. I am not a mind reader, but I can guess what you would be thinking. You know you are about to lose. The Bible is undefeated.

Archaeology is the chief body of evidence available for us to test the facts, events, and the people recorded in the Bible. Because the Bible covers a span of so many centuries, continents, and historical accounts, archaeology will either support or deny its historical truth. There have been more than 25,000 archaeological sites and digs related to facts in the Bible. All without exception support the biblical narrative. *Not one* has conclusively proven the Bible false. That record is 25,000 and 0. **Based upon this record, who should be more confident— the critic or the believer?**

Dr. Donald Wiseman, an archaeologist and professor of Assyriology at the University of London, published a book in 1958 entitled *Illustrations from Biblical Archaeology*. In this publication, he noted that more than 25,000 sites had been located in the regions covered in the Bible and dating as far back as Old Testament times that confirm the historical accuracy of the Bible. In 1997, Dr. J. Randall Price published *The Stones Cry Out*, a work disclosing that this number has probably grown to the hundreds of thousands. Through the Israeli Antiquities Authority database alone, we now have Internet access to more than 100,000 relics discovered in Israel since 1948. And the pace of discovery and confirmation has not slowed. In this chapter, we will examine one of the most famous of all biblical archaeological sites. Several others will be discussed later in Section 5.

One of the most famous of all biblical archaeological finds is that of the elusive cities of Sodom and Gomorrah. The official finding of these cities is complicated by two important things. First, the cities were completely destroyed by God with a rain of sulfur and brimstone. Second, the tendency of the archaeological community at large is professional hesitancy to officially make a conclusion. But in the mid-1960s and 1970s, the archaeological team of Paul Lapp, Walter Rast, and Thomas Schaub excavated the sites of Bab edh-Dhra and Numeira. They found both cities including surrounding walls 23 feet thick. These cities, along with three others, had been completely destroyed under seven feet of ash deposits. Mysteriously, even the burial houses located in the cemetery some distance from the town were also burned, and *from the inside out*, further proving this was not a result of some conquest. Upon further investigation, these fires started on the roofs of the buildings without exception. The archaeological team concluded that the destruction dates to the time of Abraham and Lot.

These conclusions, however, did not come without controversy. For example, the prominent critics credit the destruction to a theoretical "pocket of natural gas leading to the incineration of these cities." However, no remnant of such a "pocket" has been found. The reason they created this theory is because there are no other geological reasons that can explain the cities' destruction. It is as if the cities were destroyed . . . supernaturally. But even if they were to later discover a "pocket," incinerating pockets of natural gas do not leave seven feet of ash in their aftermath, covering several cities and burning everything from the inside out. You can be the judge of which side of the argument is best supported by the evidence.

The discovery of these cities is just one of the thousands of examples of how archaeology supports the biblical record. Other accounts for which we now have strong archaeological evidence include the walls of Jericho (discussed in more detail in Chapter 32), Noah's ark (Chapter 31), the resurrection of Jesus (Chapter 8), and the Dead Sea Scrolls (Chapter 34). When you couple archaeological evidence with the evidence of miracles (Chapter 10), prophecy (Chapter 11), and scientific discoveries in the Bible (Chapter 33), the Bible is beyond compare.

For those who flippantly refer to the Bible as just another book, I have a simple challenge. **If the Bible is just another book, then it must be on par with *many* other books. And, if so, can you just name one?** They cannot with intellectual integrity. For the Christian who flippantly says the Bible *is* the Word of God and the greatest book ever written, I also have a simple challenge. Does your Bible consumption match your words?

Chapter 10

Are Miracles Real?

C harlton Heston is one of my favorite actors. I was heavily influenced by my mother who admired him so much that she even named my brother after him. Heston is arguably one of the most iconic and principled actors Hollywood has ever seen. He has also played many roles related to the Bible, including John the Baptist in *The Greatest Story Ever Told* and, of course, his famous role as Moses in *The Ten Commandments*.

In 1997, Heston narrated a four-part documentary series titled "Charlton Heston Presents the Bible." In doing so, his intentions of supporting the Bible were obviously pure. In an effort to make the Bible more believable, however, he and the producers tried to provide natural explanations for some of the great miracles of the Bible. For example, with regards to God turning the Nile River into blood through Moses as described in the book of Exodus, they argued that the tides could have turned red due to algae. But, this natural attempt at explaining a supernatural event does not even match the biblical facts (Exodus 7:14-25). The Bible claims that God turned the river into "blood" not algae. The problem with reducing supernatural events to natural events is that you not only discredit the Bible, but you also unwittingly assist in undermining the power and glory away from God. Without real miracles, faith is powerless.

Are the miracles in the Bible just natural phenomena? Or were they actually supernatural events? Is there evidence to support the miracles of the Bible, or were they just fictional stories? If evidence supports the miracles of the Bible really took place, then additional proof exists that the Bible's supernatural stories are true.

While the Bible never gives an intentional definition of a miracle, the Hebrew word used in Exodus is *mowpheth*, which means a special display of God's power. C. S. Lewis expanded well on this definition in his book *Miracles*, when he characterized a miracle as "an interference with nature by a supernatural power." Lewis' characterization is important because it distinguishes between the natural and the supernatural. Since God created nature, God is above nature. He is supernatural. He exists primarily outside of nature, and nature is His creation. We also understand from Lewis' explanation that the natural and the supernatural are not in conflict, but work together.

God's creation of nature was a miracle in and of itself. After nature was created and put into motion, however, we still see occurrences where something outside of the natural order intervenes to change events. When we see these supernatural interferences, we should not credit them to nature since nature is not a being with a will. In other words, nature is incapable of "acting" outside of the order that God gave it.

When I witnessed the birth of my children, I was happily blown away by these amazing miracles of human birth. What I was actually witnessing was God's miracle of creation. But the creation of my children was inside the natural order that God put in motion since the beginning of time. The miracles I witnessed were truly stunning, but they were part of the overall miracle of creation as a whole. They were natural miracles. The miracles of the Bible, however, were outside of the natural order. Entire rivers do not turn into blood in the natural order.

People are not raised from the dead in the natural order. For these things to happen, God had to intervene. When this book refers to "biblical miracles," I am speaking of truly supernatural events.

The Bible contains accounts of hundreds of miracles, many during the life of Jesus, which are the primary focus of this chapter. The miracles of Jesus are doubly important since they not only prove that the Bible is reliable, but they also affirm that Jesus is God. Jesus performed so many miracles that we do not have an accurate count. What we do have are detailed descriptions of more than thirty specific miracles He performed in front of many eyewitnesses as recorded in the New Testament. These miracles were not like card tricks that can be credited to sleight of hand. For example, Jesus fed more than 5,000 people with a couple of loaves of bread and fish, raised dead people to life, walked on water, and restored sight to people who had been blind since birth. These amazing miracles were witnessed by many, documented, and the stories circulated. Eyewitnesses confirmed them. The miracles of Jesus were impossible to fake or duplicate.

As with most biblical matters, the Bible is not our only source of proof that Jesus performed the miracles of record. Jesus had many enemies in His day, and the religious leaders were by far His fiercest. In fact, their actions were central to the ultimate crucifixion of Jesus. These religious leaders constantly observed Him and also recorded their renditions of the history of Jesus in their own books. The Talmud, for example, is a historical book that is central to Judaism. This non-biblical source records events from the testimony of Jesus' enemies.

In Talmud Bavli (the Babylonian Talmud), *Tractate Sanhedrin*, Folio 43a, testimony is recorded that Jesus "practiced sorcery and enticed Israel to apostasy." The ancient Hebrew word for sorcery is *kashaph*, which is reserved for the effective practice of witchcraft or sorcery. In other words, *kashaph* does not mean tricks. *Kashaph* means supernatural. If Jesus did not perform these acts, they would never have accused him of sorcery. In other words, accusing Him of sorcery assigns to Him supernatural power.

Enticing people to apostasy (the abandonment of their religious faith) was enough to give Jesus the Hebrew death penalty at that time. The enemies of Jesus knew His miracles were obvious, were witnessed by many (including themselves), and were impossible to dismiss. They had no choice but to accuse him of sorcery, and they recorded their accusations, which now benefit us as evidence of the miraculous. We can debate whether Jesus was a sorcerer or God. But if Jesus' own enemies admitted that He performed supernatural acts, you can bet your life that He did.

In summary, both biblical and non-biblical evidence exists to support the fact that Jesus performed supernatural miracles. Jesus is God! The writings of his enemies from the same time period also confirm this truth. Therefore the Bible is reliable in this regard. In addition to archaeology, this evidence is just one more bit of testimony supporting the reliability of the Bible.

Chapter 11

Nostradamus Versus the Bible

D id someone actually predict centuries ago the rise of Adolf Hitler, and even the use of the atomic bomb? There is a growing body of people who believe that a man referred to as Nostradamus did exactly that as far back as the 1500s. Nostradamus, born Michel de Nostredame in 1503, is widely referred to as a famous prophet. His "prophecies" have enjoyed plenty of fame in the 20th and 21st centuries. As well as being the subject of hundreds of books, he has been featured in several films, and his works continue to be a subject of media interest today. In the mid-1500s, he published his most famous work, *The Prophecies*, in which he compiled hundreds of long-term "predictions" in the form of four-line poems. Other works followed. Wild claims abound about these "predictions." Some claim that Nostradamus even prophesied specifically about the attacks of 9/11.

Nostradamus himself rejected the title of prophet. By his own admission, the title was above him. He preferred the title of astrological consultant. In that light, we would more appropriately treat his "predictions" as glorified horoscopes. In fact, in most cases, his poems were less clear than horoscopes, which is difficult to imagine. For example, below is the poem in its original English translation that has been twisted and added to by conspiracy theorists to claim that he predicted the 9/11 attacks:

> Volcanic fire from the center of the earth
> will cause trembling around the new city:
> Two great rocks will make war for a long time.
> Then Arethusa will redden a new river.

This poem is far from convincing that Nostradamus had any special revelation about 9/11. It takes a lot more than the coincidence of the words, "new city," "two," and "war" together to be convincing that this is a reference to the Twin Towers falling in New York City in 2001. In fact, what this poem claims is that this event was caused by "volcanic fire from the center of the earth." The poem also concludes with a reference to Arethusa, a nymph in Greek mythology who was later transformed into a water fountain on an island in Sicily. The connection of this reference to the 9/11 attacks does not bear up under the slightest weight of scrutiny. Unfortunately, this is just one of hundreds of examples that have been distorted to try to connect these poems to modern events. Maybe we should take seriously his own rejection of the title of prophet.

The sad irony is that our society goes out of its way to glorify a vague astrologer, while it ignores the miraculous fulfillment of hundreds of biblical prophecies—in some cases hundreds of years after they were made. **What does it say when the Bible is filled with hundreds upon hundreds of prophecies that are specific and easily linked to actual events hundreds of years later? If it can be shown that non-vague prophecies written by biblical prophets actually came true, what does this suggest?** First, it would suggest that these prophets predicted future events by supernatural means. Second, it would suggest that their prophecies as written in the Bible are supernaturally inspired.

According to J. Barton Payne's *Encyclopedia of Biblical Prophecy*, there are 1,239 prophecies in the Old Testament and 578 in the New Testament for a total of 1,817 prophecies. Miraculously, none of them are false prophecies, which is an unparalleled track record. In fact, many of the prophecies of the Bible are very specific (in contrast to horoscopes).

The Old Testament prophets prophesied about the rise and fall of entire nations and people groups by name. They prophesied about famous births and deaths by name, including the manner and timing. These were not random and vague poems that could be fulfilled after their deaths. In fact, many times they prophesied about events fulfilled during their lifetimes which allowed them to be judged as either a prophet of God or a false prophet. Remember that the punishment for a false prophet was death by execution (Deuteronomy 18). For this reason, it would be easy to prophesy about matters after your death. But instead, they chose to also prophesy about specific matters to be fulfilled while they were still living. In light of the punishment, not only did this show bravery, but it also tested their credibility and found these prophets to be true.

As with the previous chapter on miracles, the prophecies we will focus on are those regarding the Messiah and Jesus. Again, these are doubly important since their fulfillment in Jesus not only proves that the biblical prophets spoke with supernatural knowledge, but it also further proves Jesus is God. The Old Testament contains more than 400 prophecies regarding the promised Messiah that relate to his life, death, and reign. The odds of a single man fulfilling just 48 of these prophecies is equivalent to 1 in 10^{157}. Because this number is hard to visualize, here is what this number looks like: 10,000,0 00,000,000,000,000,000,000,000,000,000,000,000,000,00 0,000,000,000,000,000,000,000,000,000,000,000,000,000,

000,000,000,000,000,000,000,000,000,000,000,000,000,000,0
00,000,000,000,000,000,000,000

Compare those odds with the odds of winning the lottery, which is approximately 1 in 14,000,000.

At this point, some skeptics would argue that the numbers do not matter because of their belief that parts of Jesus' story were manipulated to look like He fulfilled the Old Testament prophecies. I will address the historical reliability of the New Testament in Section 5 of this book. Here we can focus on the prophecies that were clearly outside of Jesus' control, including the following:

- He was born of a virgin (Isaiah 7:14).
- He was born in Bethlehem (Micah 5:2).
- He was born at a predetermined time (Daniel 9:25).
- He was betrayed (Psalm 41:9).
- He was crucified (Psalm 22:16).
- He was mocked, smitten, and spit on (Psalm 22:7-8; Isaiah 50:6).
- His side was pierced, but no bones were broken (Zechariah 12:10; Psalm 34:20).
- He was buried in a rich man's tomb (Isaiah 53:9).

The statistical odds of Jesus fulfilling just these eight prophecies are 1 in 10^{17}. To better understand that number, imagine the state of Texas (270,000 square miles) covered in silver dollars stacked two feet high. The number of coins equals 10^{17}. Now imagine that I marked one of those silver dollars without you knowing it. In order to find that one silver dollar, you select a drop zone somewhere over the state, skydive, and upon your first blindfolded attempt, select that one marked coin. The odds of you selecting the one I marked are the same as Jesus fulfilling just these eight prophecies, which He did.

To conclude, the odds of Jesus fulfilling eight prophecies outside of His control are 1 in 10^{17}. The odds of him fulfilling

48 prophecies are 1 in 10^{157}. Fulfilling eight or 48 prophecies would be convincing enough. Jesus however ultimately fulfills more than 400 prophecies. **What does this prove?** Unlike Nostradamus, Jesus defying all odds and fulfilling more than 400 prophecies proves that the biblical authors were prophesying with a knowledge that was above them and outside of the natural realm. The evidence of prophecy also further proves that Jesus is God.

And the prophecies do not stop there. These same prophets prophesied about you and your destiny. From Genesis to Revelation, the Bible is not only filled with Messianic prophecies. The Bible is also filled with prophecies regarding the current rise of the church, the current rise and fall of political movements, our future deaths, eternal judgment, and our eternal residence. All of these prophecies are about your future as well as mine. Read God's Word as if your future is laid out on its pages, and you will discover that it actually is.

Section 4

Logical Fallacies Commonly Used Against the Christian Faith

B efore we dive deeper into the evidence supporting the Christian faith, it is important that your critical thinking skills are calibrated. Christians are often silenced by an opponent's technique of argument and discussion. The purpose of this section is to refine your approach to defending the faith prior to introducing deeper evidence. This section, therefore, will examine a sample of common logical fallacies employed to undermine the Christian faith.

With each fallacy, I will describe it, teach you how to recognize it, and share an example of how it is commonly used against Christians. Each chapter includes questions you can use to respond to each fallacy.

Be warned. This section is devoted to critical thinking skills. It will require you to dive deep and think hard. But it is very important that you are prepared to respond to each of these fallacies if you are serious about defending the faith. Therefore, buckle up, hold on tightly, and muscle through it. The result will be worth the effort!

Chapter 12

Truth Is Relative

One day over lunch, I was reasoning with a pantheist friend about God and truth. Pantheists generally believe that everything is God and that God is ultimately one person. After he seemed to realize the evidence supporting the God of the Bible was true, he paused. He then attempted to repeat to me this dismissive quote, "Truth is relative." In other words, "What's true for you is not true for me."

Do those phrases sound familiar? I have heard them many, many times in conversations with unbelievers. They are repeated so often they have become very effective phrases for silencing Christians. Ironically, those who espouse such comments rarely seek to apply them to themselves. That is, those who repeat such phrases are preaching them as...absolute truth! The phrases themselves make no sense. They are self-contradictory. In order for a phrase to be true, it has to first be logical. If it is not logical, it is by definition false. Logic and relativism are opposites.

How do we know these phrases, and moral relativism itself, lack logic consistency? Because these statements violate the Three Laws of Logic which are universally understood and accepted by all. These laws were not invented by the church;

rather, they have long been recognized as "laws" by secular man for as long as philosophy and religion have been debated. No credible institution of man exists that defies them. If a statement violates *any* of these Three Laws of Logic, it simply cannot be true. Such a statement would be considered a contradiction or false.

The *Law of Identity* is the simplest of all and the most violated. The opening quotes about truth are certainly violations. According to this law, something is what it *is*. If something is true, it is true for all. For example, if something is wood it *is* wood. Sounds simple, doesn't it? My pantheist friend, however, attempted to say that the Christian God was true for me, but false for him. In other words, we were both right. That is relativism in a nutshell. The idea that something can be *both* true and false at the same time and in the same way. Such a belief is logically impossible.

A statement cannot be true and false and maintain its identity as truth. That is like saying wood can be wood and it can also be a 1,000-foot wall of marshmallows or that two plus two equals four and it also equals five. Distortions of identity are where most, if not all, deceptions start. We have already learned that critics confuse the nature of God with that of humans in order to attack Him. That too is a violation of the Law of Identity. God is not human. He is God.

The *Law of Noncontradiction* is that something cannot be both what it is and what it is not at the same time and in the same respect. In other words, it cannot contradict itself. Two contradictory statements cannot both be true. For example, wood cannot be non-wood. The phrase "Truth is relative" violates this law as well. Either (1) Christianity is false, (2) pantheism is false, or (3) they are both false. But they cannot *both* be true because they are logically *contradictory* (John 14:6). 1 John 2:21 reminds us that "no lie is of the truth."

The Law of Excluded Middle is that something is either what it is stated to be or it is not. For example, something is either wood or it is not wood. It cannot be both wood and marshmallows. A statement is either true or it is not. The opening phrases of this chapter violate this law because a statement must either be true or not true. By saying that the opening phrases are both true and not true, the Law of Excluded Middle is violated.

I had been teaching this subject for years when a student responded, "What about the spork?" If you don't know what a spork is, it is a combination of a spoon and a fork. It looks like a spoon with a forked edge instead of a rounded edge opposite the handle. So, for fun, let's apply the Three Laws of Logic to the spork:

> The Law of Identity: A spork is a spork.
> The Law of Noncontradiction: A spork cannot be both a spork and a non-spork at the same time and in the same respect.
> The Law of Excluded Middle: Something is either a spork or it is a not a spork.

The spork is a clever example because it looks deceptive. A spork, however, never had the identity of a spoon or a fork. It can be substituted for either, but its identity is neither because it has its own identity. The spork is what it was created to be—a spork. It does not represent a violation of the Laws of Logic; therefore, it is *not* a contradiction.

By the way, these laws are so ultimate in our thinking process that they are self-evident. We can never get around them. In order for someone to prove these laws are false, they will have to make a convincing argument. You cannot make an argument without using logic, however. Therefore, if you even attempt to prove these Three Laws of Logic to be false, you will have to use the Laws of Logic to do it. You would be *using logic* to prove that you *cannot use logic*. How foolish is that?

Aristotle pointed out this fact to the "relativists" of his day. He claimed that he could make anyone, even relativists and skeptics, prove these Laws of Logic by simply getting them to argue about anything. If they argued *for* anything, they would be using these laws to do it. The only argument that a relativist can genuinely make against logic is to remain silent. But if they say nothing, they prove nothing. In other words, to attempt to prove these laws false, you have to use logic (and deny relativism) in the process. Pantheistic teachings fall short in this very area. Pantheists teach that truth is relative while using absolute and logical terms to teach their *truth*. You will never see a pantheist claim their truth is relative and thereby agree that it is also false.

Here are a few more examples of statements that violate the Three Laws of Logic with possible responses in bold:

"Christians are wrong to judge other religions." **If it is wrong to judge, then isn't it is also wrong to judge Christians as this quote does?**

"I believe in religious tolerance and therefore reject the intolerance of others." **If you believe in tolerance, then why don't you tolerate people who are intolerant?**

"Liberals are more open-minded than and more loving than Christians. This is true because we do not claim that there is only one way to believe; we claim that every way is right. All religions are true." **You are against teaching "only one way to believe," but aren't you teaching only one way to believe?**

"I believe that abortion is wrong because a fetus is a person. Abortion should only be allowed in cases like rape." **I agree that abortion is wrong because a fetus is a person, but how is a fetus not a person in cases like rape?**

"Luke, you're going to find that many of the truths we cling to depend greatly on our own point of view." (Obi-Wan Kenobi to Luke Skywalker, *The Return of the Jedi*) **Is Obi-Wan's truth true?**

"You must experience God; you cannot try to use logic because God is beyond logic. Logic does not apply to God." **If**

logic does not apply to God, then why are you applying logic to God?

"You must learn to trust your feelings more and refrain from approaching so many issues in life from strictly an intellectual perspective. Intellect . . . is limited. Feelings are limitless." (from Shirley MacLaine's book, *Out on a Limb*). **If I must refrain from using intellect with such issues, then why are you using intellect to arrive at your own conclusion and teach it?**

"Him [Brahman] the eye does not see, nor the tongue express, nor the mind grasp. Him we neither know nor are able to teach. Different is he from the known, and from the unknown . . . the wise know him to be beyond knowledge" (Kena, in *The Upanisshads*, pgs. 30-31). **If Brahman is unknown, beyond knowledge, and unknowable, then how did we come to know these very things about him?**

"All ethics are relative . . . the contemporary man ought to avoid words like 'never' and 'perfect' and 'always' . . . as he avoids the plague, as he avoids 'absolutely'" (Joseph Fletcher, *Situation Ethics*, pgs. 43-44). **If we are not to use absolute words, as you demand, then why are you making absolute demands?**

"Since all human truth is relative, the church must surrender the idea that the Bible contains the ultimate truth . . . Christians must embrace a philosophy of uncertainty" (Bishop Spong, "Spong Calls on Church to Embrace Uncertainty," *Newark Star-Ledger*, 15 January 1984, Section One: pg. 45). **If we are to embrace uncertainty, then how are you teaching with certainty on this very issue?**

In addition to these examples, try now to think of any other examples that might attempt to prove the Three Laws of Logic to be false. As you do, keep in mind that proving the Laws of Logic false has never been done. Truth is absolute, not relative.

For the most direct example, consider the statement "Truth is relative." To assert that "Truth is relative," you must then conclude that your statement in and of itself is *both* true *and* false. If such a conclusion were true, the person making the statement is, in effect, claiming that "It is absolutely true that truth is not absolutely true." Do you see the problem? If the statement is both true *and* false, then one is forced to admit that it is *false*. If the statement is false, then the opposite of the statement is also true. If you are confused, it is for good reason. You are genuinely trying to make sense out of this statement's nonsense. The problem is not you. The problem is the statement.

The next time you hear someone cleverly say "truth is relative," respond with the question, **"Is what you just said *true*?"** But be prepared to gracefully rescue them because they will need it if they attempt to respond to your question reasonably.

Chapter 13

Is the Trinity Logical?

I n the movie *The Santa Clause*, there is a scene where a young boy named Charlie defends the idea of Santa to his stepfather Neal. Neal asks Charlie if he had ever seen a reindeer fly. "Yes," Charlie responds. Neal then loses his patience and says, "Well, I haven't!" Without missing a beat, Charlie responds, "Have you ever seen a million dollars?" "No," Neal answers. And then Charlie closes him out with the brilliant line, "Just because you haven't seen it doesn't mean it doesn't exist."

I feel like this sometimes when it comes to the Trinity. **Is God one person or three?** Can you explain the Trinity to a child or even to an adult? Can you even fully explain it to yourself? Neither can I. If there was one person who could explain it, he would be God. Just because we cannot fully understand or explain something, does not make it false. That said, this chapter is not an attempt to fully explain the Trinity. Rather we defend the fact that the concept of the Trinity is logical and, therefore, not contradictory.

In the previous chapter, the Three Laws of Logic were discussed and effectively modeled for responding to the relativists among us. If it is fair game to apply logic to relativism, pantheism, and other religions, it is fair game to apply it to the

Trinity as well. After all, the Trinity is central to the identity of God. Since God has revealed His nature in the Bible, it is in Scripture where we must first turn to see how God describes the Trinity.

Our first glimpse of the Trinity is in the book of Genesis. Genesis 1:26 says, "And God said, 'Let *us* make man in *our* image, after *our* likeness'" (emphasis added). Prior to man's creation, whom is God talking to and why would He refer to Himself in plural pronouns? Some have floated the concept that God is speaking with angels. But we know by reference to this verse and other verses that we were created in the image of God, not in the image of anything else. Further, angels do not bear God's image, and they are not co-creators of man.

No, God is speaking to the Word (Jesus) and the Holy Spirit—the other persons of the Trinity (Genesis 1:1-2; John 1:1-3). Therefore, we were made in the collective image of the Father, the Son, and the Holy Spirit. We bear the image of all three. It is challenging to see ourselves in the image of the Father or the Spirit because our mental image of them is distant from our mental image of our physical selves. It is a little easier to see ourselves in God's image when we look at Jesus. We are like a painting for which Jesus Himself posed. So naturally, since God is speaking with two other persons in Genesis 1, He is right in using pronouns like "us" and "our."

As we read further through the Bible, however, we arrive at Deuteronomy 6:4: "Hear, O Israel: The LORD our God, the LORD is one." What? The Bible said He is plural, and now it says He is singular? Yes, it did. Actually, the Bible did *both* in this verse alone. The word for "God" in the original Hebrew is the word *Elohim*. This name means God, but it is also a *plural* noun. The verse says that our God (*plural* noun) is "one."

Now fast-forward to John 1:1: "In the beginning was the Word, and the Word was *with* God, and the Word *was* God" (emphasis added). So we have God *with* the Word at the same time as the Word *is* God. That sounds plural to me. Reading further in this first chapter of John, verse 14 says, "And the Word became flesh and dwelt among us, and we have seen his glory, glory as of the only Son from the Father, full of grace and truth." Jesus, being God, had other names before He was given the name Yeshua (or "Jesus" in English). In John 1:1, His name is "the Word." And in Genesis 1, it is the Word through which all things were spoken into existence. Then later the Word became flesh and took on the name Yeshua. Are you confused yet?

Let me pause here to say that something can be logical and still not be fully understood. Calculus is logical, but I still do not completely understand it. In Scripture we see that the Trinity is revealed, we know from reason that it is logical, but we remember that we will never understand it fully. If you are experiencing confusion, just remember that we are like a pot trying to understand the potter. It probably will never happen no matter how hard we try—it is a mystery of the faith; not a mystery in the sense that it is illogical—a mystery because we lack the intellectual breadth to understand it completely.

In summary, our God (plural noun) is one. Does that summary statement sound like a contradiction? In order for this summary statement to be a contradiction, it must violate the Three Laws of Logic. The writers of these books of the Bible may not have been as intelligent as average humans are today, but they knew that three does not equal one. Moses and other biblical authors never said three equals one. If they had, this would have been a contradiction. What they taught was that three *persons* exist in one *being*. A person is always *singular*, but a being can have *plural* persons. For example, a sports team is a being made up of several persons. In God, this is the concept of triunity, from where we get the word trinity (three persons, one being). Triunity simply means unity with the diversity of three. If you look up "triunity" or "triune" in the dictionary, you will not find the words "false," "illogical," "impossible," or any other negative adjectives in their definitions. The very fact that we have accepted definitions for these words without negative adjectives speaks volumes.

The reason why we have these words is because they pre-exist in God. But God is not the only being that represents unity and diversity at the same time. In fact, "unity and diversity" has always been one of the primary pursuits of philosophy. The merger of the words "unity and diversity" is how we created the word "university." A university is a place of instruction where diversity of study is pursued in unity. **How did man get the philosophical inspiration to pursue unity and diversity?** Because we were created in the image of the One who is united and diverse. We are His reflection. If the Trinity is a logical contradiction, then so is "university."

On a side note, the lack of trinity in other religions (like Judaism and Islam) is a huge logical problem for them. These religions ultimately claim belief in a monotheistic god, which for them means he is purely singular with no diversity of persons. For example, Allah allegedly has only one personality. He is not a father, he is not a son, and he is not described like a brother. He is simply Allah. In order to illustrate the problems with a god being monistic, we will turn to another "Law" that applies to many fields of study including science and philosophy. The Law of Cause and Effect demands that in the relationship between an event (the cause) and a second event (the effect), the effect is understood as a consequence of the cause. Having a monotheistic god that lacks diversity makes it difficult to explain how unity and diversity exist in the created effect (humanity), while it does not exist in the cause (a monotheistic god).

This logical flaw creates an even deeper problem with these religions' efforts to explain how love exists in the effect (humanity) when, prior to creation, love is absent in the cause. If their creator is only one person before the creation, then this creator is alone, where it is impossible to love someone else because no other person exists. In Christian theism, the

Trinity provides for love in the cause even prior to creation (love between the Father, Son, and Holy Spirit), which explains why the effect (humanity) is able to reflect love.

Many other examples of triunity surround us all. Probably the best example is the U.S. federal government. Our Founding Fathers, most of whom believed in God, understood the benefits of emulating God in triunity and did so in the very foundation of our form of government. Our federal government has three branches: executive, legislative, and judicial. These three "persons" exist in one "being." The trinity of the federal government, modeled after God Himself, therefore bears strong resemblance to Him. In addition, in 1782, the Seal of the United States was permanently affixed with the motto, "e pluribus unum," which is Latin for "from the many, one." If the trinity of the federal government, university, and many other examples is not a contradiction, then the concept of trinity in and of itself is entirely logical. Therefore, so is a triune God. *Of course the primary difference between federal government example and God is that the being (the government) is the product or sum of the parts. The Trinity of God is **not** the sum of its parts. There are three persons in the Trinity, yet each person is "all God," not a part of God.*

Is God three persons? Yes. Is He one being? Yes. Is that a contradiction? No. Do we fully understand it? No. But understanding is not required for something to be true and/or logical. The Trinity is a logical fact that beautifully teaches us how to love.

Chapter 14

All Christians Are Hypocrites

66 All Christians are hypocrites!" Ouch! You are the rare exception if you have never had anyone hurl this charge at you or at someone you love. Your first reaction may be to verbally slap back, but I would encourage you to read on and resist the temptation.

In this section, we have been learning about common logical fallacies used against the Christian faith and how to respond to them. The logical fallacy committed with this accusation is extremely common, and *everyone* is guilty of it. In fact, I just committed the fallacy in my last sentence. It is the logical fallacy of the Hasty Generalization.

Hasty Generalization is when a general conclusion is made hastily but is based on too small a sample or one person's inadequate experience. Another form of this fallacy is when someone builds general rules from either accidental or exceptional situations or circumstances. Such conclusions have shaky foundations. Unfounded and unsupported generalizations usually become established in our minds as facts and evolve into stereotypes by which we prejudge people. And prejudging people is always wrong. Proverbs 29:20 says, "Do you see a man who is hasty in his words? There is more hope for a fool than for him."

The best way to spot this fallacy is to listen for words like "all," "none," "every," "never," "everything," or "nothing." In my next sentence, I will use one of these words but in a healthy way. *Every* time you see one of these words used in a conclusion, train yourself to pause and make sure the word is properly supported by adequate data underlying that conclusion. Notice how I did not use the word "every" to make a conclusion in that sentence. In fact, I avoided making a conclusion altogether. Too often conclusions are hastily made and unsupported. We would all be better served by making sure biblical wisdom guides our conclusions.

You might be reading this paragraph, however, and arrive at a different conclusion. You might even be a Christian and find yourself agreeing with the statement that "all Christians are hypocrites." There is a story I once heard but was never able to substantiate. A pastor was inviting a man to church. The man quipped back with this answer, "No, church people are all hypocrites." Not missing a beat, the pastor responded, "Then you should come because we still have room for one more." The pastor's choice of words may be inappropriate since he responded with prejudice, but this anecdote highlights a couple of points for us to consider.

To the person who refuses to associate with hypocrites, I ask this question, "**Where can you go to avoid them?**" I did not realize there were places and social groups that were completely void of hypocrites. I will not go as far as to say everyone is a hypocrite. Yet we know enough about the definition to realize the problem is rampant in most if not all groups, including nonreligious ones. Christians do not have a monopoly on this vice. The Christian church probably has no higher concentration of hypocrites than any other organization. That is because hypocrisy is a core problem of humanity, it is not caused by

Christianity. To prove this conclusion, we will need to define hypocrisy.

Simply, hypocrisy can be defined as preaching one thing while practicing something different. The combination in this definition is crucial. Preaching must be combined with the opposing practice. Therefore, if someone is not preaching, by definition, he is not hypocritical. So are all Christians hypocrites? Of course that is not true. I have known many Christians who totally refrain from preaching like they refrain from drinking poison. Take my late grandfather, Mertland Higgs, for example. He had an unusual name and was an unusual man. We called him "Pa." What made Pa so unusual is that he was one of the godliest men I ever knew. Before Pa passed away, he was very close to God. Pa was the kind of person you would walk in on to catch him praying—he was constantly praying. He loved God with such a passion that there was hardly an evil cell in his body. However, Pa rarely preached. When he did, it was restricted to his grandchildren and there was no doubt he practiced what he preached. I will testify to that. Was Mertland Higgs a hypocrite? No. He did not match the definition.

Now I will address those who like to judge Christians by using the words of Jesus, "Judge not" (from Matthew 7:1-5). Remember that this passage applies to everyone and not just Christians. Therefore, when you judge someone for judging that is self-refuting. Just because pastors in the church preach regularly from a church pulpit does not mean that the Christian church has a monopoly on preaching or judging either. **In fact, can you name one religion or belief structure that does not preach or judge?** Such a religion does not exist. Even overt atheists are guilty of preaching their beliefs and judging others based on their beliefs (see Chapter 56). These critics should think twice before proclaiming that they do not preach. Preaching comes in many other forms than the stereotype. So for those who take issue with Christians for preaching, I sure hope they don't preach about this as a vice. If they have a moral problem with preaching, then they should not be preaching about hypocrisy. Preaching about hypocrisy is still . . . preaching. And by preaching about hypocrisy, they convict themselves as hypocrites right out of the gate. If you think I am now judging them, remember that these critics and their own preaching beat me to the punch.

I have an agnostic friend who once accused me and other Christians of impressing our beliefs of right and wrong upon others. Here is how I responded: "It is your belief that it is wrong for me to impress my beliefs about what is wrong or right. **But, in saying so, are you not attempting to impress upon me that I am doing something wrong according to your belief? Aren't you practicing exactly what you are judging me for?**" He was startled, so I took the pressure off by saying, "Relax. I'm just showing you that most if not all people do the exact same thing. You tolerate this from everyone including yourself, but you don't show tolerance when Christians do it." He laughed and told me that I was the first person to ever explain the inconsistency logically. And we are still friends to this day.

Lastly, to my fellow Christians, I must make one parting comment. You too should refrain from judging other Christians as hypocrites. Christians often use this tactic to either guilt another Christian from holding them accountable or to silence someone that disagrees with them. In either case, this tactic is founded in bitterness and has no place in the church. We have to be careful when applying Matthew 7:1-5. This famous passage includes the command of Jesus to "judge not," but in the context of the "speck and log" analogy. Jesus is addressing the sin of judging people, not their actions. I can proclaim that stealing is wrong without judging the thief. To prove this point, notice how Jesus closes the passage: "You *hypocrite, first* take the log out of your own eye, and then you will see clearly to take the speck out of your brother's eye" (emphasis added). Jesus did say, "Judge not," but he never removed from the

Christian family the obligation to help remove sin from your spiritual brother. He did not say to take the log out of your own eye and stop. He concluded with the family obligation to "take the speck out of your brother's eye." Therefore, let's remove the logs from our eyes first but then finish the job of being family. We must also remove the speck from the eyes of our brothers and sisters.

Chapter 15

Man Is Nothing More Than Molecules in Motion

I once had a very intelligent student who was a devout disciple of science. At one point during class, she openly objected to any argument that explained any human function through means other than strict biochemistry. She proclaimed that *every* human emotion and *every* action was simply a series of chemical reactions in the brain and nothing more. How would you have responded to her viewpoint? **Is man really nothing more than molecules in motion? Is that it? Is that all we are?**

I gently asked my student, **"If a burglar murders an entire family in cold blood, were his crimes just a result of a series of chemical reactions in his brain? And if he is otherwise determined to be sane, should society hold him accountable for reactions in the brain that are strictly chemical in nature and, therefore, beyond his control?"** After all, if a burglar is simply reacting to the impulses of his biochemistry, then he has an adequate excuse to claim that he is not responsible for his crime. She argued further by attempting to change the subject.

Does the title of this chapter sound true? This is a perfect test to see if you remember the cautions from chapter fourteen about *Hasty Generalization*. Consider the statement "man is nothing more than molecules in motion" once more. There is one word in this statement that should set off alarms when you hear it, "nothing." "Nothing" is one of those strong words that you need to recognize as a marker for *Hasty Generalization*.

In addition to *Hasty Generalization*, the core logical fallacy at work in the opening quote is referred to as the *Reductive Fallacy*. This fallacy is committed when someone attempts to reduce a complex argument, idea, or thing into simple components, then attempts to explain or define the entire argument, idea, or thing by using only *one* of its components (and ignoring the others). Put another way, these arguments are single-level explanations of multi-level concepts. That is a recipe for philosophical disaster.

To conclude that a man is just a collection of molecules is to take the sum of man and redefine him as a collection of molecules and nothing else. The fact that I am typing this right now and that you are reading this page, processing the words, and feeling emotions about what you are reading simply proves this assertion to be false. Thoughts and emotions reflect something that transcends the molecules. They reflect spirit, which is not molecular. Your identity is a result of God creating you in His image. Like it or not, every human is God's image bearer. And that image is not the molecules as God added to us something that is much more than just molecules. He added spirit.

Common sense will also prove this statement to be false. **If man is nothing more than molecules in motion, then how does man contrast with other things? Aren't my potato chips also nothing more than molecules in motion?** If this is true, then apparently very little separates man from potato chips. **Does anyone reasonably believe such an argument?** While we're on the subject, **is there any material object in the universe that is *not* molecules in motion?** This reasoning sounds silly but that is because the opening statement is silly. Proverbs 26:4 reminds us, "Do not answer a fool according to his folly, or you yourself will be just like him."

We can also prove the argument that man is nothing more than molecules to be false through further analysis of man's identity. If tomorrow I die of a heart attack at work, I would be dead on the floor of my office. I would *still* be molecules, and those molecules would still be in motion. According to this statement, I am nothing more than molecules in motion today. **And, lying dead on the floor of my office, I would still be nothing more than molecules in motion tomorrow. Does that make sense? Am I the same dead as I am alive? What is different?**

Being dead is not the same as being alive. The living version of me has something that the dead version of me does not. It has life. With human life comes spirit, thoughts, emotions, and a host of other realities. Life is something science cannot fully explain, certainly not by reducing humanity to a collection of molecules. Even though we cannot explain life fully, life is a reality. Life is integral to the identity of man, and the opening quote is intellectually bankrupt for ignoring this fact.

God did something special when He created man. Among other things, He breathed life into us. He added His own breath to our moving molecules to give us life. We can even suggest that God breathed into us our souls with His own breath. Our life, our souls are more critical components to our identities than even our molecules (flesh). Those who put their faith in God must never reduce man's God-given identity by ignoring life. And nobody can credibly claim that life is not a critical component of man's identity.

It is chiefly the scientific community at large that attempts to thrust this type of reductive thinking upon the rest of us. The logical blunder of this reductive thinking, however, actually is *not* science. Science is restricted to the use of the scientific method, which is the method of research in which a problem is identified, relevant data is gathered, a hypothesis is formed, and the hypothesis is repeatedly tested. It is the method that scientists use to develop scientific conclusions. Scientists have yet to use the scientific method to prove or even observe the claims of this false quote about man and molecules. Observations of living beings actually dictate more rational conclusions. The type of reductive thinking introduced in this chapter is an example of scientists crossing over from the realm of science to the realm of philosophy. Scientists usually make horrible philosophers.

Naturalists and materialists would have us believe that we are nothing but molecular machines produced by evolution. Naturalists and materialists often provide evidence that proves the opposite is true. For example, Dr. Carl Sagan (the late author and professor of astronomy and space studies at Cornell University) reported this finding: "The information content of the human brain expressed in bits is probably comparable to the total number of connections among the neurons (about 100 trillion, or 10^{14} bits). If it were written out in English, that information would fill some 20 million volumes, as many as in the world's largest libraries. The equivalent of 20 million volumes is inside the head of each one of us. The brain is a very big place in a very small space" (*Cosmos*, pg. 278). Sagan reported his findings in terms that clearly describe the human brain as much more than just molecules in motion.

In this finding, Sagan admits there is something else that is added to the molecules . . . information. By the way, **if information was added, *who* added it?** (This line of arguing will be more fully addressed in Chapter 50). **What if we claimed that Sagan's books were nothing more than ink molecules on paper molecules? In other words, what if we used his own fallacy to reduce his work to something meaningless?** We would probably be accused of being obnoxiously shallow and rightly so.

One cannot overstate the importance of identity. Again, it is where all deception starts. I trust after reading this book your sense of identity in God will have been reinforced. I stated earlier the fact that God breathed *life* into man. Two important truths regarding our identity stem from this fact. First, God did not breathe into any other beings other than man. Second, there is only one other thing that God breathed that we are aware of from the Scriptures. In 2 Timothy 3:16, Paul writes that all Scripture is God-breathed. God breathed our souls, and then He breathed His written word. Without regularly "inhaling" and "exhaling" God's Word, we are likely suffocating our very souls. As a means of reinforcing your true identity in the future, you should regularly inhale and exhale God's Word as if your life depended upon it—because it probably does.

Chapter 16

Christians Are Weak-Minded

The late Antony Flew is probably the most famous atheist debater of recent times. For decades, he was the front man defending atheism in many public debates against Christian philosophers. Flew was a brilliant English philosopher who taught at Oxford University, among other institutions. However, in a 2004 interview with Dr. Gary Habermas, Flew changed his tune. He renounced atheism and declared that he was a deist, believing that there was a God. After continued study of the growing body of evidence supporting intelligent design of life and the universe, he said, "Although I was once sharply critical of the argument to design, I have since come to see that, when correctly formatted, this argument constitutes a persuasive case for the existence of God." He proceeded to author a book entitled *There Is a God: How the World's Most Notorious Atheist Changed His Mind*. As a result, it did not take long for *The New York Times* magazine to publish a scathing attack article alleging that Flew, their one-time friend, had "mentally declined" (article included in the November 4, 2007 issue).

Have you ever felt like the world believes that only atheists are intelligent and Christians are weak-minded? Do you ever get into conversations about God only to find people looking down on you for relying on faith as they do on "science"?

The world seems to equate faith in God with a lack of knowledge or with weakness. This treatment of Christians is best summarized in the famous words of Dr. Sigmund Freud.

"God is a psychological projection of man's fears. A child learns to lean on a real parent for psychological support. When he grows up, he must give up his parental crutch. This is too much for most people. Consequently, they create an imaginary cosmic father for security. This is why weak people believe in God."

Before you read on, pause and ask yourself how you would respond to Freud's words.

Freud was an Austrian neurologist who founded the practice of psychoanalysis. He is one of many examples of a brilliant scientist (in the field of psychology) who dabbled poorly in philosophy. Freud's mistake was that he analyzed such issues only through the lens of psychology, his area of strength. It is human nature to analyze issues through our own strengths. But wisdom demands that we examine these types of issues through more than just one lens. You cannot resolve philosophical differences solely by means of psychology. Scientists would be wise to refrain from practicing philosophy and philosophers would be wise to refrain from practicing science.

The primary logical fallacy at work in Freud's quote is referred to as the *Psychogenetic Fallacy*. This fallacy is simply when someone claims to have learned the psychological reason why their opponent favors a certain belief and then claim their opponent is psychologically biased; therefore, their opponent's belief must be wrong. However, psychological reasons are seldom, if ever, relevant to whether a widely held philosophical belief is true or false. Evidence and logic support truth, not psychology. The use of psychology in Freud's quote proves nothing either way. In fact, people can believe something that is true and believe it for the wrong reasons. But if their conclusion is true, wrong reasons do not make their conclusion false. For example, even before Christopher Columbus, there were many people who believed the earth was round for all sorts of crazy reasons. Even though their reasons were crazy, it did not mean they were wrong in concluding the planet was indeed round.

The only way to prove an idea is false is to actually prove the idea is false. You don't accomplish this by loosely claiming that everyone who believes that idea is psychologically weak. Not only is that grossly offensive, but it is not supported by available evidence. Philosophical ideas live and die on evidence and logic that either support them or do not. You must have *both* evidence and logic. In addition, in order for a philosophy to be true, it should be relevant to our experience.

C. S. Lewis, the famous novelist and English scholar of Oxford University, once illustrated the importance of evidence over psychology by way of an analogy of a bank account. If you believe that my handwritten ledger balance for my bank account is incorrect, you won't be able to fully test your belief by analyzing my psychological condition. You should test the balances, analyze the bank statements, and confer with reliable third parties. In other words, when testing someone's assertion, you should prove that what they said is wrong before you start trying to explain why you think the person is wrong. By the way, Freud would say that Lewis is an example of one of those supposed "psychologically weak" people who believe in God. But if you examine Lewis' life, his writings, his scholarship, and his reputation, nobody would declare him to be psychologically weak, even by Freud's standards.

Before we leave this subject, I hope you are not thinking that I am concluding that Christians are not weak, because we are. **In fact, who among us, Christian or not, is *not* weak?** In Paul's second letter to the Corinthians, he says, "For the sake of Christ, then, I am content with *weaknesses*, insults, hardships, persecutions, and calamities. For when I am *weak*, then I am strong" (12:10, emphasis added). In 1 Corinthians 1:25-29, Paul shares what God thinks of the weak.

"For the foolishness of God is wiser than men, and the weakness of God is stronger than men. For consider your calling, brothers: not many of you were wise according to worldly standards, not many were powerful, not many were of noble birth. But God chose what is foolish in the world to shame the wise; God chose what is weak in the world to shame the strong; God chose what is low and despised in the world, even things that are not, to bring to nothing things that are, so that no human being might boast in the presence of God."

So do not fall into the trap of claiming strength as your defense. The truth is that we are all psychologically weak, including Freud. In fact, Freud was so psychologically weak that he used his doctor to convince his daughter to assist him in committing his own suicide. But his philosophical misadventures were false not because he was psychologically weak but because they were not supported by evidence, logic, or human experience.

In addition, in some respects, faith is the opposite of knowledge. Hebrews 11:6 says, "Without faith it is impossible to please God." We do not claim to know there is a God, but we believe there is a God, which is supported by the evidence that we know. Our knowledge supports our faith. This type of interplay between faith and knowledge is also true of atheists. In fact, atheists exhibit a very strong faith. Most of them believe that everything was created by nothing—without a shred of evidence or logic supporting such a claim. That kind of faith is admirable merely because it is strong and bold. But in its lack of logic and evidence, atheism is woefully bankrupt. The blindness of atheism is multiplied when they refer to their conclusions as "science" when their ideas have never been subjected to the scientific method. If an idea has never been subjected to the scientific method, it is certainly not science.

Every person—atheist or not—operates on some level of faith. Atheists have faith that they falsely label as science. Christians have faith that we label as faith. As Antony Flew learned, the main difference between their faith and ours is that ours is more adequately supported by logic, evidence, and human experience.

Chapter 17

Is Jesus God or Just a Good Teacher?

How would you respond to that question? Do you see a logical flaw in it? **Were the teachings of Jesus good?**

I was having lunch with a friend during the final weeks leading up to the 2006 national congressional elections. We began to discuss politics. I know that many people say that it is taboo to discuss religion or politics. But I believe that if people can speak with mutual respect and maturity, they should be able to discuss almost anything—even politics or religion. In fact, these two topics represent two of the most intellectual topics that people should be able to maturely discuss. We might be better off discussing them at least to practice our maturity.

Our political discussion moved to the topic of embryonic stem cell research (not to be confused with adult stem cell research). Embryonic stem cell research is a perfect merger of both politics and religion. As you might guess, I was opposed to the idea of this type of research. I will never forget the ultimatum in which my friend tried to trap me. He said, "Either let scientists research embryonic stem cells or you condemn people to years of unnecessary suffering."

His argument was a textbook example of the logical fallacy referred to as a *Faulty Dilemma* (also referred to as the *Either/*

or Fallacy or the *Black-and-White* fallacy). Regardless of the name, look out for this trap. This fallacy is committed when an argument forces you to choose one of only two options or viewpoints to resolve a given issue, even though there are other options. While some issues do have only two options to consider, most have more. And usually when this fallacy occurs, the perpetrator is offering you two bad options. As Shakespeare wrote in *The Taming of the Shrew*, "There's small choice in rotten apples." This fallacy is also referred to as trying to "pigeonhole" people. But as a popular comedian once said, "The only thing that really fits into a pigeonhole is a pigeon."

Many historical atrocities owe their origins to the *Faulty Dilemma*. Racists of every era have used this fallacy by referencing people in one of only two groups, such as whites and non-whites or blacks and non-blacks. Hitler used it in his brand of racism by dividing all people into Aryans and non-Aryans. Communist philosophers like Marx and Lenin were infamous for black-and-white thinking in their reckless waging of class warfare. They commonly referred to the exploiters and the exploited, the haves and have-nots, the bourgeois and proletariat. In all of these cases, mankind has suffered tremendous and irreversible damage. And, yes, Christians have also been guilty of using this fallacious means of argument.

My friend's use of embryonic stem cell research was a modern-day example of the *Faulty Dilemma* because he only offered me two options. Either I support the research and the grotesque devaluing of human life that comes with it, or I condemn victims of Parkinson's disease, etc. to lives of suffering without a cure.

Christians should refuse *both* options. An undeniable truth about the first option is that there is only one source of embryonic stem cells—embryos (human beings) who are intentionally killed. The undeniable truth about the other option is that before the research is conducted, you cannot claim that it will cure or treat anything. Further, the dilemma assumes this type of research is the only chance of treating or curing the disease, which is likely false. In fact, embryonic stem cell research could be just as false a hope as all of the other drugs and research techniques that have failed to deliver cures.

In this discussion, we can pick a third option. I oppose the harvesting of human life for research but support all other known research for the cure and treatment of Parkinson's.

I learned this technique from Jesus' examples of responding to *Faulty Dilemmas* presented by those who opposed him during his earthly ministry, especially Matthew 22:15-22. This passage introduces two examples of the *Faulty Dilemma Fallacy*. Understanding the response of Jesus will help us in responding to the question posed earlier, (Is Jesus God or was he just a good teacher?).

In this passage, the Pharisees approached Jesus and said, "Teacher, we know that you are true and teach the way of God truthfully, and you do not care about anyone's opinion, for you are not swayed by appearances. Tell us, then, what you think. Is it lawful to pay taxes to Caesar, or not?" Jesus immediately saw through their faulty dilemma. They gave Him two bad options. He could either defy Caesar, which would have made Him a criminal. Or, he could side with Caesar, which would have put Him at odds with the people of Israel. In response, Jesus forced them to acknowledge Caesar's inscription on a coin and followed with His now-famous quote, "Therefore render to Caesar the things that are Caesar's, and to God the things that are God's." Once again Jesus wins. More options were available to the issue than just the two the Pharisees offered.

The second example of a faulty dilemma in this passage is implied in how the Pharisees opened their question to Jesus in verse 16. Like the title of this chapter, they tried to flatter Jesus by calling Him a good teacher, thereby subtly refusing to recognize Him as God. This type of insincere flattery of Jesus continues today. In fact, almost everyone today who does not say, "Jesus is God" would probably opt for "Jesus was just a good teacher."

Was Jesus God or just a good teacher? Is this another faulty dilemma? **If people truly believe that Jesus was a good teacher, then why are they often opposed to His teachings? And why don't they believe His teachings about Himself when He claimed to be *God* (see John 8:58, 10:31-33; Mark 14:61-62)? Would a "good" teacher claim to be God when he is not?** To quote C. S. Lewis from his book, *Mere Christianity*, "You can shut Him up for a fool, you can spit at Him and kill Him as a demon, or you can fall at His feet and call Him Lord and God. But let us not come with any patronizing nonsense about His being a great human teacher. He has not left that open to us. He did not intend to."

This example of a faulty dilemma is unlike the embryonic stem cell dilemma, where there were more than two options. The dilemma of Jesus either being God or a good teacher is faulty because He is *both*.

Chapter 18

Who Needs God?

In 1984, Warner Brothers released the movie *The Neverending Story*, which was based upon the widely loved German novel. The main character is a boy reading a mystical book about the world of Fantasia. As he reads, what happens in the real world and in his life slowly alters the story in the book. For example, as the imaginations of people dwindle in the real world, Fantasia similarly disintegrates because Fantasia is built upon the imaginations of people from the real world. The chief villain that is responsible for this destruction of Fantasia is called "the Nothing." This villain's name is clever and mildly jolting to our thinking because it is difficult to imagine that "nothing" can do anything, much less destroy something. The idea that nothing can do something might work in the world of Fantasia, but it will not work in reality. Nevertheless, many still continue to claim that everything was created *by* nothing.

Take Stephen Hawking for example. Hawking is widely considered the smartest man alive today. Born in 1942, this theoretical physicist and cosmologist received degrees from both Oxford University and Cambridge University. In 2009, he was awarded the Presidential Medal of Freedom, the highest civilian award in the United States. He was the Lucasian Professor of Mathematics at the University of Cambridge from 1979 to 2009. He also has a motor neuron disease related to ALS that confines him to a wheelchair. This disease forces him to use a speech-generating device to communicate. He has written several books, most notably *A Brief History of Time* in 1988, and in 2010, *The Grand Design*.

In his last book, he stated the following: "Because there is a law like gravity, the universe can and will create itself from nothing. . . . Spontaneous creation is the reason there is something rather than nothing, why the universe exists, why we exist. It is not necessary to invoke God to light the blue touch paper and set the universe going." In other words, creation does not need God.

Do we need God? Are the laws of science enough to create or re-create the universe? Do you see any logical problems with Hawking's conclusions?

Stephen Hawking is an extremely brilliant man, but I am about to criticize his thought process. As I do this, I freely admit I am nowhere near his level of brilliance and intellect. In comparison, I am simple-minded. His quote, however, is grossly lacking in logic and philosophical principles. It is another example of a brilliant scientist dabbling horribly in philosophy. The primary logical fallacy that Hawking is guilty of using is called *Begging the Question* or *Circular Reasoning.* Simply put, this logical fallacy occurs when someone attempts to use his own conclusion as *proof* of his own conclusion. *Begging the Question* is like tying the parts of your argument to each other, rather than to some objective and independent anchor. Each part of the argument depends upon some other part. Another classic example of *Begging the Question* occurs when a Christian says that God exists because "the Bible tells me so." Then, when someone questions why he should believe the Bible, that same person argues, "Because it was written by

God." Christians, just like everyone else, should refrain from *Circular Reasoning*.

I will highlight the logical flaws in Hawking's conclusion by way of the following questions:

- **How can something (the universe) create anything (including itself) if it does not first exist?**
- **Is it logically possible for something to create itself, especially from nothing?**
- **Isn't the law of gravity something as opposed to nothing?**
- **Can "nothing" create anything?**
- **How in his book, *The Grand Design*, can he admit that the universe is amazingly "designed," but reject the notion of a Designer?**

Hawking has not and likely will not even attempt to answer these basic philosophical questions. The lack of appropriate answers to these questions speaks volumes regarding the lack of appropriate logic in Hawking's conclusion.

Regarding the origins of the universe, most people fall into one of two camps: The universe was created by something, or the universe was created by nothing. The first camp includes all the variations of creationists and intelligent design theorists. The second camp includes Hawking and probably everyone else. It is the second camp that requires more faith than the first. Why? The theory that the universe was created by nothing violates almost every significant law of nature. In order to violate the laws of nature and still be true, a theory would require something outside of nature, or something supernatural. Hawking, however, denies the supernatural!

It is true that Christians believe in a God who is supernatural. Those in the second camp do not, yet they claim this "nothing" has the supernatural abilities to create everything without pre-existing. That is nonsense. **Which is more logical, that God is supernatural, or that nature is supernatural?**

Remember the Law of Identity? Nature by definition cannot be supernatural. Nature is natural.

It was because of this issue that Aristotle developed the concept of the "unmoved mover." He described the "unmoved mover" as the first cause (or "mover") of the universe and all that moves in it. He realized that if you keep applying the Law of Cause and Effect backwards in time, logically you would run into a problem. One cannot go backwards into infinity within the confines of nature because nature is *finite*. For example, even if you believe in the Big Bang theory, you are still left with the scientific problem of determining what caused the Big Bang to happen. It had to start somewhere. Something that was uncaused caused it. "Uncaused" is another word for infinite.

Aristotle called this infinite cause the "unmoved mover." He argued, "There must be an immortal, unchanging being, ultimately responsible for all wholeness and orderliness in the sensible world" (Book 8, *The Physics*). That is another way of saying *supernatural*. Christians call the "unmoved mover" God. People in the second camp call the unmoved mover . . . "nothing." **Which sounds more reasonable to you?**

As Christians, we must recognize when people (including ourselves) are guilty of false logic by way of circular reasoning. We must not allow ourselves to become captive to hollow thinking—even if we must challenge the thinking from the one recognized as the most intelligent person in the world. Yes, we will be accused of believing fairy tales. But, who sounds like they live in Fantasia—Christians or Hawking?

Chapter 19

Comparing Apples and . . . Goats

Several years ago, I was teaching a class on intelligent design theory (IDT). IDT is a nonreligious theory that holds that certain features of the universe and of living things are best explained by an intelligent cause, not an uncaused process. During my lesson, a student interrupted by expressing opposition to my teaching. Since I am a creationist and he claimed to be a neo-Darwinian evolutionist, I knew where he was headed before he started to speak. Instead of directly addressing the IDT-related points that the rest of the class was discussing, he decided to launch into a distracting attack on theistic creationism. While his attack was not directly relevant to IDT, I let him speak. After a while, my only "interjection" was to challenge him to make a summary conclusion. He concluded his argument this way, "The fact that there are birds that swim like fish proves that one evolved from the other."

I was shocked by his conclusion. His arguments seemingly rested on his observations about swimming birds. Later in this chapter, I will share how I responded. It is important to note that this student was well educated. I was grieved by this display of how aggressively parents and school systems are training students to think in such undisciplined ways or not to think for themselves at all. Logic was the furthest thing from this student's agenda.

The logical fallacy used by my student is referred to as a *Misuse of Analogy*. An analogy is used when someone makes a comparison of two things based upon the similarity of features. Simple analogies are often used to help people understand a more complex topic. For example, a government budget is a very complex thing to understand. So, people often use the concept of a family budget as a simple analogy to help others who struggle with the more complex topic.

Analogies are helpful as a bridge to a destination, but they are not a destination. Therefore, all analogies eventually fail. Once they have bridged you to an elementary understanding of the more complex topic, you have to stop using the analogy if you wish to progress in your study. The next step is to then dive deeper into the complex topic in order to master it. No analogy is exactly like the topic you are trying to clarify. In the budget example, a family budget helps you bridge to the more difficult discussion. But a family budget is unlike a government budget in numerous ways. In other words, analogies never prove anything—they merely clarify or partially illustrate. Secondly, an analogy is only useful if the primary similarities are strong and the differences minor.

Therefore, there are two ways to misuse an analogy. The first misuse is to attempt to use the analogy as proof instead of a mere clarification. The second misuse is to use an analogy that has weak similarities and/or strong differences. These misuses can be illustrated by closely examining the student's example mentioned at the beginning of this chapter. First, when asked to make a summary conclusion for his broad positions, he used a narrow analogy as his proof. His analogy was narrow because one example of a possible relationship between two species is not broad enough to support wide conclusions about the origin of all species. Secondly, the similarities of fish and birds swimming are weak and the differences are strong.

To demonstrate the weak similarities and strong differences in his analogy, I will share how I responded. Consistent with my own teachings, I responded with questions. First, I asked him, "**How exactly do these 'birds' in question swim like fish?**" Surprisingly, my student had never pondered this question before, which is probably proof that he had accepted a thought without applying critical thinking or healthy skepticism. All he could offer as an answer was that pelicans dive into the water, move toward their prey using the thrust of their dive, and after they catch their prey in their beaks they float to the top to eat. He would have been better served to use the example of penguins since at least penguins swim deeper than pelicans.

I initiated another question, "**Can you name one fish that uses these swimming techniques?**" He could not. You see, birds don't swim like fish. Birds swim like birds. Fish do not dive from above the water, use the thrust of their dive to propel them toward their prey, catch their prey in their beaks, and then float to the top to eat. In fact, no species of fish exhibit any behaviors even remotely similar to pelicans.

In order for a bird to swim like a fish, it would need to spend more time underwater than just a temporary dive. It would need to propel itself by side-to-side swaying motions with a vertical tail. A bird would also need gills, have the ability to breathe underwater, and be capable of swimming as deeply as a fish instead of as deep as a dive. By comparison, nothing swims quite like a fish. Sea mammals are probably the next best swimmers. The pelican was a horrible analogy. In fact, in many respects, humans swim with much more skill than birds. But my student held that fish and birds were much nearer "cousins" than fish and humans or even fish and sea mammals.

If I logically extend his thinking, all living things that swim are fishlike (the *Reductive Fallacy*, Chapter 15). Comparing the swimming of birds to the swimming of fish is worse than comparing "apples and oranges." It is more like comparing apples and goats. The similarities are weak and the differences are strong. In addition, even if birds did in fact swim like fish, this would still *not* prove that they evolved from each other. Sadly, my student had drawn an illogical conclusion, or assumed one to be true without thinking it through.

In earlier chapters, we discussed how many critics misuse the analogy of mankind and human values to compare and evaluate God. This too is a misuse of analogy (Isaiah 46:5; Psalm 89:6-8). Man cannot be understood without God. And God will never be fully understood by comparisons to man.

When you or someone you are reasoning with uses an analogy, make sure it is a strong one. Then after the analogy has helped bridge you to a destination, you might want to consider "burning the bridge" and making sure the destination stands on its own without analogies.

Chapter 20

The Bible Is Outdated

In May 2012, the state of North Carolina voted to amend its constitution to provide that "marriage between one man and one woman will be the only domestic legal union that shall be valid or recognized." As you can imagine, the debates before and after the vote were fierce, especially with regards to the practice of homosexuality. Three types of debates dominated the discussion including religious, political, and a mixture of the two. With regard to the religious debates, the most shocking were those inside the church itself. Churches may disagree politically, but they should never disagree about whether the Bible is morally outdated. It is truly heartbreaking to hear people *inside* the church claim the Bible is essentially irrelevant today to any degree. I expect this type of thinking from outside the church, but not from within. Be on your guard for this attack is unceasing from all fronts.

Is the Bible outdated or irrelevant today? How would you respond to this question? Do you see a logical flaw in conclusion that the Bible is outdated or irrelevant?

The logical fallacy attempted by this criticism of the Bible is referred to as *Chronological Snobbery. Chronological Snobbery* occurs when someone attempts to dismiss an idea because it is very old. It is a bad assumption that something is false because it is "old" or true because it is "new." Age is not necessarily a test for truth. Some old ideas are true, some new ideas are false, and vice versa.

C. S. Lewis first coined the term *Chronological Snobbery* in his book, *Surprised by Joy.* Lewis defined this fallacy as "the uncritical acceptance of the intellectual climate common to our own age and the assumption that whatever has gone out of date is on that account discredited." In other words, it is when we accept the fashionable values of today in favor of rejecting the values of the past as old without actually refuting them. He went on to counter this fallacy. "You must find out why it went out of date. **Was it ever refuted (and if so by whom, where, and how conclusively) or did it merely die away as fashions do?** If the latter, this tells us nothing about its truth or falsehood" (emphasis added). In short, this fallacy is committed when someone *labels* something as false without actually *proving* that it is.

Chronological Snobbery has never been more widely used than it is today. This is no surprise given the rise of modernism and postmodernism in our Western societies. The name alone—postmodernism—gives it away as a likely user of chronological snobbery. Postmodernism supposedly began more as a cultural mood attempting to break free of old ideas and restraints primarily for the sake of breaking free. It evolved into a movement marked by challenging all authority and following a mindset that rejects absolute truth and embraces moral relativism. Again, as we discussed and refuted in Chapter 12, strict moral relativism is the false position that right or wrong depends on the particular individual, culture, or historical period - there are no absolutes. In our churches, this false thinking has infiltrated in the form of constant challenge to God's truth, usually by convenient reinterpretations of what the Bible says.

The impact of postmodernism was evident in the 2012 religious debates concerning homosexuality. These unfortunate debates are an apt reminder of how postmodernism has ironically come full circle. Its birth was actually recorded in the Bible, and its favorite death wish is directed toward the church. Thousands of years ago in Genesis 3:1, Lucifer (or Satan) asked Eve, "Did God actually say . . .?" It was *then* that postmodernism was truly born. This movement usually takes on varying forms of this same question, which is the ultimate challenge to the ultimate authority. It was the very question that certain Christians were asking from the wrong side of the 2012 religious debates regarding homosexuality.

Deception inside the church usually starts with Christians repeating the talking points of those chiefly opposed to God. God's opponents always attempt to marginalize God's Word. Christians should not be "carrying water" for God's opposition. The answer to the enemy's question is "Yes, God did say that!" God did not stutter. He spoke with clear certainty, in black and white terms, in both Testaments, and in relevant context. To those in the church who wish to debate, God's words are not debatable.

Jesus Himself weighed in on religious chronological snobbery in John 5:46-47: "For if you believed Moses, you would believe me; for he wrote of me. But if you do not believe his writings, how will you believe my words?" It was through these "writings" of Moses that God recorded His law, which clearly forbids any form of practicing homosexuality. God also spoke with equal vigor against any form of heterosexual impropriety as well (Leviticus 20:10). God's opinions were reaffirmed after the new covenant was established in Jesus Christ (see Romans 1:26-27 for one of many examples). To my brothers and sisters in Christ, when you exalt your thinking above God's Word in any way, shape, or form, you are worshiping yourself instead of Him. We must always practice Proverbs 3:5-6 regardless of the prevailing winds of science and culture.

To my friends outside the church, the evidence actually proves that the Bible is not outdated but very relevant today. It is human experience that determines relevancy. **And what book even today exceeds the Bible in addressing and benefiting the condition of humanity?** The fact is that of all the books ever published, the most relevant book today is still the Bible. The best evidence supporting this conclusion is the quantity of Bibles that are published and distributed every year. Over the history of mankind, the total number of Bibles published is estimated to be as many as six billion. Today it is estimated that there are over 100 million Bibles sold annually. And when you include Testaments and Bible portions, the number exceeds 500 million every year. To put this number into perspective, consider the Harry Potter books, the most successful secular books of recent times. Published from 1997 through 2007, the total approximate sales of all of the Harry Potter books combined for all 11 years was approximately 450 million. The Bible's publishing record every year exceeds the entire series of Harry Potter books for all of its 11 years. **Does that sound like the Bible is outdated or irrelevant?**

The late Rudyard Kipling was a famous English poet and storywriter who was awarded the Nobel Prize for Literature in 1907. While he is probably best known for writing *The Jungle Book*, in his day he was famous for his poetry. For example, in 1919 he published the famous poem, "The Gods of the Copybook Headings," which included proverbs like "Water will wet us" and "Fire will burn" that taught virtues, such as honesty or fair dealing. In Great Britain, these proverbs were printed at the top (headings) of the pages of special notebooks called copybooks. Students had to copy these proverbs by hand repeatedly down the page. Kipling's poem foretold the decline of Great Britain. At that time, Great Britain was so vast and powerful it was said that the sun "never sets on the British Empire." Kipling attributed its future downfall to ignoring the old virtues (like the copybook headings) as outdated. His poem described how society instead chased after failed ideas that were repackaged as new or modern. And, each time society crumbled as a result, it could look back to the "Gods of the Copybook Headings" and trace its fall to ignoring their ageless wisdom and truth. This poem just might also predict what will happen to America if we continue to ignore history. I have included Kipling's poem below (pay close attention to the final three stanzas):

"The Gods of the Copybook Headings"
By Rudyard Kipling

AS I PASS through my incarnations in every age and race,
I make my proper prostrations to the Gods of the Market
Place.

Peering through reverent fingers I watch them flourish
and fall,
And the Gods of the Copybook Headings, I notice,
outlast them all.

We were living in trees when they met us. They showed
us each in turn
That Water would certainly wet us, as Fire would certainly burn:
But we found them lacking in Uplift, Vision and Breadth
of Mind,
So we left them to teach the Gorillas while we followed
the March of Mankind.

We moved as the Spirit listed. They never altered their
pace,
Being neither cloud nor wind-borne like the Gods of the
Market Place,
But they always caught up with our progress, and pres-
ently word would come

That a tribe had been wiped off its icefield, or the lights had gone out in Rome.

With the Hopes that our World is built on they were utterly out of touch,
They denied that the Moon was Stilton; they denied she was even Dutch;
They denied that Wishes were Horses; they denied that a Pig had Wings;
So we worshipped the Gods of the Market Who promised these beautiful things.

When the Cambrian measures were forming, they promised perpetual peace.
They swore, if we gave them our weapons, that the wars of the tribes would cease.
But when we disarmed they sold us and delivered us bound to our foe,
And the Gods of the Copybook Headings said: "Stick to the Devil you know."

On the first Feminian Sandstones we were promised the Fuller Life
(Which started by loving our neighbour and ended by loving his wife)
Till our women had no more children and the men lost reason and faith,
And the Gods of the Copybook Headings said: "The Wages of Sin is Death."

In the Carboniferous Epoch we were promised abundance for all,
By robbing selected Peter to pay for collective Paul;
But, though we had plenty of money, there was nothing our money could buy,

And the Gods of the Copybook Headings said: "If you don't work you die."

Then the Gods of the Market tumbled, and their smooth-tongued wizards withdrew
And the hearts of the meanest were humbled and began to believe it was true
That All is not Gold that Glitters, and Two and Two make Four
And the Gods of the Copybook Headings limped up to explain it once more.

As it will be in the future, it was at the birth of Man
There are only four things certain since Social Progress began.
That the Dog returns to his Vomit and the Sow returns to her Mire,
And the burnt Fool's bandaged finger goes wabbling back to the Fire;

And that after this is accomplished, and the brave new world begins
When all men are paid for existing and no man must pay for his sins,
As surely as Water will wet us, as surely as Fire will burn,
The Gods of the Copybook Headings with terror and slaughter return!

And, so went Great Britain just as Kipling predicted. It is not the age of an idea that makes it true or false, but its logic, virtue, and results. Albert Einstein once defined insanity as "doing the same thing over and over again and expecting different results." Postmodernism has ultimately failed us over and over again while God's Word has always prospered us through thousands of years of mankind. To ignore this and the timeless warnings of Kipling is insanity.

Chapter 21

Shooting the Messenger

V ery early in the U.S. presidential campaign of 2012, *The Washington Post* ran a story alleging that Republican candidate, Mitt Romney, hazed a male student in high school 47 years earlier. However, this article and the newspaper ignored the fact that Barack Obama, the Democrat incumbent, admitted to worse acts while in school (bullying, drugs, etc.) in his own autobiography. The truth is that all stories about school-age immaturity should be irrelevant to a presidential campaign. In spite of this truth, *The Washington Post* ran the article anyway. In light of the bias and irrelevancy, the only conclusion is that this was an attempt at "character assassination." The paper probably ran the story in order to artificially lower Romney's favorability among potential voters. This same political technique is used on Christians every day to discredit God's message.

This logical fallacy is referred to as an Argument to the Man. It is defined as attacking the irrelevant personal shortcomings of the man who is giving a message rather than addressing the validity of his message. For example, if someone declared Christianity as false because of the personal shortcomings of an individual Christian, he would be committing this fallacy. The false conclusion is based on the actions of a person, rather than the foundations of the Christian faith. One could easily demonstrate that many atheists (Joseph Stalin for example) have committed horrible crimes against humanity, which would be irrelevant with respect to the truth or falsity of atheism. In fact, we could even show that these crimes were consistent with the main principles of atheism, but that still would not necessarily indict the arguments central to atheism. Again, this fallacy is yet another form of attempting to label something as false without actually proving that it is.

In a political campaign, for instance, the candidate's present moral character is nearly always a relevant issue. Generally, we do not want dishonest political leaders in office. However, the publications on Romney and Obama regarding childhood events are not relevant to this test. In contrast, a lawyer who attacks the testimony of courtroom witnesses by questioning their character or expertise is not necessarily guilty of the argument to the man fallacy either. We expect the attorney to probe into the integrity of a witness. You are only guilty of this fallacy when you make an attack on a man's character that is irrelevant to the thing you really wish to destroy—his message.

The Bible records an interesting example of this fallacy committed by the disciples of Jesus. In Mark 9:38-41, as the disciples approached Jesus, this conversation took place: "John said to him, 'Teacher, we saw someone casting out demons in your name, and we tried to stop him, because he was not following us.' But Jesus said, 'Do not stop him, for no one who does a mighty work in my name will be able soon afterward to speak evil of me. For the one who is not against us is for us. For truly, I say to you, whoever gives you a cup of water to drink because you belong to Christ will by no means lose his reward.'"

Here is an example of someone who was not recognized as a "disciple" casting out demons in the name of Jesus. As the disciples questioned this man's ministry, Jesus corrected them for inappropriately stopping the person. Jesus' point was clear: focus on the *message* and not the *person*.

When others attack you personally, there is a silver lining. The attacks usually mean they are unable to refute your message. They have given up on intellectual reasoning and resorted to personal attacks. If a personal attack is their last resort, you have probably done such a good job of reasoning that your arguments were winning the day. Looking across the course of human history, I cannot think of one example of an *ir*relevant personal attack that was appropriate.

That said, when you are attacked personally, you should avoid the temptation to return the favor. In keeping with the earlier chapters in Section One that dealt with how to defend the faith, attacking someone is never appropriate. Reasoning is our appropriate response. Remember, we are on the defense, not the offense. First Peter 3:9 says, "Do not repay evil for evil or reviling for reviling, but on the contrary, bless, for to this you were called, that you may obtain a blessing." It is very difficult for anyone to reject genuine love in the form of blessings.

When reasoning with others who argue to the man instead of the message, lovingly point them back to the principles of the message. Try to redirect attacks away from the messenger. Still, do so with gentleness and respect: "Let your speech always be gracious, seasoned with salt, so that you may know how you ought to answer each person" (Colossians 4:6).

As those who continually bask in the glorious overflow of God's never-ceasing grace and favor, we have no other inspiration but to likewise pour this grace on those whom God places into the flow of our lives.

Chapter 22

The Majority Never Really Rules

I will never forget the day several years ago when my son came home from school laughing uncontrollably. His teacher was giving a lesson about animals and showed them a video of lemmings following each other over a cliff to their drowning deaths. Lemmings are mouse-like rodents that live primarily in northern European regions and are known for their mass migrations. These migrations sometimes result in mass drowning. As a young boy, my son found this to be hysterically funny. He even had great difficulty telling me about the video because he could not stop laughing. For animal lovers, this would have been a sad video to watch. But for those less sensitive or who are young, it was humorous. What is less humorous, however, is how today many of us behave much like lemmings intellectually.

I work in the pharmaceutical industry. As a result, I work with many highly educated scientists who discuss science constantly. Once, when having lunch with a colleague, the discussion wandered into the origin of the universe. I unintentionally dropped the word "design" into the discussion. My colleague was stunned that I actually believed and supported the notion of creation. He even started to talk down to me as if I needed some instruction like a lesser-educated high school pupil. In my industry, those who hold to design-based theories of origin make up a small minority. The nature of his reaction was borne from disbelief that I would ignore the "obvious consensus of scientific opinion" regarding evolution.

This logical fallacy is referred to as an *Appeal to the People*. It is an attempt to prove something true based upon the number of people who believe it to be true: "If most people, scientists, teachers, etc. believe something, it must be true." Those who argue in such a manner are attempting to establish their position by appealing to popular sentiments instead of relevant evidence. Even if it was popular to believe that 2 + 2 = 5, it would not change the fact that 2 + 2 = 4, even if only a few people believed it. Popular opinion does not necessarily reflect truth by default.

Immanuel Kant once said, "Seek not the favor of the multitude; it is seldom got by honest and lawful means. But seek the testimony of the few and number not voices, but weigh them." That is good advice. As C. S. Lewis was fond of saying, "Counting noses may be a great method of running a government (even there it has limitations), but it is no necessary criterion for truth."

For example, consider what might have been the result if you had taken a poll in Nazi Germany in 1941 on the question, **"Should the Jews be removed from German society?" Would the errant majority in such a poll have proved blatant racism to be righteous?** Today we praise the minority in Germany who opposed the Nazis and tried to help the Jews at the risk of their own lives. And why do we now praise that minority? We praise them because they were right.

In the lunch conversation with my work colleague, I let him speak, followed by my usual round of probing but respectful questions. My questions of him used scientific laws to make him think beyond his posture. **For example, using the Law of**

Cause and Effect, what source caused the existence of the first atom and the material that it was made of? I have never found a challenger who has adequately answered that one in a logical fashion. As a result of this question and other questions, he got very flustered and visibly frustrated. I found a creative way to change the subject. He has not talked down to me since.

This interchange with my colleague highlighted something atheist philosopher Friedrich Nietzsche once said, "Public opinion is nothing but private laziness." In other words, public opinion is a lazy way of thinking. It is a means of avoiding the hard work of independent reasoning by letting other people do your thinking for you. It is never right to conclude something is true based upon the stated positions of the majority. Consensus thinking often leads to incorrect conclusions because it usually refuses to employ critical thinking and healthy skepticism.

Too many times the views of the minority are dismissed as lacking critical thought. But more often, it is the case that the majority is more highly concentrated with people who bypassed critical thinking. This does not mean the minority is always right either. The only way to determine which is right is to use critical thinking and healthy skepticism to appropriately analyze evidence that then leads to a logical conclusion. Not using critical thinking and healthy skepticism is what Nietzsche meant by "private laziness." This is one of the few times that I agree with him. Private laziness is probably why lemmings do what they do.

My personal conclusions in support of creationism are based upon deep archeological and scientific research coupled with highly critical thought. I have researched and answered the question that I posed to my colleague. In contrast, my colleague had apparently never done the same. Rather, he relied on the "obvious consensus of scientific opinion." I have an answer to the cause for nature's existence. Nature's existence requires an eternal Creator whose existence is supernatural and independent of the scientific laws that govern nature.

Every person I have ever encountered in such discussions has always displayed intellectual frustration due to their inability to answer the tougher questions of ultimate origin. Scientific consensus is the crutch that fails them.

The statistical support for creationism in the scientific community is fairly low. In the general population, according to yearly polling by Gallup, over the past 30 years the percentage of Americans who believe that God created human beings pretty much in their present form at one time within the last 10,000 years or so is trending downward from a high of 47% down to a present low of 40%. The trend continues. The number of creationists in America decreases on an annual basis. There is good news, however, minority opinion does not mean wrong opinion.

Jesus also exposed the "appeal to the people" as a fallacy. In Matthew 7:13-14, Jesus said, "Enter by the narrow gate. For the gate is wide and the way is easy that leads to destruction, and those who enter by it are many. For the gate is narrow and the way is hard that leads to life, and those who find it are few." I realize that Jesus' analogy of "the narrow gate" was referring to answering the ultimate philosophical question of whether or not you will follow God, but all answers to the ultimate philosophical question begin with origin. If you answer the questions of origin incorrectly, the path you have chosen does not point in the direction of "the narrow gate." The wrong path points to a wide gate that ultimately leads to a fatal cliff fall from which none have survived. Entering the wrong gate does not mean you cannot later turn back towards the narrow gate. It just means the further you walk the wrong path, the odds that you will turn back are dramatically reduced.

Robert Frost was a famous American poet of the early 20th century who was awarded the Pulitzer Prize for Poetry. I am not sure of his religious positions, but his poetry encourages my faith. My two favorite Frost poems include "God's Garden" and "The Road Not Taken." I encourage you to read both of these short poems together with this chapter. He summed up this discussion well in the famous final stanza of "The Road Not Taken." I have included the poem in its entirety below:

"The Road Not Taken"
By Robert Frost

> Two roads diverged in a yellow wood,
> And sorry I could not travel both
> And be one traveler, long I stood
> And looked down one as far as I could
> To where it bent in the undergrowth;
>
> Then took the other, as just as fair,
> And having perhaps the better claim
> Because it was grassy and wanted wear,
> Though as for that the passing there
> Had worn them really about the same,
>
> And both that morning equally lay
> In leaves no step had trodden black.
> Oh, I marked the first for another day!
> Yet knowing how way leads on to way
> I doubted if I should ever come back.
>
> I shall be telling this with a sigh
> Somewhere ages and ages hence:
> Two roads diverged in a wood, and I,
> I took the one less traveled by,
> And that has made all the difference.

Following God and His Word will place you in the minority. But on this road less traveled, take comfort. You are in good company for this is the road on which Jesus—our God, Creator, and merciful Savior—walks with us.

Chapter 23

You Can't Prove There is a God

S everal years ago, I had been meeting a friend regularly for coffee for the purpose of reasoning together about God and faith. One of those mornings, he brought along a friend who was a stranger to me. I don't normally like to interrupt a longstanding personal dialogue with a newly introduced stranger. But since it was important to my friend, I agreed to proceed. I quickly learned that the stranger was an aggressive atheist. We hardly got two minutes into the conversation when he began to assert aggressively that I was foolish for believing in the God of the Bible. Realizing a brick wall when I see one, I tried to change the subject. Before I could successfully do so, he launched his final attack, "If there is a God, prove it. You can't prove there is a God."

With this attack, the atheist committed a logical fallacy called the *Appeal to Ignorance*. Those who claim they are right just because their opposition is unable to prove an opposing position commit this fallacy. They assume that their position "wins" by default. The idea of any theory winning by "default," however, is foolish. You may be able to win by default in tennis, but not in philosophy. In order to prove your position is right, you actually have to prove your position is right, not just prove that your opposition cannot defend their thesis. Even if winning by default were possible, one would still have to prove that there were only two possible theories that could be correct. If there are more than two, winning by default can never be an option.

It would be silly for a person to claim victory when he had eliminated only one alternative theory while others were not yet addressed. Even if we assume that we have only two possible theories, the failure to prove one does not necessarily prove the other.

The best way to illustrate the *Appeal to Ignorance* is a fallacy is with an analogy of proving guilt in a criminal court case. In the American legal tradition, the accused does not have to prove that he or she is innocent. Rather, the accused is always innocent until proven guilty. In a court of law, we require the prosecution or the accuser to prove guilt beyond reasonable doubt. In fact, the accused has the right of remaining silent. Therefore, the one who asserts (the prosecutor) has the burden of proof. If courts should suddenly shift the burden of proof to the accused, the courts would be committing the logical fallacy of an appeal to ignorance.

In all argumentation it is important that we know where the burden of proof lies. In general, the burden of proof is on the person who makes an assertion. As in the example with my friend, the atheist was making all of the assertions and then asking me to offer proof for my opposing position. It was his duty however to offer proof for his assertions. The burden of proof was actually his and not mine. In the short two minutes of conversation, as you can imagine, I restricted my approach to asking respectful questions. Therefore, I never made any assertions. Questions asked well are not usually received as assertions. This is an additional benefit of the Socratic Method (Chapter 3).

Ironically, I can think of no better example of this in the area of philosophy than an argument famously made by an atheist named Dr. Bertrand Russell. Russell is known for the Celestial Teapot analogy. Russell was a British philosopher, logician, mathematician, and historian as well as a renowned atheist. In 1952, in response to assertive Christians hypothetically trying to pass the burden of proof to their skeptics, Russell wrote that if he claimed that a teapot were orbiting the sun somewhere in space between our planet and Mars, it would be ridiculous for him to expect others to believe him on the grounds that they could not prove him wrong. And, here is one of the few times that I agree with Russell. But this analogy applies to non-Christians in the same measure that it applies to Christians.

However, not too many years after Russell shared this analogy, the late Dr. Stephen J. Gould (1941 – 2002), a Harvard paleontologist, was famously guilty of the same logical error. In responding to whether the theory of evolution is proven true, Gould seriously asserted, "Well, we are here, aren't we?" This statement ignorantly assumes that the theory of evolution is the only possible cause for our existence. His argument would naively hold that evolution must be a fact of life because we exist. Bertrand Russell, if he were alive at the time Gould said it, would beg to differ.

Norman Macbeth, an expert on jurisprudence, points out that many highly trained scientists have a strange difficulty in recognizing the burden of proof when they argue for the theory of evolution. Many champions of evolution assume that because they believe creation has no scientific proof, evolution wins by default. Not only is the assumption that scientific proof is lacking for creation *not* true (covered in detail in Section 8), evolution can never win by default. It can only win if it is true.

When the atheist was attempting to attack me over coffee, I kept reminding myself of Ephesians 4:18: "They are darkened in their understanding, alienated from the life of God because of the *ignorance* that is in them, due to their hardness of heart" (emphasis added). "Ignorance" in this passage is not a negative adjective that means unintelligent as the word is often used in modern speech. "Ignorance" in this verse means what the word actually means—intentionally ignoring something. It is a hardness of the heart that leads to this type of ignorance. And the longer the heart stays hard, the more blind the person becomes to the truth. Only God and His love can soften such hearts and cure such blindness. All we are called to do is simply love and obey.

So, can I prove there is a God? Of course I can't. Neither can anyone prove that there is *not* a God. Either way, this in itself proves nothing. I *believe* there is a God (faith). Everything that I *know* (from extensive study of the evidence even outside the Bible) supports my *faith*. By the way, this book is secondarily meant to support your faith—not prove it. Replacing our faith with knowledge on this side of eternity is not a good thing. Remember the words of Hebrews 11:6, "Without faith it is impossible to please Him."

Resist the temptation to replace all faith with sight. Remember what Jesus told Thomas in John 20:29: "Blessed are those who have not seen and yet have believed." Keep the faith!

Chapter 24

Was 9/11 an Act of Religion?

D r. Richard Dawkins is one of the most outspoken atheists of the 21st century. He is a British evolutionary biologist and author who is a retired fellow of New College in Oxford, England. Prior to that, he was Oxford University's Professor for Public Understanding of Science from 1995–2008. In 2006, he published a famous book, *The God Delusion*, which was a broad attack on religion in general. In interviews promoting the book, Dawkins explained that the terrorist attacks of September 11, 2001 were an act of religion and a good example of the harm that religion causes. He went on to say, "Many of us saw religion as harmless nonsense. Beliefs might lack all supporting evidence but, we thought, if people needed a crutch for consolation, where's the harm? September 11th changed all that."

By claiming that "September 11th changed all that," Dawkins believed the argument changed on that day. But his argument is definitely nothing new and nothing changed. Long before 9/11, critics have used historical atrocities like the Crusades and the Spanish Inquisition as cases against Christianity and religion in general. The Crusades were a series of brutal expeditionary wars blessed by the Catholic Church (from the 11th–13th centuries) with the stated goal of restoring access to the holy places in and near Jerusalem that were under primarily Islamic control. The Spanish Inquisition was a series of 16th-century religious tribunals in Spain marked by the extreme severity and cruelty of its proceedings.

This logical fallacy is referred to as *Special Pleading* or *Selective Reasoning*. *Special pleading* occurs when someone opposes a position by emphasizing the material that confirms their position while neglecting or even denying the obvious material that *disproves* their position. *Special pleading* is more than reasoning from one side of an issue. It is not a logical fallacy to defend your own claims about what is true. Should you choose to address the positions and claims of others, however, you need to be careful that your statements acknowledge the obvious evidence that opposes your arguments.

For example, a witness in a court proceeding must take the oath to tell the whole truth because partial truth can be very misleading. The omission of a single fact can lead to a false verdict. In a story about a terrible train wreck, a certain brakeman testified at a hearing that he had signaled by vigorously waving his lantern. He gestured dramatically to the jury to prove his point. After the questioning was over, he looked relieved and said, "Whew! I was afraid that the other lawyer was going to ask me if the lantern was lighted!"

Extending the horrible acts of modern-day militant Islamic extremists to Christianity as Dawkins indirectly did is more than a stretch. On the other hand, the Crusades and the Spanish Inquisition are fair game when discussing Christianity since the "Christian" church was central to and operative in those events. There is a significant and obvious disconnect between these horrible events in history and the gospel of Jesus Christ. That is, while the "organized church" of that day supported those atrocities, Jesus, himself, did not. In those events, the church was operating politically, even militarily, but not spiritually—it was a tool of the state for the political ends of earthly kings. When that happens, the church is no longer operating as a tool and bride of its one true King, Jesus Christ.

The Crusades and Spanish Inquisition were not evidence of true Christianity in action. Rather, they were examples of sinful humanity at its worst. It is impossible to connect the teachings of Jesus with these actions in history; therefore, it is special pleading to cite these events as proof of Christianity's "errors" while ignoring this clear disconnect. Further, the global church today, which is mostly unbridled from centralized political control, unanimously denounces these events and clearly proclaims that they were disconnected from Jesus and His gospel. And any fair reading of Jesus' own words supports such a conclusion.

Matthew 22:23-33 contains an example of the Sadducees confronting Jesus, but employing *special pleading* as they do. Jesus provides a wonderful example of how to handle such a situation. The Sadducees were a Jewish religious group that did not believe in a future, bodily resurrection, so they asked Jesus a question: "Teacher, Moses said, 'If a man dies having no children, his brother must marry the widow and raise up offspring for his brother.' Now there were seven brothers among us. The first married and died, and having no offspring left his wife to his brother. So too the second and third, down to the seventh. After them all, the woman died. In the resurrection, therefore, of the seven, whose wife will she be? For they all had her."

Their question is an example of special pleading. By posing the hypothetical question, they were ignoring a great deal of biblical evidence. Notice how Jesus responded: "You are wrong, because you know neither the Scriptures nor the power of God. For in the resurrection they neither marry nor are given in marriage, but are like angels in heaven. And as for the resurrection of the dead, have you not read what was said to you by God: 'I am the God of Abraham, and the God of Isaac, and the God of Jacob'? He is not God of the dead, but of the living.' And when the crowd heard it, they were astonished at his teaching."

Jesus exposed the special pleading of the Sadducees by citing the clear examples of scriptural evidence. The Sadducees had chosen to ignore God's own words on the matter.

Interestingly, since the publishing of *The God Delusion*, Dawkins has watered down some of his militant claims. In the 2008 documentary, "Expelled: No Intelligence Allowed," he admitted in an interview with Ben Stein that intelligent design theory (IDT) was actually plausible. Later in 2012, during a lively debate with the Archbishop of Canterbury, he confessed that he was no longer a militant atheist but an agnostic. He admitted, "I can't be sure God does not exist." For this, we should all applaud him and be further encouraged.

To avoid being attacked with special pleading, we should learn to ask the following of others and ourselves, **"And what are the arguments on the other side of this question?"** or **"Have you addressed the problems that are obvious to your position?"** Again, respond with respectful questions and re-member to ask these questions of your own positions before you seek to advance them. Argue with yourself and not others. Make your assertions in the form of respectful questions.

For almost every religion and philosophy, there are ex-amples of followers who committed horrible acts. In most cases, these acts had nothing to do with their religions' claims. Remind those you reason with that discrediting a belief re-quires that you discredit its central claims. In order to discredit central claims, you must evaluate the central figures of each religion and each philosophy along with their claims. In the case of Christianity, that figure is Jesus Christ. Therefore, in order to discredit Christianity, you must discredit Him and His claims. If you are a Christian, take comfort in the truth that discrediting Jesus and His claims has never been done.

Chapter 25

Hitler the Straw Man

As introduced in the previous chapter, in 2008 Ben Stein co-wrote and starred in the documentary "Expelled: No Intelligence Allowed." The movie examined the issue of academic freedom and exposed how there really is no academic freedom when it comes to the teaching of intelligent design theory (IDT). In his response to critics who expressed that teaching IDT is somehow "dangerous," Stein pointed out the dangerous correlation between the central principles of Darwinian evolution and the goals of the Holocaust. As you can imagine, this ignited a firestorm of debates concerning Hitler and Christianity. Stein, who is Jewish, was accused of calling the evolutionists and atheists Nazis. Some of those who reacted to Stein's assertions even claimed Hitler was actually a Christian and that the Holocaust was inspired by his faith.

The logical fallacy committed by both of these extreme accusations is the fallacy of *Extension*, which is also known as "*creating a Straw Man*." In the heat of controversy, most people are often tempted to paint their opponent's position in the worst possible light. The fallacy of extension is committed when someone attempts to "extend" their opponent's true position into something more than it really is and then attack the extension rather than their true position. They create a *Straw Man*, which is not really the opposing position, and then tear down the Straw Man with their arguments and claim philosophical victory. When the Straw Man is destroyed, listeners are inclined to think that the original position was also destroyed. Unfortunately, what has often happened is that the person creating the Straw Man has put words in their opponents' mouths that were never there to begin with. This fallacy pops up in almost every single significant philosophical debate of record.

If someone takes a non-extreme position on an issue, it is very easy to distort their belief so that it looks much more extreme. Here are some examples:

- If you oppose a particular war, you can be accused of pacifism.
- If you oppose gay marriage, you can be accused of hate or phobia.
- If you oppose tax cuts, you can be accused of Marxism.
- If you oppose abortion on demand, you can be accused of misogyny.
- If you oppose gun control, you can be accused of being an anarchist.
- If you oppose expanding Social Security, you can be accused of supporting euthanasia.

All of the above examples are illogical and inappropriate.

The proper defense against the fallacy of extension is to carefully restate the true issue under discussion, making sure that it is not parodied or blown up into another issue. A position stands or falls on its own merits—not those of its parody.

Therefore, with regards to Stein and his documentary, he was incorrectly demonized. First, Stein was responding to aggressive critics claiming that teaching IDT is *dangerous*. It is hypocritical to attack Stein in this manner and be offended when he reciprocates. Regarding the first Straw Man accusation against him, Stein was not calling anyone Nazis, including Darwin. Stein's counterpoint is that Hitler's racism was foundationally built upon the concept of survival of the fittest. Consistent with his family's "religious tradition," Hitler's driving belief was that the Aryan race was superior to all others. Therefore the Aryan race would be right to exterminate the weaker races before they further diluted the Aryan gene pool. In his humanistic and evil ambitions, Hitler believed such a course of action was for the betterment of the human species as a whole. He was wrong on all counts.

With regards to the second Straw Man accusation against Stein, we can draw two conclusions. First, Hitler was certainly not operating under the principles of Jesus Christ or any inspiration from the church. Second, the principles that were his foundation were dangerously correlated with Darwin's theory of the survival of the fittest. This conclusion does not imply that all or even many atheists or evolutionists are Nazis. I have never met an atheist or evolutionist (or any other person for that matter) who would support Hitler's policies in any way whatsoever.

Discussions about Hitler do not answer the questions we are asking. The flawed inspiration of one man does not prove that Darwinian evolution is false. Darwinian evolution is false due to failings of logic and evidence (see Section 8), not due to failings of those who may have been falsely inspired by its principles. Stein was not engaging in the fallacy of extension; he simply demonstrated the fallacious reasoning of men like Dawkins by drawing an obvious philosophical correlation that demonstrated they had created a *Straw Man*

It is blatant absurdity to claim that Christianity inspired Hitler. In my life, I have had numerous discussions involving reasoning through issues of faith with people who opposed me.

I believe I have seen or read about almost every form of attack that can possibly be made. Most of the questions people have about faith are fairly common and reasonable. I say they are reasonable because most of the time people are questioning from an incomplete set of information. Either they are unaware of information that answers their question or they are blinded to it. In either case, it is possible to reason with such people. On the other hand, I have yet to encounter anyone that tries to argue that Hitler's actions were a product of Christian teaching who is open to reason and dialogue. I am not saying these people do not exist. I just haven't found them.

Christians should also refrain from calling people Nazis unless those people actually claim to be Nazis. It is one thing to correlate the dangers of philosophical views with historical events and yet another to accuse the holder of that view of something as extreme as Nazism. Christians should avoid the business of accusation.

Another less provocative example of the fallacy of extension is this famous quote by Jean-Paul Sartre: "The very notion of God is contradictory . . . The theist believes God caused everything. Therefore, God is His own cause, which means that He would have had to exist in order to cause His existence . . . This is impossible." Sartre was a French philosopher, writer, and literary critic and one of the leading figures in the 20th century in the areas of philosophy and Marxism. He was awarded the 1964 Nobel Prize in Literature. In his attack on theism, he was guilty of creating a Straw Man argument.

Christians do not believe God is self-caused, nor do Christians believe that God caused everything. Everything means everything. In other words, everything includes God. Christians actually believe that God is uncaused and infinitely eternal (covered in Section 2). Christians believe that God caused everything *except Himself*. It is entirely illogical for anything to cause its own existence because something that does not exist yet would have to exist in order to cause its existence.

Sartre not only cleverly attempted to put words in Christians' mouths, he made no effort to demonstrate how or where such a conclusion was taught by Christians or the Bible.

The Scriptures provide an example of how to deal with the creation of a Straw Man argument. In Matthew 26:59-61, the Bible records the illegal trial of Jesus: "Now the chief priests and the whole council were seeking false testimony against Jesus that they might put Him to death, but they found none, though many false witnesses came forward. At last two came forward and said, 'This man said, 'I am able to destroy the temple of God, and to rebuild it in three days.'"

How did Jesus respond? He said *nothing*. He did not empower the false accusers with a response. He recognized that the trial was not an opportunity to "reason together." Additionally, he knew that His destiny was the cross and He was willing to receive our guilt in spite of his innocence. Thank you, Lord!

It is important to know what you believe and to anchor your words to those beliefs. If someone accuses a true Christian of being a Nazi, that accuser should be ignored as someone with whom you cannot reason. On the other hand, if someone puts words in your mouth during the course of dialogue, humbly respond by asking, **"When did I say that?"**

Chapter 26

Can't We All Just Get Along?

Have you ever seen the bumper stickers that cleverly use different symbols in place of the individual letters that spell "COEXIST"? These symbols supposedly represent Islam, peace, male/female, Judaism, Wicca/Pagan/Bahai, Taoism/Confucianism, and Christianity. This is probably the most popular symbol for universal "tolerance" today. It's another way of saying, "Can't we all just get along?" While it seems innocent, this phrase has been used many times on Christians to blunt religious conversation—but only in one direction.

The primary logical fallacy committed by such an approach is called *Cliché Thinking*. *Cliché thinking* occurs when someone uses a well-known saying as their proof or position. Webster's Dictionary defines a cliché as "a sentence or phrase, usually expressing a popular or common thought or idea that has lost originality, ingenuity, and impact by long overuse." A cliché should rarely be the basis for an important position.

Far too many of us rely on canned statements like clichés. Granted, clichés have some power to persuade us for a number of reasons—they are pointed, are easily remembered, and often are recognized to contain general wisdom. Most clichés, however, have exceptions and are in need of proof themselves.

Clichés are usually too simple to include exceptions to the rule. Additionally, many clichés exist that oppose other clichés. Consider the following popular proverbs that have become cliché. Each has an opposing proverb that states an exception.

"Many hands make light work," *but* "Too many cooks spoil the broth."

"Great minds think alike," *but* "Fools never differ."

"Haste makes waste," *but* "he who hesitates is lost."

"Nothing ventured, nothing gained," *but* "better to be safe than sorry."

The COEXIST message is equally flawed on multiple levels. The first flaw is on its surface. As if clichés were not shallow enough, this one is a one-word cliché. Even worse, this cliché, taken literally, says nothing at all. Inspiring people to coexist is like inspiring them to breathe. They already do that without effort.

The second flaw of COEXIST is in its ultimate meaning, which is almost never discussed. Coexisting is pretty easy, as long as you do not stop anyone else from existing. The last time I checked, however, there are only one or two groups on the bumper sticker that are truly and deadly militant. Although proponents will claim that the bumper sticker is directed at all of the groups represented, their actions differ. In my own experience, the COEXIST bumper sticker is often directed at nonmilitant Christians and Jews.

The sad irony is that of all the groups listed, only Christians and Jews are today being routinely threatened, jailed, tortured, and killed as martyrs by the thousands on a weekly basis. Regarding martyrs, it is an important side note to recognize that Islamic extremists who use suicide bombs on innocent victims are not martyrs but murderers. A martyr is "a person who willingly suffers death or torture at the hands of others rather than renounce his or her religion." In 2010 alone, almost 160,000 Christians were killed for their faith, and this number does not include those who were threatened, jailed, and tortured. Sadly, the pace is quickening, and this comes with nearly zero outrage from my COEXIST friends. Christians and Jews should be the last groups at which COEXIST should be directed. They should instead be at the top of the list of those recognized as victims. For these reasons alone, the cliché carries little philosophical weight.

In spite of this reality, many still insist upon using COEXIST against Christians or Jews. For some reason, it is widely believed that Christians and Jews make it impossible for everyone to get along. This position ignores the facts. Authentic Christian faith loves every person and does not "wrestle against flesh and blood," but restricts "warfare" to the spiritual realm (Ephesians 6). For this reason, the Christian faith is not physically militant but loving. Therefore, an authentic Christian does not prevent people of other faiths from existing as some other faiths attempt to do.

The third flaw in COEXIST is in its practice. The primary message that is conveyed has very little to do with the word itself and more to do with a false definition of tolerance. The "tolerance" preached by COEXIST is one that tolerates most groups in communicating their moral beliefs, while refusing to tolerate others in doing so. Of course, such an approach is gross hypocrisy. **If you express COEXIST as your moral ideal, on what basis can you urge Christians away from peacefully expressing their moral ideals? If you believe in the ideals of COEXIST, is it logically consistent of you to call others to abandon what their religion calls them to do?**

In contrast, Christian faith is tolerant as long as tolerance is not redefined as changing your own faith to please people who do not like it. The idea of tolerance does not mean that everybody must be recognized as right even when they are not. Sadly, this flawed definition of tolerance is now creeping its way even into the church in the form of urging tolerance of any "god" or any behavior.

For example, I have lost count of how many times Christians incorrectly cite the Apostle Paul as saying, "All things are lawful for me." Many use this verse to defend unwise behavior. The problem is that Paul implied something completely different with that statement. The passage in 1 Corinthians 6:12 actually reads, "'All things are lawful for me,' *but* not all things are helpful. 'All things are lawful for me,' *but* I will not be dominated by anything.'"

Look closely and you will see that the phrase "All things are lawful for me" is in quotation marks. Paul is quoting someone else, not himself. He is actually exposing this quote as a destructive cliché. He was not proclaiming a newfound ideal of spiritual lawlessness. Paul's letter to the church in Corinth addressed many pagan behaviors by its members that were tolerated by the church he had planted there.

He was warning them against their unwise behaviors, not defending them. He was specifically urging them to stop living by worldly clichés and calling them to live by the Spirit and God's Word instead. The context of the verse, clarifies that the guiding standards of spiritual freedom are helpfulness and avoiding domination by anything except God's Spirit. That is a far cry from assuming any behavior is acceptable because "All things are lawful for me."

The remedy for cliché thinking is to translate the saying into practical language. Take for example, "Silence is golden." This cliché loses much of its charm if you express it as "Saying nothing is the best thing to do." **That no longer sounds so worthy to follow in many cases, does it? In the case of "All things are lawful for me," isn't worshiping Satan included in "all things"?** In the case of COEXIST, that too loses its charm if you express it as "believe everyone is right even if they are wrong."

As Christians, we must recognize when cliché thinking has taken the place of sound, logical arguments. We must respond to others with gentleness, respect, and most of all, wisdom.

But inside our own minds, when a cliché is presented, it must be stripped bare and exposed for what it usually is—a shallow thought. We have the mind of Christ, not the mind controlled by Christless sound bites.

Chapter 27

Didn't God Create Evil?

I was teaching a class on the nature of God when one of my students asked, "Didn't God create evil?" I was impressed. I had heard this question before from many who have attacked the faith, but up to that point, I had never heard this genuinely asked by one of my students.

The logical fallacy in this question is a language trick called *Equivocation*. Equivocation occurs when a word has several unequal definitions that are substituted for each other as if they were equal and equally applicable. While this fallacy sounds intentional, many times the person making the argument is unaware he or she has committed such a mistake in logic. Here is an illustration of equivocation that may help the reader understand how it occurs:

1. Nothing is more important than life.
2. Holes in doughnuts are nothing.
3. Therefore, holes in doughnuts are more important than life.

The "nothing" used in #1 has a definition that means almost everything. The "nothing" used in #2 has a definition that actually means "nothing." Then in example #3, the second definition is used *equivocally* for the first statement, an obvious example of *equi*vocation. Ephesians 5:6 gives us a warning about language tricks like equivocation: "Let no one deceive you with empty words, for because of these things the wrath of God comes upon the sons of disobedience."

The opening question is a less obvious example of equivocation. It treats "evil" as an object when in fact "evil" is actually an adjective. In the dictionary, the first and primary definition of evil is an adjective. There are secondary definitions of "evil" as an abstract (nonphysical) noun. But when you read them carefully, you will see that these definitions never describe evil as a separate and willful "thing." Likewise, the Hebrew word for evil is *ra*, which is also primarily an adjective. *Ra* also has secondary noun definitions that are limited to meaning distress, misery, or injury, which are all abstract nouns and not separate and willful "things."

In fact, all definitions for evil in standard dictionaries and the Bible always assume an evildoer. An evildoer is assumed because evil acts do not happen on their own. And, when we say Lucifer (Satan) is evil, we are describing him with an adjective and not a noun. In truth, evil is not a literal beast or separate created being that goes around destroying peoples' lives by wielding a will of its own. By comparison, consider evil's opposite, good. **Is good a separate and willful "thing"?** Of course not and neither is evil.

Evil is the adjective that describes our actions (humans and angels) when we abuse the gift of free will to rebel against God (the Giver). In addition to God giving us free will, He also gave humanity dominion over His physical creation. Since Lucifer is also an angel, "evil" is used to describe his rebellious actions. Sometime after Lucifer's rebellion, we followed in rebellion and surrendered our God-given dominion over the world to Lucifer by submitting to him instead of remaining faithful to God. Evil never describes God's actions. The opening question ignores all of this history by using an abstract noun. By doing so, the question implies that evil is a separate, willful, and created thing so as to trick the listener into thinking God created it since we hold that God created all created things. This language trick is a trap.

To further illustrate how adjectives, abstract nouns, and physical nouns are not equal, consider the adjective "brown." **Have you ever seen the noun "brown" as a separate and physical thing?** Of course not—it is an adjective that describes nouns. You have seen brown mud and brown eyes along with many other nouns that are characterized with color. The only place you can refer to it as a noun is in the abstract (nonphysical) when we refer to it as "the color brown." In this case, it is being referred to as a noun in speech only. And abstract nouns are not observable things apart from nouns that they describe. You have never seen a color without it being an adjective or a trait of an object or noun. In short, adjectives, abstract nouns, and physical nouns cannot be substituted for each other without significantly modifying the question.

We also know that "evil" is not a creation of God from a common sense review of the order of events in Genesis. All of God's original physical creation of the universe ended with the sixth day. After that day, God rested and did not resume original creative activity. By "original," I mean creating man and the universe for the first time as opposed to using the created natural order to create offspring in the days afterward. Genesis 1:31 says, "And God saw everything that He had made, and behold, it was very good. And there was evening and there was morning, the sixth day." Note that "everything" He made in the universe was finished at this point in time. Original creation was completed, and everything He had made "was very good." Therefore, no evil acts by man had yet taken place. God then rested after the completion of His work. Sometime after the seventh day and after original creation, mankind rebelled. Since God had finished His creation on the sixth day, any distortions of His creation thereafter bear the fingerprints of men and angels.

If you insist on thinking of "evil" as a thing, then credit this "thing" to its true creator. If "evil" is a thing (and it's not), then Lucifer and humanity are its creators, not God. Additionally, keep in mind that the fact that God created Lucifer does not change this logic. At the completion of Lucifer's creation, he too had free will and was good.

This discussion reminds me of a famous and possibly true story about a teacher that told his students he could prove that God was evil. The teacher offered, "If God created everything, then he created evil. If he created evil, then he is evil." One of his students raised his hand and asked, "Teacher, does darkness exist?" "Of course it does," replied the teacher. The student followed, "No sir, it does not. According to the laws of physics, darkness does not exist. Darkness is actually just the absence of light. Light is something that we can study, but we are not able to study darkness." The student continued, "Evil also does not exist as a thing as you say. It is similar to darkness. God did not create evil. Evil is what describes our actions when we leave God out of them." The student used a brilliant analogy to make an irrefutable point. Evil, like darkness, is not a separate and willful thing that we can study. However, it does exist as an adjective that describes our rebellious actions.

Chapter 28

Creationists Are Intellectual Baboons

In 1925, the state of Tennessee prosecuted John Thomas Scopes for teaching evolution in his classroom in violation of Tennessee's Butler Act. This landmark case is famously referred to as the Scopes Monkey Trial. What most people today do not realize is that Scopes and his famous attorney, Clarence Darrow, actually lost the trial. The state of Tennessee along with William Jennings Bryan prevailed. But during the course of the trial, Darrow attacked creationists by saying, "We have the purpose of preventing bigots and ignoramuses from controlling the education of the United States." Since then, the tables have turned so radically that science classrooms today teach evolution as fact and practically ban the teaching of creationism as an alternative theory under threat of government prosecution. However, even though Darrow lost the case, his inappropriate attack has only strengthened over time by his successors.

For example, in 2012, after lobbying by the Caleb Foundation (an evangelical lobbying group), the National Trust of Great Britain called for a museum to recognize alternative views (including creationism) on the universe's origins in its exhibitions along with evolution. In response to this decision, Dr. Richard Dawkins said that the National Trust should not have buckled under pressure from the "intellectual baboons of young earth creationism." Dawkins also said that it was regrettable that the Trust had "paid lip service to the ignorant bigotry." "Bigots," "ignoramuses," and "baboons" are the words used from 1925 to today in order to attack those who dare believe in creationism.

The logical fallacy included here is another language trick referred to as emotional language. Emotional language is when people attack a position by using language that is deliberately designed to arouse negative emotions instead of reasoning through the evidence. Such emotional attacks are distasteful no matter who uses them. From Darrow to Dawkins, creationists have continually been labeled as non-intellectuals and incapable of understanding complicated scientific theories. Nothing could be further from the truth.

Usually when emotional language is used, evidence is ignored. For example, below is a list of famous creationists who stand as some of the forefathers of modern science. As you read the list below, ask yourself if these people are "bigots," "ignoramuses," or "baboons":

- Johannes Kepler (1571–1630): Physical astronomer credited with the foundational laws of planetary motion
- Blaise Pascal (1623–1662): Pioneer in projective geometry and inventor of the mechanical calculator
- Robert Boyle (1627–1691): Recognized as the first modern chemist and founder of modern chemistry
- Isaac Newton (1642–1727): Widely regarded as the most influential scientist of all time and formulated the laws of motion and universal gravitation
- Michael Faraday (1791–1867): Discovered electromagnetic induction, diamagnetism, and electrolysis

- Louis Pasteur (1822–1895): Discovered the principles of vaccination, microbial fermentation, and pasteurization (a modern process that bears his name)
- William Thompson also known as Lord Kelvin (1824–1907): Mathematical physicist who contributed to the formulation of the laws of thermodynamics (in his honor absolute temperatures are stated in units of kelvin)
- James Clerk Maxwell (1831–1879): Formulated a set of equations that describe electricity, magnetism, and optics as manifestations of the electromagnetic field

These are just a few of the many examples of Christian intellectuals over the course of scientific history. For a more exhaustive list that includes modern creation scientists, go to www.answersingenesis.org/home/area/bios/. The list of creation scientists that span history is certainly not a list of people to be mocked with emotionally charged epithets. Remember the warning of Ephesians 5:6, "Let no one deceive you with *empty words*, for because of these things the wrath of God comes upon the sons of disobedience" (emphasis added).

It is common in the scientific community for those who believe in evolution to claim some false intellectual higher ground and to speak in a condescending manner to those who disagree with them. The truth is that they have no such higher, intellectual ground. They are no more intelligent and no more intellectual than their creationist counterparts. Evolutionists and creationists are simply looking at the exact same set of incomplete data, yet coming to completely different conclusions as to what the data suggests. Emotional language may stir the pot, but it does not settle the debate.

Another language trick often occurs in debates such as those referenced above. It is known as using *Prestige Jargon*. Prestige jargon is employed when someone takes a potentially simple concept and describes it with large words and compound sentences that artificially make them sound more intelligent or acceptable. Many times, using prestige jargon is also meant to give the false appearance of commanding a higher intellectual ground.

Trying to sound intellectual, however, often gets in the way of teaching and learning. For example, if a professor's highest calling is to educate students, then he or she should do whatever it takes within reason to transfer knowledge to them. The best way to do so is to communicate in terms that are effectively understandable to the highest percentage of students, not the lowest percentage. You can be intellectual and still communicate in ways that others can understand you. In fact, if you are truly intellectual, you should certainly be capable of doing just that. Instead, I find that too often prestige jargon is used in order to hide something. Albert Einstein put it best when he said, "If you can't explain it simply, you don't understand it well enough."

Read the following paragraph and see if you can spot the use of prestige jargon.

"We do respectively petition, request, and entreat that due and adequate provision be made, this day and the date hereinafter subscribed, for the organizing of such methods of allocation and distribution as may be deemed necessary and proper to assure the reception by and for said petitioner of such quantities of baked cereal products as shall, in the judgment of the aforesaid petitioners, constitute a sufficient supply thereof."

Did you figure out what it says? That paragraph says, "Give us today our daily bread." Remember that Jesus created intelligence and "Give us today our daily bread" were His words (Matthew 6:11). The creator of all human intelligence chose a much simpler communication style. When others use unnecessary words, maybe they do not know how to communicate simply. Or, it may mean they are deliberately trying to hide something and/or make you think they are intelligent.

No matter the reason, it is unnecessarily deceptive and not a display of true intellect.

Whenever you hear a position expressed in complicated language, just wait politely until the person is finished and then say, **"Yes, that's interesting, but may we now get down to the evidence?"**

Emotional language and prestige jargon have long been tools of deception against the truth. We must recognize them when they are used, see through them, and respond appropriately. As you do, remember that you represent the one who is the source of all intelligence and science. You are the ambassador of the one who is the smartest of all.

Chapter 29

Are Facts Stubborn or Are People Stubborn?

Many years ago, I was reasoning with a Hindu colleague over lunch. We were discussing some of the principles of Hinduism. I was quite young in my faith and mental maturity at the time. This conversation was my first meaningful one-on-one discussion with a devout Hindu. I asked her to explain to me in her own words the concepts of karma and reincarnation. To paraphrase her, in Hinduism, karma is the destiny that is determined by your own actions in this life—good or bad. Reincarnation is the belief that each soul is reborn after death into a new body/life based upon their karma in the prior body/life. As she described these principles, she was passionate about the importance of life and the preservation of all life including insects and fish.

To be honest, I was startled by her absolute position on all life. I genuinely asked her if, in light of her beliefs, she refrained from killing mosquitoes or taking antibacterial medications. She laughed at me and responded in a way that I will never forget. She said, "Religion has to be practical!" When her stated position was questioned and potentially exposed as faulty, she admitted to the error but continued in her way of thinking.

The logical fallacy committed in this example is referred to as the *Ultimate Fallacy*. This fallacy is committed when a person refuses to accept a position that has been proven true by adequate evidence. The *ultimate fallacy* often is simply a logic error. Sometimes, however, the ultimate fallacy can also reflect a moral error. When this fallacy is expressed in moral error, we call it stubbornness. Frederick Nietzsche, a famous atheist philosopher, was guilty of this fallacy when he admitted famously in his book *Antichrist*, "We deny God as God. If one were to prove this God of the Christians to us, we should be even less able to believe in him." In other words, even if we prove to him that we are right, he would reject it even more. His admission is nothing short of stunning, and it also explains much about the atheistic posture of Nietzsche's works and the suicidal ending to his life.

H. G. Wells, the British science fiction author, felt that it was "in the power of scientists to produce a world encyclopedia for dissemination of their knowledge to all, which [would] compel men to come to terms with one another." As Nietzsche's admission proves and the Bible teaches (Romans 1:16-32), Wells was naive to assume that knowledge would compel anyone. Knowledge does not always compel people to accept the truth. People often know the truth and routinely violate it, ignore it, or suppress it. In fact, the main lesson we learn from history is that we rarely learn from history.

Samuel Johnson said of those who commit the ultimate fallacy, "I have found you an argument; but I am not obliged to find you an understanding." Johnson's response is rather terse, but his response faithfully portrays the old proverb, "You can lead a horse to water, but you can't make him drink."

Returning for a moment to the conversation with my Hindu colleague, I asked her two primary questions. First, **according to what authority must religion be practical? Second,**

shouldn't religion be *true*?" She had no answers at the time. We have lost touch over the years. Looking back, my immature handling of the conversation did not allow me the opportunity to fully understand how she processed our discussion.

Sometime after that conversation, I came across the famous confession of Aldous Huxley. His admission was a revealing display of what most people think who commit the ultimate fallacy. Huxley said, "I had motives for not wanting the world to have meaning; consequently assumed that it had none, and was able without any difficulty to find satisfying reasons for this assumption . . . For myself, as, no doubt, for most of my contemporaries, the philosophy of meaninglessness was essentially an instrument of liberation. The liberation we desired was simultaneously liberation from a certain political and economic system and liberation from a certain system of morality. We objected to the morality because it interfered with our sexual freedom."

In other words, Huxley objected to morality solely because it stood in the way of his desires. How's that for an honest confession? Huxley clarified further by saying, "Most ignorance is vincible ignorance. We don't know because we don't want to know." What Huxley implied was that an error or lie can be just as satisfying as the truth because errors and lies often appeal to our fallen nature.

Consider the introduction of Computer Generated Imaging (CGI) in movies. CGI was not well received many years ago in the initial movies where it was tried. At first, it was mocked because some images looked unrealistic and fake. The reason the images looked fake was because they lacked imperfections. For example, human faces in reality are not perfectly symmetrical. However, early CGI human faces were symmetrical. Therefore, the images were rejected by the imperfect human viewers as fake. Similarly, in philosophy, we have grown so accustomed to error that when faced with perfect truth, our first reaction is often skepticism or rejection.

This mental bias toward imperfection presents us with a dire warning. Even after we have learned about the many common logical fallacies, we must still cultivate the desire to avoid error. Pursuit of perfect truth is our goal. Such a pursuit is not only noble, but it is the only path that promises a destination of intellectual honesty. Knowing how to spot logical fallacies is no guarantee to a life of wisdom or reason. Sir William Drummond, a Scottish politician and philosopher, once said, "He that will not reason is a bigot; he that cannot reason is a fool; and he that dares not reason is a slave." Avoiding this brand of slavery demands a constant pursuit of and compliance with known truth.

One of the starkest examples of such philosophical slavery can be found in Luke 16:19-31. In this passage, Jesus gave us the famous parable of "Lazarus and the Rich Man," which also dealt with the biblical afterlife. In this parable, both Lazarus and the rich man died. In the afterlife, the rich man was burning in judgment while Abraham comforted Lazarus in Paradise. The two were separated by a chasm that they were unable to cross, but they were able to see each other and communicate. The rich man called out to Abraham and begged him to send Lazarus back from the dead to go witness to his family. He wanted his family to repent and avoid the burning judgment.

But in Luke 16:31, we read this chilling response, "He said to him, 'If they do not hear Moses and the Prophets, neither will they be convinced if someone should rise from the dead.'" **How hardened and philosophically enslaved do you have to be to not even be convinced by a man that you watched die and then rise from the dead?** These words reveal the true depth of human stubbornness. It is the ultimate fallacy. Sadly, even though this story of Abraham and Lazarus is a parable, it is not hypothetical.

If you are reasoning with others and they respond by ultimately refusing to accept a position that has been proven true by adequate evidence, take comfort in the fact that you probably did such a good job of reasoning with them that they quit. Unfortunately, it does not mean they are going to change their thinking immediately, but at least you lived up to your commitment to reason with them. Only your commitment to compassion and prayer remain.

Section 5

Evidence the Bible Is the Most Reliable Book of History

F or centuries, critics have attacked the Bible in remarkably predictable ways. These attacks range from claiming that the Bible is merely written by men to claiming the Bible was edited by men and therefore full of errors. The truth is that the Bible is the most historically authentic and reliable book of antiquity. Any contemporary person who attempts arguments against the reliability of Scripture is guilty either of an astounding measure of ignorance or laziness. The purpose of this section is to share just a sample of the evidence that confirms the reliability of the Christian Bible.

In these next chapters, we will show that the Bible is supported as a collection of historically accurate stories. We will continue to look at the evidence from archaeology and how it supports even the more miraculous Bible stories including Noah's ark and the battle of Jericho. We will examine in considerable depth the pervasive display of scientific intellect throughout the Bible that exceeded the knowledge of its simple authors. Lastly, we will show through the discovery of the Dead Sea Scrolls and early church letters how the Bible has remained intact and unedited from its original writing to the copy in your hands or on your shelf.

All the tests scholars use to determine historical reliability have been used against the Bible. It is the most scrutinized work of all time, yet it has never failed to stand up to these tests. In the arena of historical books, God's Word stands as "best in class" even to the extent of being in a class of its own. The Bible is truly the most reliable book of history.

Chapter 30

Isn't the Bible Full of Legends?

I was on a Monday morning flight with two work colleagues when one of them launched us into a discussion about the church service he attended the day before. He was disturbed by the sermon preached in his church. The sermon in question centered on Rob Bell's infamous book, *Love Wins*. In this book, Bell claimed that the idea of a literal and eternal hell was not supported in the Bible. This book was more than sufficiently refuted by Francis Chan in *Erasing Hell*. What disturbed and frustrated my colleague about Bell's book, however, was the fact that a pastor could take an obviously biblical teaching from the very mouth of Jesus Christ and *deny* it. What was more interesting was the reaction of the other colleague to our mutual frustration. This colleague rarely attended church. His response was this, "But, isn't the Bible full of legends?"

In Section 3, I briefly addressed the archaeological evidence supporting stories in the Bible as well as some of the writings of non-biblical authors of those time periods who confirmed the resurrection and miracles of Jesus, proof those stories were not legends. This chapter, however, will focus on the general criteria for how a story typically grows into a legend and how the Bible contrasts with other books of comparable history using these criteria.

The word "legend" is defined as a non-historical or unverifiable story handed down by tradition. Based on this definition alone, the Bible is certainly not a book of legends since it is both historical and verifiable. While difficult to measure consistently, due to living eyewitnesses, stories generally take more than two generations to be exaggerated into legends. Critics of this measure will point to a handful of examples of singular stories that developed into legends over shorter periods of time, but we are not evaluating singular or discreet stories. We are evaluating the Bible, which is a grand anthology of stories spanning thousands of years that is *supported* by eyewitnesses, archaeology, and prophecy. **So, if the development of legends generally requires a time gap of more than two generations between the event and it's recording, then how do biblical writings compare to such a measure?**

We will start with the New Testament, as this is central to the gospel of Jesus Christ. The earliest copies of the main texts of the New Testament are generally dated as follows:

- Matthew: A.D. 70 to 80
- Mark: A.D. 50 to 65
- Luke: A.D. early 60s
- John: A.D. 80 to 100
- Paul's letters: A.D. 55 to 66

Given that the resurrection of Jesus is dated at approximately A.D. 30 to 33, your first reaction might be that time gaps of 20 to 70 years between the events and their earliest recordings seem long. But this initial reaction requires further research and comparison. If we excluded John, the gaps are 20 to 50 years. If we further use only the earlier dates in the ranges, the gaps are 20 to 37 years. Given that a generation is widely understood as approximately 30 years, these gaps are still collectively a far cry from more than two generations (60 years).

The dates of the earliest copies are also not necessarily the dates of the originals. Since we do not have the originals, in many cases we do not know the actual dates of the first writings. Logically, the originals are dated closer to the events than the copies, but we are bound by discipline and conservatism to use the date of the earliest copies for this evaluation.

It is also important to note that these writings were distributed while the eyewitnesses were still alive and therefore able to confirm the written accounts. The primary reason why it usually takes more than two generations for a story to grow into a legend is that exaggerations can go unchecked if the eyewitnesses are deceased. Eyewitness confirmation alone sets the Bible apart from other comparable books of history.

The more important question is how do those "other comparable books of history" compare to the Bible using such measures? How do they contrast with the Bible regarding time gaps for legend development and eyewitness confirmation? Below is a list of comparable works and their time gaps between the events and their earliest recordings:

- Home's *Iliad*: time gap of 400 years
- Livy's *History of Rome*: time gap of 400 to 1,000 years
- Pliny Secundus' *Natural History*: time gap of 750 years
- Caesar's *Gallic Wars*: time gap of 1,000 years
- Tacitus' *Annals*: time gap of 1,000 years
- Thucydides' *History*: time gap of 1,300 years
- Plato (all of his works): time gap of 1,300 years
- Herodotus' *History*: time gap of 1,350 years
- Demosthenes (all of his works): time gap of 1,400 years

Keep in mind that these are some of the best examples from comparable secular history books on which we currently rely. The time gaps only become more distant as you descend the secular list further. You would think critics of the Bible would contrast these time gaps before criticizing the Bible's. **Now, how do you feel about the time gaps for the copies of the New Testament writings?** The Bible's time gaps of less than 20 to 70 years are truly "best in class." Even the most critical scholars have all but conceded that the reliability of the New Testament is beyond all other books of comparable history.

Another nail in the coffin of the legend criticism is the fact that many of the great stories of the Bible have been confirmed by other non-biblical writers of those same time periods. In Section 3, we discussed the non-biblical writings of Flavius Josephus and the Talmud with regards to the resurrection of Jesus and His miracles. On the broader discussion of the entire Bible, however, the list of non-biblical authors is expanded to include Thallus, Pliny the Younger, Emperor Trajan, Lucian, Mara Bar-Serapion, Tacitus, Julius Africanus, Origen, Celsus, the Mishnah, and Pontius Pilate.

Archaeologists have also unearthed in various countries many physical structures on which ancient pagans carved historical records that also agree with the Old Testament accounts. A partial list of such discoveries recorded by pagans is as follows:

- Israel campaign by Pharaoh Shishak (1 Kings 14:25-26) is also recorded on the walls of the Temple of Amun in Thebes, Egypt.
- Revolt of Moab against Israel (2 Kings 1:1, 3:4-27) is also recorded on the Mesha Inscription.
- Fall of Samaria to Sargon II, king of Assyria (2 Kings 17:3-6, 24; 18:9-11), is also recorded on his palace walls.
- Defeat of Ashdod by Sargon II (Isaiah 20:1) is also recorded on his palace walls.

- Campaign of the Assyrian king Sennacherib against Judah (2 Kings 18:13-16) is also recorded on the Taylor Prism.
- Siege of Lachish by Sennacherib (2 Kings 18:14, 17) is also recorded on the Lachish reliefs.
- Assassination of Sennacherib by his own sons (2 Kings 19:37) is also recorded in the annals of his son, Esarhaddon.
- Fall of Nineveh as prophesied (Zephaniah 2:13-15) is also recorded on the Tablet of Nabopolasar.
- Fall of Jerusalem to Nebuchadnezzar (2 Kings 24:10-14) is also recorded in the Babylonian Chronicles.
- Captivity of King Jehoiachin (2 Kings 24:15-16) is also recorded in the Babylonian Ration Records.
- Fall of Babylon to the Medes and Persians (Daniel 5:30-31) is also recorded on the Cyrus Cylinder.
- Freeing of captives in Babylon by Cyrus the Great (Ezra 1:1-4, 6:3-4) is also recorded on the Cyrus Cylinder.

In the discussion with my colleagues, I walked them through some of the facts above. The colleague who asked the question about legends had never heard of any of this evidence. Instead, he had heard the repeated but unsupported attacks on the Bible made by those who surrounded him during his formative years. He was stunned to hear that the Bible had such historical support.

In conclusion, the evidence supports the fact that the Bible is the most reliable book of comparable history known to man. Over the centuries, God's Word has faced its fair share of criticism and passed every test without fail and with high scores making it the valedictorian of history books. If it is a book of legends, then there exists no book of comparable history on which we can rely because all other such books do not even come close to the Bible on every measure of reliability. This is just one more significant way in which our faith is supported by undisputed evidence.

Chapter 31

World Flood Versus World Flood

I n 1996, I advised a company whose factory was flooded by two feet of excessive rainwater during Hurricane Fran. The damage was expensive. They filed a claim with their flood insurance company only to find it was initially denied. The insurance company cleverly replied that although the company was covered for "floods," this was not a "flood." By their definition, a flood is when a body of water overflows, and this water was "surface water looking for a body of water to flow to." My client did not find this humorous. The company fought and won the claim. Before then, I had no idea there was more than one definition of a "flood."

Have you ever been mocked in conversations about the biblical account of Noah's flood? The irony is that there is probably not a soul on our planet who does not admit there was a world flood. I realize that statement sounds too far-reaching—but just bear with me and you will eventually agree. The critics of the Bible criticize it for having a world flood story while at the same time they have created or embraced their own loosely supported world flood story.

Amid the scientific community, most believe that more than 65 million years ago an exploding meteor 6 miles wide hit the Yucatan Peninsula near the Mexican town of Chicxulub leaving a crater 110 miles wide. They claim the impact was so enormous that it blanketed the entire earth with a cloud of dust and ash that the sun was unable to penetrate for approximately 1,000 years. This may not sound like a world flood because there is no mention of water. But, the impact is very similar. You don't need an insurance company to realize that with a meteor ash flood everything is submerged and everything probably dies. If the sun cannot penetrate the global ash cloud for 1,000 years, there would be no photosynthesis and the vast majority of life—if not all life—would eventually cease.

This story has some insurmountable problems, however. First of all, such an extinction of all life would require that evolution start all over again almost from zero. Even atheists agree that global macroevolution (the mutation of species into entirely different species over long periods of time - discussed more fully in Section 8) is statistically very unlikely. In fact, it is either highly improbable or impossible. Believing it happened the first time on a global scale is hard enough. Add to this the belief that 65 million years ago practically all life was supposedly made extinct by this meteor makes it worse. If this meteor ash flood story is true, global macroevolution would had to have happened again and with the same result.

Secondly, the timing of the meteor only allows evolution to happen over the last 65 million years from ground zero, if you will. It is widely held in scientific circles that evolution from nothing to what we have today required several billion years. When you link this meteor ash flood story with the assertion that evolution requires billions of years, a damning inconsistency emerges.

In addition, **if practically all life was made extinct 65 million years ago, then why do we see identical fossils for the same animals existing both before and after this meteor**

ash flood? For example, the scientific community holds that the Coelacanth fish existed almost 400 million years ago, but they also believe this fish was made extinct by the Chicxulub meteor 65 million years ago. This evolutionary speculation sounded reasonable until 1938, when a living Coelacanth was caught off the coast of South Africa. And, in almost 400 million years, it had not evolved in the slightest. **Are we to believe that the Coelecanth took several billion years to evolve, existed 400 million years ago, became extinct 65 million years ago, then re-evolved in its identical form swimming the oceans today?** This is just one of many species that blows holes in evolutionary theory and the assertion of a 1,000 year meteor "ash flood." The meteor ash flood story lacks logical consistency.

Why then did the scientific community create such a bizarre world flood story? They had no other choice. The fossil record is so global and plentiful that it points to a world flood very clearly. Today it is very rare for a fossil to be created. For that to happen, three requirements are needed: death, immediate covering with mud, and ideal uninterrupted conditions for a long period of time. If an animal dies in the woods, it does not become a fossil because it will be eaten, it will decompose, or both will happen. The same is true if a dead animal is buried in soil. The earth, however, is littered with fossil remains on every continent, in every region, both high and low, including fish fossils on mountain peaks.

The fossil record is proof of a world flood. Because this fact is irrefutable, scientists that deny a world-wide flood as described in the Bible were forced to develop a theory to explain the evidence and match the fossil record. The same community that promotes the bizarre meteor ash flood story attacks the Bible's claims of a world flood story.

That said, there is one favor that our friends in the scientific community have done for us. They have reluctantly admitted that the fossil record clearly supports a world flood. **The question is whose flood story does the evidence support?**

We have already discussed just a few of the many reasons why the meteor ash world flood story is illogical and unsupported. Now, let us turn our attention to the evidence for the biblical flood story.

What if Noah's ark had been found? What if pictures and news reports from secular reporters at the site of the ark supported the find? What if that relic matched the dimensions of the ark in the Bible? What if the location and condition of the find matched the Bible and what we would expect of a relic this old? If so, would you be encouraged that the Bible is in fact supported on this subject?

The truth is that Noah's ark probably has been found, but not necessarily on Mount Ararat. For decades, numerous groups have been searching this single mountain for the boat based upon a possible misreading of Genesis. The Bible never said the boat rested on Mount Ararat. Genesis 8:4 says, "The ark came to rest on the mountains of Ararat." Notice that the verse says "mountains" (plural) and not "mountain" (singular). Ararat actually was and is a large region in Turkey with many mountains. This region was named after its largest mountain, Mount Ararat. A boat-shaped object has been found on the slopes of one of the region's other mountains, Doomsday Mountain, a sister mountain approximately 15 miles south of Mount Ararat but still in the Ararat region.

What remained of the lower hull of the alleged boat had been covered over with dirt for hundreds of years, resulting in the wood being mineralized. Like fossils, had this not been covered with dirt, it too would have disintegrated like any other exposed wooden object over thousands of years. A series of earthquakes loosened the soil around it to reveal its form and the grain of the timbered structure. The structure is boat-shaped, symmetrical, and has the approximate dimensions as recorded in the book of Genesis. The mineralized wood was tested and confirmed to have a high concentration of organic carbon, consistent with ancient mineralized wood. Manmade iron deposits were found, tested, and confirmed. When these deposits were mapped on the site, the visible support structure of the boat was further revealed—complete with symmetrical cabins and cages.

Within several miles of the boat are several eight-foot anchor stones, many of which were carved with eight crosses probably representing the eight members of Noah's family who survived the flood. Further, the region is known by local inhabitants as "The Region of the 8," and several neighboring towns and villages are named for parts of the Noah's flood story. The boat and anchor stones are resting several thousand feet above sea level. On June 20, 1987, the Turkish government announced to the world this discovery of Noah's ark and built an official museum next to the site that still stands today. While some have dismissed these claims, the ABC News show *20/20* aired an investigation confirming all of the facts mentioned above, among others. This was followed up by similar confirming investigations by CNN, the Discovery Channel, and TLC. The find is not without controversy, as is the case with most archaeological finds. But the facts stated herein remain consistent.

All archaeological discoveries provide ample opportunities to question because archaeology is almost always an incomplete set of data. Therefore, being a critic of a given discovery is as simple as attacking holes and inconsistencies between claims and pointed assumptions. However, these same opportunities to question exist even more so with the meteor ash world flood story. In fact, there is far less evidence supporting the meteor story than the Noah's ark discovery. The inconsistencies in the meteor ash story are not the result of comparing claims with evidence. Worse than that, its inconsistencies are the result of comparing claims with claims. If critics would apply the same level of scrutiny to the meteor story as they have applied to the Noah's ark discovery, these same critics would have dismissed the meteor ash story first.

The failings of the meteor ash story remind me of when I was raising my younger children. The easiest way to catch my children when they were concealing a wrongdoing was to analyze how they reported the events to me. I would successfully reveal their deceit usually when their story was not plausible, inconsistent and/or lacked appropriate evidence. Like my children's loose-knit cover-up stories, the meteor ash story's fails all three of those tests. This failed story is one of only two predominant stories on how the world was undeniably flooded. The other is the Bible's world flood story, which is plausible, consistent and supported. As are you when you stand up for it even in the face of mockery.

Chapter 32

The Walls of Jericho Found

U ntil the early 1900s, there were many critics of the Bible crowing about why the great city of Jericho and its famous walls had never been found. Before these critics were silenced by archaeological evidence, their criticisms ranged from claiming the story was entirely untrue to the claim that it was just another exaggerated story. This pattern continues to repeat itself even today. A missing city mentioned in the Bible is used as fodder for mockers until archaeology has a chance to silence them.

As mentioned in earlier chapters, archaeology has supported the Bible more than any other book of history. The city and walls of Jericho are no exception. Before we examine the evidence, a reminder of the content of the story will be helpful.

According to Joshua chapter six, after the Israelites marched around the city once a day for six days, on the seventh day they circled the city seven times. After the seventh time around, the priests blew their trumpets, the people shouted, and the walls fell down. The Israelites stormed into the city, raided it, killed almost everyone, and set the city on fire as commanded. One more important detail is that the house of Rahab was rewarded for assisting Israel's spies. Based on the spies' instruction, she hung a scarlet cord from the window of her house, which was built into the wall. With this sign, she was promised protection. Prior to the 1900s, the chief question of critics was "**Does archaeology support the main parts of the Jericho story?** Today, we know that the answer to that question is "yes."

The first major excavation of the site of Jericho was carried out by a German team between 1907 and 1909. This team was the first to find piles of mud bricks at the base of the mound the city was built upon. Later in the 1950s, Kathleen Kenyon, a British archaeologist, also excavated the site using more modern methods. She determined that these bricks were from the city wall that had collapsed when the city was destroyed. Kenyon also found evidence for a massive destruction by fire as in a conquest just as the Bible recorded. She wrote in her excavation report, "The destruction was complete. Walls and floors were blackened or reddened by fire . . . in most rooms the fallen debris was heavily burnt" (Bryant Wood, "Did the Israelites Conquer Jericho? A New Look at the Archaeological Evidence," *Biblical Archaeology Review*, 1990, pg. 56).

In 1997, two Italian archaeologists, Lorenzo Nigro and Nicolo Marchetti, working in concert with the new Palestinian Department of Archaeology, revisited Kenyon's work. While they did not oppose Kenyon's physical conclusions about Jericho and its walls, they took exception with the dating of the destruction. There are many who suspect, however, that these disagreements were meant to disconnect the find from Jewish interests in order to protect Palestinian interests. Regardless of the conclusions about the date of destruction, they were just that—disagreements about the date—*not* about the facts supporting the destruction of Jericho. Regarding the evidence that proves this location is Jericho, as recorded in the Bible, archaeologists agree.

These findings, however, have not stopped the critics. They also have turned their attention to offering up "natural" explanations for the city's destruction, most notable of which is a hypothetical earthquake. But there are more than a few problems with this theory. First, there is no other evidence in the region of such a massive earthquake taking place. Second, it is extremely unlikely that an earthquake would cause the entire city to burn as it did. The burn evidence points to a military conquest.

Third, an earthquake of that magnitude would probably not allow a portion of the city wall on the north side of the site to remain standing while 100% of the rest of the city was reduced to rubble. This part of the ruins points to Rahab. Since Rahab's house, which was part of the wall, was obviously spared while the rest of the city wall fell, these interpretations of the story might explain the remains of a wall section that did not fall. The preserved city wall on the north side of the city was found to have had houses built against it. This evidence supports the biblical account. It does not support the hypothesis of an earthquake.

Interestingly, the destruction of the wall appeared to happen simultaneously. Even for a conquest, this would typically not make physical sense. Conquests usually focused on breaching one part of a city wall because it would have been unnecessary to breach the entire wall. Also after a nation conquered a city, its citizens would want to keep the wall for their own future protection. **And, if a conquest had the goal of destroying the entire wall, then why leave Rahab's portion of the wall standing?** Again, the evidence supports a supernatural destruction of the wall followed by a conquest as recorded in Scripture.

Other problems also plague the earthquake hypothesis. As mentioned earlier, the archaeologists documented that the wall's bricks were found at the base of the mound the city was built upon, which means that the wall was found fallen outward, which is significant at two levels. First, this evidence is inconsistent with what we know about earthquakes, conquests, and the laws of physics. Earthquakes cause structures to collapse inwardly—not outwardly. Likewise, a typical conquest that results in a physical breaching of the city wall would also push walls inwardly.

Biblical evidence paints a picture of the walls falling toward the outside of the structure. Joshua 6:20 reads, "As soon as the people heard the sound of the trumpet, the people shouted a great shout, and the wall fell down flat, so that the people went up into the city, every man straight before him, and they captured the city." The only way for walls to fall "flat" is if they fall outward. If walls fall inward, they collapse into an obstructive pile on top of each other and the buildings close to the walls. The only way for "every" one of the more than 40,000 soldiers and priests (Joshua 4:13) to rush "straight before them" into the city is if the walls fell outward with spaces to rush in as opposed to if they fell inward. This archaeological confirmation of the supernatural is like finding the fingerprint of God.

Once again, archaeology continues to support the biblical record. I am reminded of Luke 19:40, where Jesus responded to the Pharisees who asked Him to silence the praises of his disciples during his triumphant entry into Jerusalem. Jesus responded, "I tell you, if these were silent, the very stones would cry out." If you struggle with the argument that the Bible is not supported adequately, I strongly urge you to become more acquainted with the archaeological record. In addition to other chapters within this book, you might consider reading Randall Price's *The Stones Cry Out: What Archaeology Reveals about the Truth of the Bible.* What you will find is what has already been long established. There is no other book of history that is more supported by archaeology than the Bible. Thanks to archaeology, the "stones" are crying out in frequency and in unison that the Bible, God's Word, is *true.*

For reference, below is a partial list of other documented archaeological finds confirming the Bible's historical reliability:

- The palace at Jericho where Eglon, king of Moab, was assassinated by Ehud (Judges 3:15-30)
- The east gate of Shechem where Gaal and Zebul watched the forces of Abimelech approach the city (Judges 9:34-38)
- The Temple of Baal/El-Berith in Shechem, where funds were obtained to finance Abimelech's kingship and where the citizens of Shechem took refuge when Abimelech attacked the city (Judges 9:4, 46-49)
- The pool of Gibeon where the forces of David and Ishbosheth fought during the struggle for the kingship of Israel (2 Samuel 2:12-32)
- The pools of Heshbon, likened to the eyes of the Shulammite woman (Song of Solomon 7:4)
- The royal palace at Samaria where the kings of Israel lived (1 Kings 20:43, 21:1-2, 22:39; 2 Kings 1:2, 15:25)
- The pool of Samaria where King Ahab's chariot was washed after his death (1 Kings 22:29-38)
- The water tunnel beneath Jerusalem dug by King Hezekiah to provide water during the Assyrian siege (2 Kings 20:20; 2 Chronicles 32:30)
- The royal palace in Babylon where King Belshazzar held the feast and Daniel interpreted the handwriting on the wall (Daniel 5)
- The royal palace in Susa where Esther served as queen of the Persian king, Xerxes (Esther 1:2; 2:3, 5, 9, 16)
- The royal gate at Susa where Mordecai, Esther's cousin, sat (Esther 2:19, 21; 3:2-3; 4:2; 5:9, 13; 6:10, 12)
- The square in front of the royal gate at Susa where Mordecai met with Halthach, Xerxes' eunuch (Esther 4:6)
- The foundation of the synagogue at Capernaum where Jesus cured a man with an unclean spirit (Mark 1:21-28) and delivered the sermon on the bread of life (John 6:25-59)

- The house of Peter at Capernaum where Jesus healed Peter's mother-in-law and others (Matthew 8:14-16)
- Jacob's well where Jesus spoke to the Samaritan woman (John 4)
- The pool of Bethesda in Jerusalem where Jesus healed a crippled man (John 5:1-14)
- The pool of Siloam in Jerusalem where Jesus healed a blind man (John 9:1-4)
- The tribunal at Corinth where Paul was tried (Acts 18:12-17)
- The theater at Ephesus where the riot of silversmiths occurred (Acts 19:29)
- Herod's palace at Caesarea where Paul was kept under guard (Acts 23:33-35)

Chapter 33

Modern Science in the Ancient Bible

Have you ever been in a conversation about God's Word when someone attempted to dismiss the Bible as just another book written by men? Is the Bible just another book written by men? Or was it inspired and breathed by God? If you believe the latter, why do you believe it?

What if it was possible to prove that there is intelligence in the Bible that was beyond the human authors? Modern scientific discoveries are littered throughout its pages. They were later discovered by modern scientific pioneers who were credited with the discoveries. **What does it suggest when uneducated biblical authors write with scientific knowledge that is discovered by man as scientific breakthroughs hundreds and sometimes thousands of years later?** Either these simple authors were scientifically accurate men of their day, or they were writing with knowledge beyond themselves. The modern science in the ancient Bible is proof that it is breathed by God Himself and that the Bible is in fact God's Word.

Approximately 40 authors wrote the 66 books of the Bible over a span of 1,500 years dating as early as the 1400s B.C. to A.D. 100. While some of the authors were intelligent in their day, most were the likes of shepherds, fishermen, soldiers, peasants, tax collectors, poets, and musicians. The closest we come to a biblical author being a scientist is Luke, who was a physician. Keep this fact in mind as we discuss a few of these scientific discoveries penned by these simple and pre-modern men. The natural tendency is to read these discoveries from our current knowledge of science and forget how much more educated we are today than these men who lived in biblical times. **We must take ourselves back to biblical time periods and review what they knew at that time.** Here are just a few of the many examples:

1. In Genesis 2:1-2 we read, "Thus the heavens and the earth were finished, and all the host of them. And on the seventh day God finished his work that he had done, and he rested on the seventh day from all his work that he had done." In 1860, Rudolf Clausius and William Thompson were credited with the First Law of Thermodynamics. This law simply holds that the energy of an isolated system is constant. More simply, the quantity of matter and energy in the universe is always the same. It never decreases or increases but just changes forms. It is "completed." While Moses was not revealing a new scientific law, his writing was consistent with scientific conclusions that were not reached for thousands of years.

2. In Psalm 102:25-26 we read, "Of old you laid the foundation of the earth, and the heavens are the work of your hands. They will perish, but you will remain; they will all wear out like a garment. You will change them like a robe, and they will pass away." In 1824, Sadi Carot was credited with formulating the Second Law of Thermodynamics. This law, also known as entropy, states that systems left to themselves will trend toward disorder. In other words, our system, the universe, is in a constant state of decay. It will "wear out." The

psalmist wrote of this reality centuries before Carot was even born.

3. Jeremiah 33:22 records, "I will make the descendants of David my servant and the Levites who minister before me as countless as the stars of the sky" (NIV). Hundreds of years later in the second century, Ptolemy counted the stars at 1,056, making Jeremiah look seemingly foolish. But in 1608, Galileo invented the telescope. We now know what God meant by the stars being countless. Our galaxy, the Milky Way, is estimated to contain more than 100 billion stars, and the universe is estimated to contain more than 100 billion galaxies. **But how could Jeremiah have known that without a telescope?**

4. Consider Job 38:31, "Can you bind the chains of the Pleiades or loose the cords of Orion?" We now know that of all the constellations, the only ones in which the stars and planets are gravitationally bound to each other are Pleiades, Orion, and Hyades. With regards to the mythical stories of Pleiades and Orion, neither story involves "chains" or "cords." These figurative references are pointing to the bounded characteristics of these particular stars in these particular constellations. In this passage where God is speaking to Job, He is directly revealing science that would not be known until thousands of years later.

5. Job 26:7a teaches that God "spreads out the northern skies over empty space" (NIV). **Did the science of Job's day hold that outer space was empty? Without the ability to explore outer space, how could he have known this scientific fact?** In his lifetime, outer space was believed to be filled with a hypothetical gas like ether. Modern space exploration has confirmed that the majority of space is in fact "empty." Who knew?

Certainly such knowledge was out of reach of a simple farmer like Job.

6. Job 26:7b teaches that God "hangs the earth on nothing." **How could Job, a simple farmer thousands of years ago, know that without more modern knowledge about the cosmos?** In fact, the science or mythology of the day held exactly the opposite—including the heavens being held up by men, or the earth resting on the backs of turtles, and so on. Job is speaking in ways none of his peers could even understand. But thousands of years later, scientists proved him sane.

7. Isaiah 40:22 describes the earth: "It is he who sits above the circle of the earth." Prior to 1492 and Christopher Columbus, most believed that the world was flat and square. **Did you know that Columbus cited this Bible passage as his inspiration?**

8. Luke 17:31-34 teaches us, "On that day, let the one who is on the housetop, with his goods in the house, not come down to take them away, and likewise let the one who is in the field not turn back. Remember Lot's wife. Whoever seeks to preserve his life will lose it, but whoever loses his life will keep it. I tell you, in that night there will be two in one bed. One will be taken and the other left." This is my favorite: Jesus is describing the rapture of the church. We know later from 1 Corinthians 15:52 that the rapture happens in a single "moment" as quickly as a "twinkling of an eye." Yet Jesus refers to this event as happening at both "day" and at "night." Jesus is telling us that the world is round—half shrouded in night while half lit by day at the same time. This fact was not widely known or understood at the time. This is the very fingerprint of God in His Word from the mouth of Jesus.

9. Psalm 8:6-8, "You have given him dominion over the works of your hands; you have put all things under

his feet, all sheep and oxen, and also the beasts of the field, the birds of the heavens, and the fish of the sea, whatever passes along the paths of the seas." **Did you know that Matthew Maury (1806–1873) cited this passage as his inspiration?** Maury was the father of modern oceanography and naval meteorology and the first to map the global sea currents. His nickname was "Pathfinder of the Seas."

10. Ecclesiastes 1:7 records, "All streams run to the sea, but the sea is not full; to the place where the streams flow, there they flow again." Job 36:27-28 says, "For he draws up the drops of water; they distill his mist in rain, which the skies pour down and drop on mankind abundantly." The hydrologic cycle was credited to Bernard Palissy and Pierre Perrault thousands of years later. This cycle describes the continuous movement of water on, above, and below the surface of the earth.

11. Ecclesiastes 1:6 provides further evidence, "The wind blows to the south and goes around to the north; around and around goes the wind, and on its circuits the wind returns." There are six major wind belts that encircle the earth. All six belts move north in the northern summer and south in the northern winter. These wind belts move in circular motions as they cycle the planet. **Given his travel limitations, how could Solomon have even known this without this knowledge being imparted from God?**

12. In Leviticus 17:11, we read, "For the life of the flesh is in the blood." In 1668, Dr. William Harvey discovered that blood carries oxygen and other nutrients required for life throughout the body. After Harvey's discovery, the horrendous practice of bloodletting quickly died out. Before his discovery, doctors used bloodletting because they wrongly believed that blood was one of the four basic substances in the body called humors.

They believed that all diseases and disabilities resulted from an excess or deficiency of one of these four
humors. In attempts to restore health, they would drain
blood from the patient.

13. Leviticus 12:3 records, "And on the eighth day the flesh
of his foreskin shall be circumcised." We now know that
the ideal time for a baby's blood to clot is approximately eight days after birth. **Did Moses learn this through
trial and error or was it revealed by God?** Given the
evidence presented so far, it is clear the latter is true.

14. Consider Leviticus 13:45-46, "The leprous person who
has the disease shall wear torn clothes and let the hair
of his head hang loose, and he shall cover his upper
lip and cry out, 'Unclean, unclean.' He shall remain
unclean as long as he has the disease. He is unclean.
He shall live alone. His dwelling shall be outside the
camp." What Moses is describing is the concept of
quarantine. During the Great Plague of England in the
1500s, concerned Christians started the practice after
consulting this passage in the Bible. Their actions ended
the plague, and quarantine became a modern practice
used to this day.

Is the Bible just written by men? **Does the evidence
suggest that these men had knowledge beyond themselves?**
The examples discussed in this chapter are just a few of the
many modern scientific discoveries in the ancient Bible. For
the critic who insists that the Bible is written solely by men,
these examples are fairly inconvenient. That is probably why
these discoveries are generally avoided as if they don't exist.
The evidence supports the fact that the Bible was breathed
by God with intelligence above these simple and pre-modern
authors. Be confident in your faith in God's Word.

Chapter 34

Was the Bible Edited?

In 2003, Dan Brown published his bestselling novel *The Da Vinci Code*, which was later made into a successful movie. Of course, what most people ignored was the fact that the novel was almost entirely fiction. And the few "facts" that were loosely used could never pass the slightest weight of scrutiny. One of the ridiculous claims made in the book was that the Bible was essentially edited by Emperor Constantine and his Council of Nicaea in order to establish Roman Catholicism as a global religion for controlling the masses. This novel was not the first endeavor at ignoring the facts in a desperate attempt to claim the Bible was scandalously edited.

Can we prove the Bible was not edited? Since it was written so long ago, can we be sure it was not manipulated? How comfortable do you feel that the Bible is historically authentic?

Brown did not invent the false theory of the Bible being edited. It happens to be a popular criticism in atheist and agnostic circles from ages past to today, especially among the educational elite. **But before we address whether or not the Bible was edited, we should ask why so many people claim that it was.** Critics make this claim because they have no other choice. As mentioned in other chapters, the Bible stands alone among books of ancient history when it comes to historical authenticity. To have 66 books written over 1,500 years covering 4,000 years of history by 40 different authors who produced an amazingly consistent story regarding God and the universe would seem to be an impossible task. This reality really forces one to choose from a few possible conclusions: this unlikely compilation is the result of sheer luck, the Bible truly is God's miraculous Word, or the Bible was edited to make it look like it was miraculous. It is reasonable to understand why the biased critic must hold to the last conclusion. **But what does the evidence say?**

The charge of the Bible being edited is based upon two primary premises. First, critics claim that the text was edited in transmission from the originals to us. Second, they claim that the books were selected for inclusion with bias.

With regards to the first criticism, in order to test a document for historical reliability, it is generally agreed that three tests must be employed: the bibliographical test, the internal evidence test, and the external evidence test. The latter two tests are the subject of other chapters. In this chapter, we will focus on the bibliographical test. This test is an examination of how a book's original text was transmitted to us. If the Bible was edited as Brown's novel fictionally claimed, then God's Word would fail this test.

The New Testament alone is preserved in more than 5,600 ancient Greek manuscripts that were consistently copied by hand from the second through fifteenth centuries. In addition, there are more than 10,000 ancient manuscripts in Latin Vulgate and at least 9,300 other early versions, totaling approximately 25,000 ancient manuscript copies of portions of the New Testament in existence today. No other document of historical events comes close to this. The closest competitor is Homer's *Iliad* with only 643 manuscripts that still survive. Many of these New Testament portions are dated prior to the reign of Constantine (A.D. 306) and the Council of Nicaea (A.D. 325). In fact, the early church leaders (also primarily before the reign of Constantine) wrote letters to each other and therein quoted portions of the New Testament. From these written quotes alone, we can re-create the entire New Testament except for a handful of verses. These New Testament texts could not have possibly been edited by Constantine and the Council of Nicaea unless they used a time machine. F. E. Peters is Professor Emeritus of Middle Eastern and Islamic Studies and History at New York University. He summarized the comparisons this way: "On the basis of manuscript tradition alone, the works that made up the Christians' New Testament were the most frequently copied and widely circulated books of antiquity."

How about the Old Testament? With regards to its textual transmission, the critics had free reign in their skepticism until 1947. Between 1947 and 1956, one of the greatest archaeological finds ever was uncovered on the northwestern shore of the Dead Sea. A shepherd boy was exploring some caves in the region and threw a stone into a mysterious cave only to hear a piece of pottery break. Upon further exploration, the boy and later teams of archaeologists found what we today refer to as the Dead Sea Scrolls. Among these scrolls were found approximately 972 manuscripts dated between 150 B.C. and A.D. 70. They were deposited there by ancient Jews and forgotten. Among these manuscripts were copies of the texts of the Hebrew Bible. The texts of the Old Testament books of the Bible were identical to . . . the Bible. Since the Dead Sea Scrolls were deposited in caves over 200 years prior to Constantine, he and the Council of Nicaea could not have possibly edited the Old Testament texts either.

Therefore, the Bible passes the bibliographical test like no other book of history. And if critics wish to cling to their false theories, then they must denounce *every* book of history since none pass this test as clearly as the Bible does. What you have as your copy of the accepted Bible text generally matches the vast majority of the aforementioned manuscripts. In the cases of a handful of minor differences, the earlier manuscripts are used since earlier manuscripts are considered to be more reliable than later manuscripts.

The second criticism claims that the books of the Bible were selected for inclusion with bias. This claim is actually true. Imagine what the critics would say if it were not true. Bias was used in selecting the books, but the bias used was a public bias and not a secret bias. If every book that addressed something to do with biblical events had been included, not only would the book be unmanageably large, but it would also include books of discredited heresy and historically false accounts.

In order for a book to be included in the New Testament, there had to be accepted proof of divine inspiration. In order to prove divine inspiration, the following criteria had to be met: (1) written by an apostle, (2) universally accepted by the early churches, (3) read regularly in early church gatherings, and (4) consistent with other accepted Christian writings. If a work met these requirements, it was considered divinely inspired and therefore included in the Bible. If one of these requirements was not met, it was excluded.

And by the way, with the exception of obvious heresy, exclusion from the Bible did not necessarily mean that the excluded writings were bad or evil. It just meant that they were not found to be divinely inspired. The main comedy of this criticism, however, is that even if the excluded writings were included, the message of Jesus Christ being God and the Savior of the World would remain intact.

The evidence clearly shows that the text of the Bible was not altered as Dan Brown fictionally claimed. But where the critics may have a point is how the Bible has been *verbally* altered by you and me. If you think I have been harsh to Brown and those who ignorantly accept his fiction as fact, you are mistaken. I reserve my harshest criticism for those whom I call spiritual brothers and sisters who daily participate in the fleshly and verbal altering of God's Word and adding to its revelation for their own purposes. Their actions have been much more damaging to the Bible than anything else critics have done. I challenge you to treasure God's entire Word explicitly for what it is—the very breath of God. We would all be better served by erring on the side of reading whole passages of Scripture verbatim, and therefore allowing the Bible to speak for itself.

Section 6

Apparent Contradictions in the Bible Addressed

It is a favorite hobby of many biblical critics to comb through the Bible for contradictions. If they can find a contradiction, then they can persuade others that either the Bible contains errors and/or that it is not God's Word. If they can indict the Bible for errors, then the Bible can be deemed unreliable. Therefore, for hundreds of years, critics have repeatedly recycled the same old criticisms without paying attention to how they have all been repeatedly dismantled. In truth, there are no new criticisms of the Bible that have not already been heard thousands of times and dismissed thousands of times. But every generation marches out with new self-proclaimed heroes opposing the Bible and ready to re-expose what has already been exhaustively vetted. Since this cycle of recycling unsuccessful attacks will likely never cease, this section is devoted to displaying the folly of these efforts. Please know that there has never been a criticism of the Bible that has not been adequately dismissed.

Chapter 35

Does the Bible Contain Contradictions?

Have you ever wondered how Moses was able to record his own death and burial in the Bible? Moses is credited with authoring the first five books of the Bible. If he did, then in Deuteronomy 34:5-7 he apparently recorded his own death and burial. For this reason, I have had many students ask me, "How could Moses write a book that records his own death? Isn't that a contradiction?"

What I have found over the course of my research and teaching this material for many years is this—that if you want to find a contradiction in the Bible, you can easily create one that really isn't there. All you have to do is perform inadequate research before making your conclusion. In other words, if you examine biblical issues with the depth of study that they require, you will find that a seeming contradiction on the surface is not a contradiction beneath the surface. For any matter of high importance, proper research and conclusions must be sufficiently in-depth.

To that end, this chapter includes fifteen guidelines for researching "apparent" contradictions or discrepancies in the Bible. My challenge to those seeking the truth is to research each of the issues you encounter by properly exhausting these guidelines:

1. **The unexplained is not necessarily unexplainable.** For example, how did Moses seemingly record his own death and burial? This is not explained, but it is explainable. Joshua could have easily written this portion of the book as an obituary without compromising Moses' general authorship.

2. **False interpretations do not mean false revelation.** There are passages in the Old Testament that poetically say, "The world is established; it shall never be moved" and "The sun rises, and the sun goes down, and hastens to the place where it rises." This poetry was falsely interpreted by the early church to literally mean that the earth was the center of the universe. As Aristarchus and others later proved, this is scientifically false. The false interpretation has been used by critics to claim that the Bible contains false revelation. The passage is not a false revelation, however, when evaluated in its poetic form. (Also refer to guidelines #6, #10, and #12.)

3. **Understand the context of the passage.** Psalm 14 contains the phrase "there is no God." Using this fragment of a passage, one could claim that the Bible says there is no God. But if you read the entire passage, you will see that the psalmist is quoting a fool.

4. **Interpret difficult or vague passages by using clear ones.** In Philippians 2:12, Paul implores the reader to "work out your own salvation with fear and trembling." These words can be misinterpreted to vaguely imply having to earn your salvation through works. But Ephesians 2:8-9 (and many other passages) clearly say, "For by grace you have been saved through faith. And this is not your own doing; it is the gift of God, not a result of works, so that no one may boast." What we know

from other verses is that Philippians 2:12 was referring to sanctification and not justification. Justification is an immediate and free gift. Sanctification is the subsequent lifelong refinement of our flesh and its behaviors.

5. **Don't base teaching on obscure passages.** In 1 Corinthians 15:29, Paul wrote, "Otherwise, what do people mean by being baptized on behalf of the dead? If the dead are not raised at all, why are people baptized on their behalf?" In this passage, Paul is defending "resurrection" to the Corinthian church by highlighting their errant practice of being baptized for dead people. This was a practice they mingled in from their pagan culture. But Paul is not approving of it. The Mormon Church, however, mistakenly adopted the practice based exclusively on this one obscure verse.

6. **Humans use human expressions.** Isaiah 11:12 references the "the four corners of the earth." This was a common human expression of his day rather than the Bible declaring the earth was flat or square.

7. **Just because a report is incomplete does not mean it is false.** Mark 5 and Luke 8 speak of an encounter with one demoniac, while Matthew 8 records the same event mentioning two demoniacs. Mark and Luke were likely using the firsthand report of the incident and giving a partial report that focuses on the more prominent demoniac of the two. All three accounts are complementary and supply more information when taken together.

8. **New Testament citations of the Old Testament do not need to be exact.** In John 19:37, John paraphrases Zechariah 12:10-11 by saying, "They will look on him whom they have pierced." The exact wording from Zechariah is "when they look on me, on him whom they have pierced." There is no factual contradiction in the paraphrase.

9. **The Bible does not necessarily approve of all it records.** For example, the Bible records various men of God practicing polygamy, but God opposes polygamy (such as Corinthians 7:2).

10. **The Bible uses non-technical, everyday language.** In Joshua 10:12, Joshua commanded the sun to "stand still." While his command sounds unscientific, this is no more unscientific than to refer to the sun "rising." Modern-day meteorologists and most humans for that matter still refer to daily events like "sunrise" and "sunset."

11. **The Bible may use round numbers.** Second Chronicles 4:2 records the measurements of a basin in the temple: "It was round, ten cubits from brim to brim . . . and a line of thirty cubits measured its circumference." We know from geometry that circumference divided by diameter equals the number "π" (or "pi"), which is approximately 3.14. From the passage, "thirty" divided by "ten" equals exactly 3. This passage, however, was not attempting to refer to a perfect circle or establish geometric principles. The fixture could have simply been an oval, which is also round but does not conform to pi.

12. **Note when the Bible uses different literary devices.** When Psalm 36:7 speaks of us resting under the shadow of God's "wings," the psalmist is not referring to God literally as a winged being.

13. **An error in a copy does not mean an error in the original.** When we refer to the inerrancy of Scripture, we are referring to the originals and not necessarily the copies. For example, in a few cases, biblical scholars have later discovered an older copy that does not contain a verse that was later added to a newer copy. They had relied on the newer copy until they discovered the older copy. In the NIV translation, there are

17 such verses that are excluded in the New Testament (such as Matthew 17:21). In all 17 cases, doctrine is not affected when these verses are left out of the NIV.

14. **General statements don't necessarily mean universal promises.** Proverbs 16:7 says, "When a man's ways please the Lord, He makes even his enemies to be at peace with him." Obviously this did not happen for Jesus Christ or the Apostle Paul as they were executed by their enemies.

15. **Newer revelation supersedes older revelation.** When God created the human race, He commanded that they eat only fruit and vegetables (Genesis 1:29). But later, when conditions changed after the flood, God permitted them to also eat meat (Genesis 9:3). This change is progressive revelation, and not a contradiction.

If you can research biblical issues while reasonably honoring these fifteen guidelines coupled with common sense and healthy skepticism, you should arrive at reasonable and in-depth conclusions. These next chapters will not go through all of the Biblical issues ever raised, but we will discuss a few in order to illustrate these fifteen guidelines. The rest of the research, as always, is up to you.

I have been researching "biblical contradictions" for decades. Without exception, not one of them would alter the message of the Bible, its doctrines, or the gospel of Jesus Christ. They have also all been shown to not be contradictions, but mostly surface misunderstandings. I can understand imperfect humans presuming that God's Word being "penned" by man is likewise imperfect. Imperfection is a key part of our present human existence. But when characterizing God and His Word, proper research has not and will not allow such a presumption to stick.

Chapter 36

Does the Bible Have Two Conflicting Creation Stories?

I had a former student return to my class one day for advice. He had just heard something from his fellow students in a secular college Bible class "proving" an "obvious contradiction" in the Bible. His fellow students had claimed that the order of creation events in Genesis 1 contradicted the order described in Genesis 2. In their opinion, the two accounts apparently have the creation sequence listed in differing orders. Among other things, they pointed out that Genesis 1 described how plant life was created on Day 3 and humans were created on Day 6. In contrast, Genesis 2:5-7 states the following: "When no bush of the field was yet in the land and no small plant of the field had yet sprung up—for the Lord God had not caused it to rain on the land, and there was no man to work the ground, and a mist was going up from the land and was watering the whole face of the ground—then the Lord God formed the man of dust from the ground and breathed into his nostrils the breath of life, and the man became a living creature."

Therefore, in their opinion, Genesis 2 implies that humans were created before these bushes and plants, which seems to be in contradiction with Genesis 1.

In the previous chapter, I shared fifteen guidelines for properly researching "apparent" biblical contradictions or discrepancies. In this chapter, we will examine together this popular contradiction about two creation stories by using a more detailed analysis thereby modeling a thorough research approach. This issue seems like a discrepancy in the Bible, but once you dig deeper, you will quickly find that it is not.

The first step is to read the context of the verses in each chapter. It is important to gain an understanding of the obvious purpose of each passage. Also be sure to note how each passage complements one another instead of contradicting one another.

Genesis 1 is a chronology of all six days of God's creation of the entire universe from beginning to end. Genesis 2, however, is not a chronology at all; it is simply a detailed flashback to Day 6. Remember that Day 6 was the climax of creation. Genesis 2 does not even address Days 1 through 5. Since these days are not addressed, the obvious conclusion is that Genesis 2 cannot serve as a chronology. Rather, it is only a detailed narrative of that one day. And, more specifically, what Genesis 2 is detailing is the creation of the Garden of Eden and how God filled it with man, bushes, and plants. It is nothing more than that. It is not a narrative addressing the creation of the entire universe or even the entire earth.

To illustrate this point further, Genesis 2 says nothing about the creation of the heavens and the earth, the atmosphere, the seas, the land, the sun, the stars, the moon, or the sea creatures. The exclusion of these other creations supports the fact that the focus of the chapter is narrowly upon the creation confined to the Garden of Eden. By comparison, to illustrate how Genesis 1 has a much broader focus, Adam and Eve are not even mentioned by name. The naming of Adam and Eve is left to later chapters that elaborate further. Genesis 1 also never mentions the Garden of Eden because the author knows this will be discussed in Genesis 2. And, Genesis 2 mentions only things directly related to the creation of the Garden, Adam and Eve, and the life in the Garden God prepared especially for them.

In fact, Genesis 2:1 opens by bridging the reader from Genesis 1 by saying, "Thus the heavens and the earth were finished, and all the host of them. And on the seventh day God finished his work that he had done, and he rested on the seventh day from all his work that he had done." Clearly, the author is not signaling to the reader that he is about to repeat the whole of Genesis 1 with the verses that follow. Any clear, complete, and reasonable reading of both chapters leads to these conclusions. The two chapters are meant to complement one another and that is precisely what they do.

Now, more reasonable critics will probably concede that Genesis 2 is not a chronology, but they might continue that it still shares facts that seem to contradict Genesis 1. This brings us to the mention of the "bushes" and "plants." Notice that the discussion in Genesis 2:5 is restricted to only those bushes and plants "of the field" that needed a man to tend them. In contrast, Genesis 1:12 refers to *all* plant life, not just those of the field. The broader creation of all plant life in Genesis 1 included trees, plants, and others that did not require the help of mankind. This is clear evidence that Genesis 2 is strictly dealing with the Garden of Eden and not the entire earth. Since Genesis 2 is covering only the Garden of Eden, this flashback does not preclude these same "bushes of the field" and "plants of the field" already existing outside the Garden on Day 3. In addition to their being created on Day 3, God chose to not plant them inside the Garden until Day 6 or thereafter.

The other word in Genesis 2:5 that is misunderstood by critics is "land." This is the Hebrew word for soil in the context of the Garden, and not a reference to all land on the entire earth as the criticism implies. This fact is further supported by the limited reference to only bushes and plants of the field. If this reference to land referred to the entire earth, the reference to bushes and plants should have been much broader. This is not the only Hebrew word in this passage that causes problems for those who don't research further than the surface. But each and every Hebrew word is just as easily explained.

Lastly, let's not forget that both chapters have the same author: Moses. Moses was educated as a prince in Pharaoh's palace for the first 40 years of his life and then received a personal education by God Himself for another 40 years. He was not so stupid as to contradict himself on the second page.

In conclusion, the sum of the evidence is very clear. Genesis 1 and 2 do not contradict each other; in fact, they complement each other. On this controversy, one thing I can say in defense of the atheist scholars that I follow is that this is not a contradiction that they generally are willing to argue. **In light of that, what does it say when "students" tout this issue while their atheist professors generally won't?** Here is where I give credit where credit is due. With only a few exceptions, on this topic, my atheist counterparts have dismissed this criticism because they have done their research. I challenge every Christian and every person to similarly perform adequate research before jumping to such conclusions.

Chapter 37

Bible Contradictions – The Top Ten

B laise Pascal, the French mathematician and physicist, once said, "Contradiction is not a sign of falsity, nor the lack of contradiction a sign of truth." Depending on the subject, that may or may not be true. But how does Pascal's quote apply to so-called "contradictions" in the Bible?

In prior chapters we demonstrated that the "apparent" contradictions in the Bible are not contradictions at all, not when adequately researched and understood. In this chapter, I will address the *Top Ten* contradictions I have encountered. These are the ones that seem to be repeated the most by critics of the Bible. From this sample, you will begin to understand how inadequate research leads to false conclusions. You will also see a model for how to mentally process such issues. For the sake of brevity, I will only dismiss each one in a summary fashion. Of course, my complete responses would be much more detailed as in the prior chapter, but I hope you still find my summary approach helpful.

The Most Repeated Claims of Contradictions in the Bible:

1. "The creation accounts of Genesis 1 and Genesis 2 conflict with one another?

Answer: We addressed this contradiction in Chapter 36.

2. Where did Cain find a wife if God created only Adam and Eve, who only had two sons?

Answer: Cain probably married one of his many sisters. Remember, incest was not forbidden by God's command until centuries later. Also, human lives spanned up to 969 years (Genesis 5:27) at that time, which allowed for much more procreation over much longer generations. Lastly, contrary to popular misreading of Scripture, Cain did not find his wife in Nod but was married *before* migrating there (Genesis 4:16-17).

3. In one place the Bible says Noah took one pair of animals on the ark (Gen 6:19), in another it says he took seven pairs. How many pairs of animals did Noah take on the ark?

Answer: These adjacent passages clearly point out that Noah brought one pair of every "unclean" animal and seven pairs of every "clean" animal. Chapters 6 and 7 are two sequential parts of the story that should not be separated from each other.

4. Moses said, "Eye for an eye," but Jesus said, "Turn the other cheek." Which is correct?

Answer: Moses was writing the law for the national theocratic government of Israel. Jesus was addressing individual followers, not the government. Jesus implored followers to individually behave with holiness that exceeds the minimum of the law. For example, Jesus implored us not to just avoid committing adultery as the law provides. Rather, he taught us that commandment applied to lust as well.

5. If God is good, why did he command the Israelites to kill an entire people group (the Canaanites)?

Answer: This question implies that man can judge God and that man determines good and evil. Both are false. God determines good and evil, not man. Man is incapable of properly judging man, much less God. No reality exists where a creator answers to his creation. God is also not bound by the law that He gave to His creation to govern it. He is above all law. Therefore, all that He decides to do is always right and by definition can never be wrong. God is the giver and taker of all life. He did not just approve of killing the Canaanites. He has approved and presided over the taking of every life that has ever been taken and ever will be taken. This was His forewarned consequence that we opted for when we rebelled against Him. God is justly following through with the option we chose. He also takes life in various ways. Some He allows to die in their sleep, others by disease, and the Canaanites by the sword. The manner in which God allows a life to be taken in this temporary world is not something that we should place levels of value upon. Only the manner in which we live should be valued in such a way. Everyone enters eternity through the same filter (judgment) where they won't be concerned with how they died, since all of their concern will be reserved for how they lived. Physical death is not the ultimate punishment. The true and eternal punishment awaits in the afterlife. I am sure that as we speak, the Canaanites, awaiting eternal punishment, are not crying foul about their manner of death. Neither should we.

6. How can God forgive some people of major sins (David) and not others of minor sins (Lot's wife)?

Answer: There is no evidence that Lot's wife was either forgiven or unforgiven. God is good, and man has never been a righteous judge of that which is good. Every such question and answer must assume an eternal perspective coupled with the sovereignty of God. God has mercy on whom He chooses to have mercy and takes life when He chooses to take it. We are unable to properly judge His actions because we are not God and know only a small fraction of the story. God is God; He alone knows the full story. The death of Lot's wife was an earthly consequence of her sin, which in reality was far less consequential than those David faced for his sins. But again, everyone enters eternity through the same filter (judgment) where they won't be concerned with how they died, since all of their concern will be reserved for how they lived. We do not know Lot's wife's ultimate judgment. If an eternity in heaven awaits her, she is forgiven and she might see her "untimely" death as a favor. If eternal punishment awaits her, I am sure she is not complaining about her manner of death. Her manner of death is overshadowed by her eternal residence.

7. How could both God (2 Samuel 24:1) and Lucifer (1 Chronicles 21:1) incite David to conduct the same census?

Answer: Adam and Eve gave Lucifer temporary dominion over this world, but he has no dominion over God. Lucifer is still unable to act beyond that which God's sovereignty allows. God first desired to incite David to conduct a census to reveal David's pride and to discipline him for it. God used Lucifer to carry it out. The desired result of David's humility was achieved. God can use everything and everyone to His ultimate ends.

8. Why is Luke's genealogy of Jesus different from Matthew's?

Answer: They are two different but complementary genealogies. Matthew's genealogy is the genealogy of Joseph. Luke's genealogy is the genealogy of Mary. This is not a contradiction.

9. How did Judas die—by hanging himself (Matthew 27:5) or by falling on rocks (Acts 1:18)?

Answer: Judas died by hanging himself. He was left there as cursed, and no one was willing to remove him. Eventually, his rotting body fell upon rocks and burst open as described. But the hanging certainly killed him. The Acts passage never claimed a cause of death, just the demise of his dead body.

10. Why are there differences in the post-resurrection accounts of Jesus between the gospels?

Answer: They are different because the accounts are from different points of view. Each of the different accounts, however, complements the others like a harmony. Ironically, had each account been identical, this would have certainly incited criticisms about the lack of objectivity and authenticity.

Other "contradictions" that I have not addressed also fall short for similar reasons to these Top Ten. Attacking the Bible by citing apparent contradictions is nothing new; it has been going on for centuries. And people will continue to repeat the same attacks as if they are something new. But as Solomon said in Ecclesiastes 1:9b, "There is nothing new under the sun." That statement certainly applies to this issue. Yes, the same attacks get recycled, but I have yet to find one attack that equates to a "smoking gun" that disproves the Bible.

In addition to the Bible being the most corroborated book of history and spirituality known to man, it also happens to be the most consistent as well.

Chapter 38

Does the Bible Approve of Slavery?

When it comes to the issue of the Bible and slavery, one of the most popular attacks involves Exodus 21:7-11. Many accusers claim that this portion of Mosaic Law instructed the Israelites on how to sell their children as sex slaves to other men. This attack has led many believers into doubt. But, such doubt and the criticism that inspires it are grossly misplaced.

Claiming that the Bible approves of slavery may be the most distorted of all the attacks from critics. They process this attack by using this very narrow stereotype of historical slavery, specifically when Western nations were stealing Africans against their will in order for them to serve in subhuman conditions as forced labor for pre-Abolition plantation owners. But westernized slavery in the sixteenth-nineteenth century is by no means a complete picture of all types of slavery—either in the past or the present. In order to properly address this issue, we need to make sure our definition is the same as that used in the Bible. In this chapter, we will clarify God's position on the subject by using His own words.

In an earlier chapter, I shared fifteen guidelines for adequately researching biblical "contradictions." On the topic of slavery, we will focus on three of those guidelines:

- Understand the context of the passage (#3).
- Interpret difficult or vague passages by using clear ones (#4).
- The Bible does not necessarily approve of all it records (#9).

By using these guidelines, we will focus on the most frequent attacks on Bible passages regarding slavery, including Exodus 21, Leviticus 25, Ephesians 6, 1 Timothy 6, and Luke 12. The first truth to understand is that God hates slavery. The entire message of God is the good news of the gospel of Jesus Christ that frees mankind from our chosen bondage to sin. God is constantly and willingly setting people free from all bondage, and He has never changed.

During the years prior to and after the giving of the Mosaic Law, the Israelites rebelled against God and adopted pagan behaviors from the nations surrounding them. In fact, the most famous mention of slavery in the Bible is when the Egyptians brutally enslaved the Israelites for 400 years prior to the giving of the Mosaic Law. The resulting plagues that God unleashed on the Egyptians recorded in Exodus 7-11 offer a clear indication of God's sharp disapproval of slavery. That said, from these foreign influences the Israelites learned about slavery, polygamy, and many other vices. Unfortunately, they adopted these practices into their own culture against God's warning, and God's disapproval was the result.

In biblical times, there were various types of slavery that fall into one of two broad categories: involuntary and voluntary. The more modern stereotype of African slaves is one example of involuntary slavery. But in biblical times, voluntary slavery was very common. People even sold themselves as slaves to creditors when they could not pay their debts. This is an example referred to as "indentured slavery." Sometimes doctors, lawyers, and even politicians were slaves of others. In addition, some people actually volunteered to be slaves so as to have all their needs met by wealthy people. This is certainly not identical to an involuntary slave.

Before we evaluate voluntary slavery with the fervor we rightfully direct at involuntary slavery, consider the obvious implications for voluntary live-in maids and other forms of voluntary servants in both past and present cultures. These were included in the biblical definition of a "slave" or "servant." And to illustrate God's providence toward even voluntary slaves, God forced the Israelites to free them within seven years or in the Year of Jubilee, whichever came first, regardless of whether they had an unpaid debt. It was also common for voluntary slaves to request to remain as slaves and reject freedom. The Bible even gives guidance for these occurrences as well.

But more to the point, God's Word specifically condemns the practice of "man-stealing" in Exodus 21:16: "Whoever steals a man and sells him, and anyone found in possession of him, shall be put to death." Similarly, in 1 Timothy 1:8-10, slave traders are described as "ungodly and sinful," and they are listed in the same category as parent killers, murderers, and adulterers. God clearly opposes such slavery. These verses also begin exposing the distortion in the opening attack because those who sell their children as sex slaves would certainly violate these two passages, among others.

Many have also attacked the Bible because it instructs slaves in maintaining a good attitude toward their masters, which is often distorted as biblical approval of involuntary slavery. But the Bible likewise instructs an innocent prisoner to have a good attitude toward his warden and his government. Nobody modeled this better than Jesus Himself. Therefore, the Bible instructing us to keep a good attitude in the face of injustice does not mean that the Bible approves of that injustice.

With that background, we now more directly address the opening accusation regarding the passage in Exodus 21:7-11. This passage is certainly not an example of sexual trafficking of children. Rather, it is a reference more likened to the ancient custom of paying a reverse dowry for an arranged betrothal and marriage. The rules for these customs in the surrounding passages clearly support that interpretation over the distortion.

But since we are on the subject, let's focus on the biggest plight on mankind regarding slavery today: prostitution. Prostitution is arguably the largest final frontier of modern slavery abolition. The following facts easily support this assertion:

According to the United Labor Organization, up to 96% of women in prostitution want to escape but are trapped against their will regardless of whether they voluntarily entered the practice.

Involuntary entry into prostitution begins with human trafficking. Human trafficking obtains the "product," and prostitution and pornography is where the "product" is sold.

According to the United Nations, human trafficking is a $58 billion-per-year industry across 161 countries.

According to the U.S. Department of Justice, the average age of entry into commercial sex slavery in the United States is 13 years old.

According to UNICEF, a child is trafficked every 30 seconds.

According to the Internet Filter Review, pornography is also a $96 billion-per-year industry.

Today more than 27 million people are otherwise enslaved around the world. This is more than double the number of Africans enslaved during the Trans-Atlantic slave trade.

There are approximately 40 million women trapped and enslaved in prostitution where it is legal and regulated in 22 countries, including the United States.

This kind of slavery is horrific and indefensible! **But what are we doing about it? For those who accuse the Bible of approving slavery, do your own opinions and actions regarding** modern pornography and prostitution approve of the worst form of slavery known to man? Do you see prostitution and pornography as victimless? Do you similarly oppose and fight your government over these issues as you do against the Bible? Are you part of the problem or the solution? Who is man to point the finger at the Bible or at God? On prostitution, God's opinion is similarly clear (Deuteronomy 23:17-18).

In fact, God offers the solution to this form of slavery as well as every form of slavery. The primary purpose of the Bible is to point the way to salvation, not to reform society. But reformation is a clear byproduct of salvation. If a person experiences the free grace, love, and forgiveness of God by accepting Jesus Christ and His salvation, God will reform their soul. A person who has experienced reformation of the soul will realize that enslaving another human being is wrong and will instead be gracious toward others as well as defend and work to free the enslaved. This is the Bible's primary prescription for ending slavery.

When it comes to a position on slavery, I gladly defend God's position over man's any day.

Chapter 39

Is the Bible Sexist?

When my son was in his late teens, he was approached in the mall by a religious group who engaged him alone in a conversation. They asked him several questions about God. They quickly began twisting Bible verses to try and convince him that God is female. They implied that without "their interpretations" the Bible is sexist or chauvinist. In other words, since their scriptural distortions are not actually in the Bible, the Bible is sexist. Critics today from many fronts are quick to claim that the Bible supports and even prescribes sexism.

Sexism is defined as "discrimination or devaluation based on a person's sex." According to that definition, the critics of the Bible are guilty, not God. The critics are valuing earthly function with more importance than God-given royal identity. If you single out women and only define them by an earthly function or ambition, you ignore their higher identity in God. This results in a prideful pursuit for earthly position beneath their true identity.

According to the Bible, daughters of God are thereby daughters of the King of kings, princesses, and eternal coheirs to His kingdom, and nothing less. The worst displays of sexism, in fact, are to either treat women as something less than this standard and to suggest women pridefully pursue some lesser function disregarding their identity from God. Regarding discrimination, if you encourage daughters of the King to ignore their royalty for the pursuit of earthly positions, you have engaged in the worst kind of discrimination. And, regarding devaluation, anyone who treats a woman as something less than royalty is practicing the worst kind of devaluation. Even voluntarily stooping down in blinding ambition for earthly positions is self-devaluation. In truth, both chauvinists and feminists are the worst peddlers of sexism.

Compared with all other belief structures, the God of the Christian faith places the highest value on women. In contrast, atheism places one of the lowest values on women by seeing them as nothing more than a cosmic accident or animal mutation that can be treated in manners not confined by moral law. For example, atheism generally favors "abortion on demand," which places zero value on the unborn woman. According to God, women (born or unborn) are His image bearers and coheirs of His kingdom:

"So God created man in His own image, in the image of God He created him; male and female he created them" (Genesis 1:27).

"There is no male or female, for you are all one in Christ Jesus" (Galatians 3:28b).

"Likewise, husbands, live with your wives in an understanding way, showing honor to the woman as the weaker vessel, since they are heirs with you of the grace of life, so that your prayers may not be hindered" (1 Peter 3:7).

"If we have died with Him, we will also live with Him; if we endure, we will also reign with Him" (2 Timothy 2:11-12).

It is against this backdrop that the biblical motivation for all Christians here on earth is to race each other to the low place—not the high place. And Jesus Himself modeled this example for us (Philippians 2:3-11). Jesus, being God, was willing to take the most extreme low place when He willingly emptied Himself and descended to taking the form of a man, down to being a lowly servant, unjustly tried as a criminal, convicted while innocent, brutally executed, and buried by His creation. **If we have this mind of Christ, what will our earthly ambitions look like as women (or men) following His example?**

In spite of this obvious scriptural teaching, critics still attack Ephesians 5:22-24 as sexist when it says, "Wives, submit to your own husbands, as to the Lord. For the husband is the head of the wife even as Christ is the head of the church, His body, and is Himself its Savior. Now as the church submits to Christ, so also wives should submit in everything to their husbands." First, this attack conveniently ignores verses 25-33 that command husbands to sacrifice everything for their wives, including themselves, as Jesus did for us. Secondly, this attack, along with chauvinist Christians, also ignores the verse just before it—Ephesians 5:21—which says, "Submitting to one another out of reverence for Christ." Men and women are to be "submitting to one another." We both should race each other to the low place. But like any team, to achieve the marital unity that God designed, women are called to regard their husband as their leader but without forfeiting their eternal royalty. Remember, Jesus took an even lower place than that and never forfeited His eternal royalty.

Humility, or pursuing the low place, is the Christian standard, not the prideful grasping of earthly position and/or power. This pursuit of the low place also comes with a promise in eternity: "So the last will be first, and the first last" (Matthew 20:16). Therefore, men and women who faithfully and humbly seek the low place on earth will be exalted to the high place in God's kingdom for eternity. **Would you rather have the functional high place for the short duration of your earthly life resulting in the assignment to the "lower" place for eternity?** The alternative is much more appealing. If women follow the

Scriptures and model Christ by racing men to the low place, then in eternity it will be they who will have the high place above the prideful chauvinists.

Another favorite attack regarding sexism is aimed at 1 Timothy 2:9-12: "Women should adorn themselves in respectable apparel, with modesty and self-control . . . Let a woman learn quietly with all submissiveness. I do not permit a woman to teach or to exercise authority over a man; rather, she is to remain quiet." First of all, women during those times were inappropriately treated like property and virtually uneducated. God did not approve of this since women bear His royal image. The commands toward modesty and quietness, however, were addressing the disorderliness of these specific church gatherings where apparently certain women were disruptive for the reasons mentioned in 1 Timothy. But these same standards also apply to men. **Should men be modest? Should men learn in quietness? Should men be humble and seek the low place?** The answer to all of these questions is obviously "yes."

At the beginning of this chapter, I described how my son was approached by a religious group who believed that God was female. Their attempt was first of all guilty of trying to change God's nature to human. In John 4:24, Jesus taught us that "God is spirit," which means that God is not flesh. He is referred to in the masculine, but that does not reduce him to a man. Since both men and women bear God's image, they both have qualities they received from God's nature. For an example of God's motherly sensitivities, in the book of Isaiah, God is compared to a mother comforting a child. In Deuteronomy, God is said to have given birth to Israel. But these verses do not reduce Him to a woman either. He is God, which makes Him neither man nor woman. The fact that He is referred to in masculine terms should not offend someone unless that someone is self-governed by pride over humility. Those who wish to distort such scriptural realities have some strong opposition because it was Jesus Himself who was referred to as the "Son" not daughter, and who (as God) chose to refer to God as His and our Heavenly Father, not mother.

In conclusion, the Bible is not sexist, nor does it demean women. God displays far more respect for women than all feminists combined. He created women wonderfully and gave them His breath and image. He also sacrificed His life to give them a royal eternity. Those who oppose Him on this issue selfishly seek to devalue a woman's royal identity in pursuit of lesser and temporal earthly functions and power. It is God who constantly affirms His royal image in us and seats the humble in the high places of His kingdom for eternity. I have yet to find a critic of the Bible who personally ascribes more value to women than God.

Section 7

The Problem of Evil and Suffering

O ver the centuries, critics of the Christian faith have used the "problem of evil" rather successfully to persuade those in doubt into full-fledged non-belief. We are taught from childhood that God is so incompatible with evil that He cannot be in the same room or coexist with it. We are also taught that God is good and would never allow evil to go unchecked. These teachings, however, paint a picture of life that is in fact an unbiblical fairy tale. So when we grow up to find it was human-embellished fiction, we become jaded and vulnerable to the darkest of deceptions.

This "god" we are taught is actually not the God of the Bible. While the God of the Bible absolutely hates evil, He also chose to summon Lucifer into His presence on multiple occasions. While the God of the Bible will not allow evil to go unchecked, He also gave us a timeline of when the "checks" will come due. And His timeline does not necessarily coincide with our demands of Him. It is good to a certain extent to shield the innocence of children from the harsh realities of modern evil. But when it introduces them to a fictional god, we are only setting them up to believe in a cosmic Santa Claus.

Critics have thrived upon dismantling such childish fairy tales. But the irony is that in the process, they have weaved a fiction of their own. In particular, the fiction of atheism is rarely tested by the likes of the religiously jaded.

This section is devoted to explaining evil and good. We will expose evil, not as a problem of God, but as a problem and product of sinful man. We will define evil, good, free will, and God's sovereignty by using God's own words as opposed to our often insufficient terminology. These next chapters will also show how Christianity offers the only credible and logical solution to understanding the coexistence of both evil and good. Christianity also goes the extra mile beyond atheism to actually offer a practical solution for solving the problem. And that is something its critics never do.

Chapter 40

Atheism's Problem with Evil

I n 2008, Dr. Bart Ehrman authored a book entitled *God's Problem: How the Bible Fails to Answer Our Most Important Question—Why We Suffer*. Ehrman is a famous agnostic who is the James A. Gray Distinguished Professor of Religious Studies at the University of North Carolina at Chapel Hill. Ironically, his spiritual journey began as an evangelical Christian. After his graduate studies, he became an agnostic through struggling with the philosophical problem of evil (or pain and suffering). I have attended and watched several of his lectures over the years. While he professes agnosticism, his book unintentionally promotes atheism. His central argument can be summarized with the following question: How can we reconcile a good and all-powerful God with the terrible evil and suffering we see in this world?

In Chapters 6 and 27, I dealt with the fact that evil is not a separate and willful thing and that God has defeated the enemy in such a way as to freely extend grace and forgiveness to as many people as possible. In this chapter, I will expand further to address the central criticism put forth by Ehrman and atheism. Before I do, there is a much better book on the subject that I highly recommend entitled *If God Is Good* by Randy Alcorn. Here and in related chapters, I borrow significant inspiration from Alcorn's work.

Ehrman, in the title of his book, cleverly states that evil is "God's problem," but such a conclusion is misleading. A more accurate title would state that evil is "man's problem." First and foremost, humanity is responsible for the evil in the world. It is by our unforced hands that these horrific acts are carried out. Christian theism additionally argues that man even ushered in natural disasters. Since creation was our dominion, when man fell due to rebellion, we forced our entire dominion to fall with us. **Under any worldview, who are we to point our accusing finger and call this God's problem when we are the ones doing the evil?** That is the equivalent of a child stealing cookies and shifting blame to his parents for leaving the cookie jar on the kitchen table.

For this reason, we can turn the tables on Ehrman and atheism. We can instead place the burden of proof not on God or Christianity, but on man. If atheism is correct, then it is atheism that must also answer for why there is evil in the world. **If God doesn't exist, why is atheism's argument always directed at God and never directed at mankind who conducts evil acts?** Atheism and its preachers are generally very good at questioning, but fail to offer credible solutions to their own questions. By failing to answer their own questions, the typical atheist's approach to the problems of evil is the most lacking among all worldviews.

To illustrate, let's assume atheist argument is right in saying that there is no God. **If God doesn't exist, then by what objective basis can we measure morality? Where do we get the universal standard of goodness by which we judge evil to be evil?** When atheists claim that something is evil, that is an admission of the existence of objective morality. The fact that atheists use objective morality, even though they have no basis for it and deny it even exists, is self-refuting because their assertion of a universal standard is evidence of the very God they deny. Atheism is not a credible, moral framework. C. S. Lewis, once an atheist who became a famous Christian apologist, said, "My argument against God was that the universe seemed so cruel and unjust. **But how had I got this idea of just and unjust?** A man does not call a line crooked unless he has some idea of a straight line. **What was I comparing this universe with when I called it unjust?**"

Atheism logically calls for the dismissal of known foundations of morality as either having no basis or at best being subjective. When God and objective morality are ignored as if they do not exist, no basis remains for the recognition of even basic human rights. It is no irony that atheism was the centerpiece of the rise of Soviet and Chinese communism wherein its leaders murdered more than 100 million people. **So, why are atheists outraged by such evil? Should they be outraged by evil if our world is just a place of random chance and survival of the fittest—beliefs that are central to a purely naturalistic worldview such as atheism?**

As another example, consider Jeffrey Dahmer, the notorious sexual predator and cannibal, who asked rhetorically in an interview, "**If it all happens naturalistically, what's the need for a God? Can't I set my own rules? Who owns me?** I own myself." **How can atheism logically respond to those questions using naturalistic arguments?** We don't express moral outrage when polar bears kill and eat their young. **Employing atheism, why are human "animals" any different?**

On a broader scale, as Americans reeled from the events of September 11, 2001, I don't recall anyone explaining the terrorists' actions from a naturalistic worldview. I also don't remember anyone arguing that it was merely natural selection at work. People knew in their gut that such evil transcended naturalistic explanations. **What universal moral authority can atheism use to condemn Dahmer or the 9/11 terrorists?**

With that backdrop, we may pose even more questions for atheists. **Why do the great majority of suffering people want or fight to go on living despite their circumstances? Why is there so much good in the world despite the evil? Since atheism argues that Christianity does not adequately account for evil, then how does atheism adequately account for good? If the existence of evil provides evidence against God, then isn't the existence of good evidence for God? Wouldn't the existence of good be evidence *against* atheism?** The circular reasoning of atheism's argument is obvious.

Since evil was caused by man, the central question before us is what is man doing to remedy it? Blaming God for allowing evil is the first step in the wrong direction because it assumes we are not guilty or responsible for our own actions. If God does not exist as atheism posits, there is no one else to blame for evil, except us. It is beyond disturbing when people use evil to deny God's existence while personally either doing nothing about evil or further enabling mankind to avoid responsibility for it.

Perhaps the biggest problem with Ehrman's work is his attempt to "attack" God for not doing enough to diminish suffering. He then offers this conclusion, "I think we should work hard to make the world—the one we live in—the most pleasing place it can be *for ourselves* . . . We should make money and spend money. The more the better. We should enjoy good food and drink. We should eat out and order unhealthy desserts, and we should cook steak on the grill and drink Bordeaux . . . We should drive nice cars and have nice homes. We should make love, have babies, and raise families. We should do what we can to love life—it's a gift and it will not be with us for long."

Aside from the fact that Ehrman calls life a "gift" while arguing for the nonexistence of the "Giver," he also uses the word "should" eight times in that short paragraph. Using "should" is another appeal to objective morality, which is something he assists in denying. What's even worse is how

Ehrman submits a solution that promotes self-indulgence and not self-sacrifice. This approach is a classic case of being part of the problem and not part of the solution. For these reasons alone, Ehrman's work is woefully flawed and lacks intellectual integrity, as does the atheism that he inspires.

Scottish theologian James E. Stewart, once said, "It is the spectators, the people who are outside, looking at the tragedy, from whose ranks the skeptics come; it is not those who are actually in the arena and who know suffering from the inside. Indeed, the fact is that it is the world's greatest sufferers who have produced the most shining examples of unconquerable faith."

Does any worldview or religion make a credible case that the universe, including its goodness and evil, has a meaning and a purpose that one day we may understand? Christianity does. Atheism does not. As stated earlier, the atheist who abandons belief in God because of the problem of evil assumes that a good and all-powerful God cannot have good reasons for creating a universe in which evil and suffering temporarily exist. **Shouldn't such an assumption require some proof?** Such an assumption has never been proven. In my opinion, it is false. **Could not God create a universe in which He knew people would commit evil and temporarily suffer, if such a reality was necessary to achieve a far greater eternal result?** Of course He could. That issue will be addressed further in upcoming chapters.

We should blame man for evil. We should also embrace God's beautiful, self-sacrificing remedy for it.

Chapter 41

The Story of Our Evil and God's Good

I heard a story about a wise rabbi and a soap maker who went for a walk. The soap maker said, "What good is preaching about God and goodness? Look around you. You see continuing trouble, misery, and wars. All this evil still exists." Then they noticed a child covered in mud playing in the gutter. The wise rabbi said, "Look at this child! What good is it to make soap? With all the soap in the world this child is still filthy." The soap maker answered, "But rabbi, soap can't do its job if it isn't used!" Like mud and soap, it can also be said that evil exists because humanity fails do its job of being good. In previous chapters, we began to address the philosophical "problem of evil." As we did so, we pointed out that atheism cannot account for the existence of good. To explain this issue with more clarity, it is necessary to explain how good and evil interact in humanity's story.

Evil (or moral evil) describes our actions on earth when we refuse to accept God as God or place someone or something else in God's place. A good analogy of this distortion is the manner in which rust forms. Metal does not need rust, but rust needs metal. Likewise, good does not need evil, but evil is the attempt to distort good. By the way, this indirectly means that good can, did, and will one day exist without evil. Good has an eternal existence. Evil, on the other hand, had a beginning and will also have an end.

Just like the fruit of rust is decay and malfunction, the fruit of evil is pain and suffering. Pain and suffering follow moral evil like a train caboose follows the engine. There is no such thing as moral evil that does not produce pain and suffering. The Scriptures sometimes refer to suffering from natural disasters as evils. To distinguish this from moral evil, the moral evil of the earth's stewards (man) resulted in God allowing the earth (man's dominion) to fall as well by subjecting it to natural disasters and their resultant pain and suffering. It must be said, however, that natural disasters are not necessarily directly linked to the sins of individuals who perish or suffer in them. Rather, they are linked to the evil actions of us all.

In addition to the evil of our actions, we also demonstrate evil with our inaction. Albert Einstein once said, "The world is too dangerous to live in—not because of the people who do evil but because of the people who sit and let it happen." Apart from God's Spirit in us, we are not that different from every notorious murderer and ruthless dictator. Blaming our complicit selves for what mankind collectively does is a lost art that we need to recover. It is only from a true sense of personal responsibility coupled with God's eternal perspective that the "problem" of evil ultimately will be resolved.

One of my biggest disappointments when explaining the interaction of evil and good is when certain Christians diminish the value of good. When the value of good is diminished, subsequent discussion about God's goodness becomes almost pointless. If we accept the false argument that the highest value of the universe is short-term human happiness in the form of immediate fulfillment of our desires, then we cannot defend Christianity because we ourselves have departed from it. God's goodness transcends this temporary life. In fact, "good" encompasses an eternity reigning over our heavenly inheritance.

For these and other reasons, "good" in our present day can be mischaracterized. God is the giver of all good gifts (James 1:17). That said, not every good gift seems good while in the midst of a suffering world. Consider the analogy about a three-year-old boy who swallowed poison. The father called the Poison Control Center and the person who answered says, "You have to get him to the hospital immediately. And, whatever you do, don't let him fall asleep. If he falls asleep, he'll die." On the way to the hospital, the boy's head starts to drop. His father slaps him in the face. The boy cries. His head starts to drop again. The father slaps him again and again, all the way to the hospital. The child can't understand why his father is slapping him. He's only three years old. With tears falling down his face, his father says, "I love you, son." But, the boy doesn't want any more of his father's harshness. **Isn't the father being good to his son?** What the boy considers harsh is actually love and goodness. **Is it possible that God also sometimes shows His love and goodness toward us in the midst of our own self-poisoning and, like the three-year-old, we sometimes fail to understand his actions?** As the soap maker learned, people don't need help feeling good—they need help being good.

If the good-evil story line is still fairly unclear to you, consider another analogy. Imagine that you were rewriting the story of mankind from scratch. **How would you rewrite mankind's story?** Almost everyone likes a story with good and evil where good wins. Ironically, that same conflict is apparently what we wish to avoid in real life even though it is exactly what we love about stories. The greatest human character virtues we know would never appear in a story without evil. Writers of fiction do not ask their characters for permission to let them face evil because, as authors, they know the best ending for the story. **If you were authoring humanity's story, would**

you give the characters the pen? Even if we could do that, I cannot think of anyone who wishes his own story was about a choiceless and powerless life.

In our present story, we are living between "Paradise Lost" and "Paradise Restored." Recalling the story's beginning and knowing its ending gives perspective to our lives in the middle. As we presently muddle our way through the fog of spiritual war, it is our origin and destiny that brings clarity. In this spiritual war we know that God has won. One day in heaven (our destiny) we will view our present suffering with very different eyes. Mother Teresa once said, "In light of heaven, the worst suffering on earth, a life full of the most atrocious tortures on earth, will be seen to be no more serious than one night in an inconvenient hotel." If any modern figure held credibility on this subject, it was Mother Teresa.

The truth is that the story of our redemption began before God created the world. Before creation fell, God decided exactly what He would do to renew it. His plan involved the postponement of worldwide judgment to give more of us time to repent and turn to Him for redemption. In the larger story, this may not seem to us to be the best possible world. To God, however, it is the best possible means of achieving the best possible world. He knows, because He sees from a grand perspective and knows the ending in detail. The glorious ending to this story is in a new heaven and a new earth that is breathtaking partly because there is no more evil.

Finally, God does not leave us alone in our story of struggle with suffering. In fact, God has not immunized Himself from the pain we suffer. Whenever you feel tempted to ask God, "Why did you do this to me?" please look at the cross and instead ask, "Why did You do that *for* me?" Our God is the one true God. When compared with all others, He is the only one who came to suffer with us and in our place. This truth separates Him from all others and should silence reasonable critics. John R. W. Stott, the famous Anglican cleric, said...

"I could never myself believe in God, if it were not for the cross ... **in the real world of pain, how could one worship a God who was immune to it?** I have entered many Buddhist temples in different Asian countries and stood respectfully before the statue of Buddha, his legs crossed, arms folded, eyes closed, the ghost of a smile playing round his mouth, a remote look on his face, detached from the agonies of the world. But each time after a while I have had to turn away. And in imagination I have turned instead to that lonely, twisted, tortured figure on the cross, nails through hands and feet, back lacerated, limbs wrenched, brow bleeding from thorn-pricks, mouth dry and intolerably thirsty, plunged in God-forsaken darkness. *That is the God for me!* He laid aside his immunity to pain. He entered our world of flesh and blood, tears and death. He suffered for us. Our sufferings become more manageable in light of his. There is still a question mark against human suffering, but over it we boldly stamp another mark, the cross, which symbolized divine suffering. The cross of Christ ... is God's only self-justification in such a world as ours." (emphasis added)

Every day that God delays his final judgment against Lucifer and those who follow him is one more day to extend His free grace and salvation to more who need it. It is also one more day in humanity's story for God to demonstrate through Christ His tremendous love for a lost and dying world, a work for which we will praise Him in a perfectly good eternity.

Chapter 42

Man's Choice Versus God's Choice

One of my colleagues used to have a plaque on his desk that read, "What would you attempt to do if you knew you would not fail?" When I asked him how this phrase had impacted him, he responded, "The question is impractical because it doesn't exclude the impossible. Should I attempt to jump off a tall building and fly? There is no way to know that I would not fail at something." This is a great analogy for explaining free will. **How *free* is "free will" when we consider man's limitations and God's sovereignty? Is "free will" totally free in light of all things being under God's control? Are we responsible for evil or is God responsible?**

Man's free will is not limitless, but it is man's poor exercise of his "free will" that results in unforced evil actions. Our free will is limited first because we are finite and second because of our sin nature. Jonathan Edwards defined free will as "the ability to choose as one pleases . . . A man never, in any instance, wills anything contrary to his own desires, or desires anything contrary to his own will." Therefore, every person has free will. **But given our sinful nature, are we free to desire righteousness or live righteously without God's empowerment?**

Whatever our malcondition, isn't it still a consequence of our own sin? Truthfully, even the most wicked among us have the knowledge of good and sometimes act on it. God is not preventing us from doing good activities or forcing us to do evil activities. We do what we generally desire to do.

The struggle to explain the interrelationship between God's sovereignty and humanity's free will has been argued probably since the beginning of time. The Bible actually teaches both free will and God's sovereignty. It is wise to examine humanity's free will through the lens of God's sovereignty, and not vice versa. The universe began and will end with God, not humanity. If we attempt to examine God strictly through the lens of humanity, we are bound to distort Him into something He is not.

The structure of a world in which God allows free will is necessary if man is to have meaningful choice. Ironically, some who most value this freedom to choose are often quickest to attempt to judge God for allowing evil to happen. If we say we wish God had made humans without the freedom to do evil, we also say humans should not have freedom. That is like saying that humans should not be human. Eliminating meaningful choice or its consequences would mean the end of marriage, family, culture, and meaningful life. **Is any reasonable critic willing to pay that price?**

Alvin Plantinga, Professor of Philosophy Emeritus at the University of Notre Dame, wrote the following about the true source of moral evil, "A world containing creatures who are significantly free (and freely perform more good than evil actions) is more valuable, all else being equal, than a world containing no free creature at all. Now God can create free creatures, but He can't cause or determine them to do only what is right. For if He does so, then they aren't significantly free after all; they do not do what is right *freely*. To create creatures capable of moral good therefore, He must create creatures capable of moral evil; and He can't give these creatures the freedom to perform evil and at the same time prevent them from doing so. As it turned out, sadly enough, some of the free creatures God created went wrong in the exercise of their freedom; *this is the source of moral evil*" (emphasis added).

When we attempt to explain God's sovereignty, we must confine our explanation to God's terms from Scripture (Ephesians 1:9-11 for example). **From that perspective, is it possible for God to plan for something He knows without forcing that thing to happen?** God didn't force Adam and Eve to do evil, but He did create them with freedom and permitted Lucifer in the garden, fully knowing they would choose evil and that His redemptive plan would serve a greater good. We still experience our will as free and unforced. Therefore, no reasonable person can deny personal responsibility for evil. "God made me do it" is an absurd defense.

God does not commit moral evil. He overcomes all evil for good purposes. Because He has almighty power, no one—including demons and humans—who choose to violate His moral law can thwart His ultimate purpose. Though evil had no part in God's original creation, it was part of His original plan. God did not devise His redemptive plan arbitrarily. Evil did not take Him by surprise. God is not the author of evil, but He is the author of a story that includes evil. He intended from the beginning to permit evil and then defeat evil to the praise of His glory (see Chapter 41).

While this initially sounds difficult, remember that God's plan included the difficult death of His one and only Son on our behalf. God did not spare His own Son when working to deliver us from our own failures. **Doesn't the same God who took evil and turned it for good in the life of His own Son do the same in the lives of His other children as well?** Romans 8:28 says, "Yes." Take Joseph, for example. Not only did God permit Joseph's journey to Egypt, He sent him there through his brothers' evil deeds (Genesis 50:20). But through Joseph, God spared the world of one of the fiercest famines in history.

For those who bristle at the notion of God's ultimate control, consider this point. If anything in the universe can happen outside of God's control, then ultimately we cannot trust God's promises. For God to promise something in the future and be trusted to fulfill His promises, He must have control in order to maintain that trust. God hates sin and judges it, yet He has predetermined a plan in which He uses everything to accomplish His purposes and fulfill all of His promises. Scripture teaches both God's sovereignty and meaningful human choice. In fact, they both sometimes appear in the same passages without contradiction. For example, in the Exodus story, "God hardened Pharaoh's heart" seven times. But Pharaoh also later hardened his own heart several times. God's sovereignty and man's meaningful choice worked together as they do today. No contradiction exists between praying, "God please protect our family on this road trip," and then putting on seat belts.

Evil aside, we must be careful to not always condemn the existence of pain and suffering. God uses them to our benefit. Proverbs 27:21 says, "The crucible is for silver, and the furnace is for gold, and a man is tested by his praise." Regarding this test of man's character, there is a beautiful example in Job. After all was taken from him, he said in Job 19:25-27, "For I know that my Redeemer lives, and at the last He will stand upon the earth. And after my skin has been thus destroyed, yet in my flesh I shall see God, whom I shall see for myself, and my eyes shall behold, and not another. My heart faints within me!" I believe this is why Romans 5:3-4 says, ". . . But we rejoice in our sufferings, knowing that suffering produces endurance, and endurance produces character, and character produces hope." We tend to define our good in terms of what brings us health and happiness now. But God defines our good in terms of what makes us more like Jesus. And His definition is the only definition of good that ultimately matters.

Consider too that even though God later rebuked Job, He primarily faulted him for attempting to judge the wisdom and goodness of his infinite Creator. We would be wise to learn from this rebuke. What we call the "problem of evil" is actually the problem of our limited and distorted understanding. For example, God may already be restraining 99.99% of evil, suffering, and tragedies. In our eagerness to see miraculous intervention, we disregard "natural processes" as minor and secondary, missing God's marvelous daily and constant interventions on our behalf. Common grace is God's means by which He gives people innumerable blessings even apart from salvation. Not every person experiences saving grace—but all people, without exception, experience common grace daily. If humanity lacked all goodness, we could not survive.

We should be profoundly grateful for the freedom to choose, God's restraint of evil, His delay of judgment, and His gift of Himself in our fallen world.

Section 8

Science Supports Origin by Creation

One of Satan's primary attacks on Christians is in the area of identity. As stated in prior chapters, the enemy is constantly focused on attacking God's identity as well as our own. If he can successfully devalue either or both in the minds of God's followers, then he can succeed in separating us from our faith. Therefore, Christians must maintain a firm foundation in both the identity of God and their identity as God's children.

The identity of humanity begins and has its foundation in our origins. Our origin is the very first defining intersection between God and man. As we know from Scripture, we are the only created beings who are created in the image of God. This origin is the beginning and foundation of who we are. Therefore, if the enemy can convince us that God did not create us and/or that there is no God whose image we share, he begins the much easier process of leading us to transfer our faith away from God. It is through the clever blurring of the boundaries between science and philosophy where he has proven to be most successful.

This blurring between science and philosophy is accomplished in seemingly small, incremental steps. First, move science away from the scientific method by employing fiction and opinion but still insist it is still the practice of science. Second, declare the fiction and opinions to be scientific facts. Once fiction and opinion are transformed into facts, science begins to dictate philosophy, and the philosophy that it feeds is atheism under the deception of impartiality.

It is absolutely necessary that Christians be prepared to interact in scientific discussion as they relate to the origins of the universe and humanity. This section will help you to do just that. First, we will establish the irreconcilable differences between the Bible and evolutionary philosophy regarding the origins of humanity and show that Christianity offers the only credible meaning for life. We will then expose modern scientists for violating scientific laws and methods.

Additionally, we will deal directly with the truth about the dating and aging of fossils, rocks, and sediments. We will examine the evidence of the fossil record to interpret it clearly with regard to the absence of transitional fossils of animals and humans. We will also explore explanations for the existence of genetic information in the simplest life form and see how that life form is far from simple. We will study irrefutable evidence supporting the inference of design in the natural universe and it's fine-tuning. And along the way, we will expose as fictional myths those opinions that have been declared "scientific facts."

The goal of this section is to reinforce your faith by (1) reinforcing your identity as God's special creation and (2) confirming the origins of humanity. I encourage you to keep a skeptical mind as you read through this section, but let your skepticism be of the healthy variety. Healthy skepticism requires that you apply equal measure of skepticism to all philosophies. As you do, you will realize which philosophy truly stands up to legitimate scrutiny.

Chapter 43

Did God Actually Say "Six Days"?

I n 1996, Pope John Paul II famously said the following regarding the differences between biblical creation and evolution: "There is no conflict between evolution and the doctrine of the faith . . . some new findings lead us toward the recognition of evolution as more than a hypothesis. In fact it is remarkable that this theory has had progressively greater influence on the spirit of researchers, following a series of discoveries in different scholarly disciplines. The convergence in the results of these independent studies—which was neither planned nor sought—constitutes in itself a significant argument in favor of the theory."

In other words, the late Pope John Paul II said that evolution and the Bible probably do not need to be reconciled and are probably in agreement. Is there no conflict between evolution and the Bible?

I realize that some in the church hold the words of the Pope as "infallible." But with all due respect, he is a man and what he said is false. Biblical creation and Darwinian evolution are impossible to reconcile. They cannot both be true as I will explain further, but this has not stopped even some in the church from insisting that they are.

The following theories actually attempt to force Scripture to agree with Darwin's hypothesis: theistic evolution, day-age creationism, and the gap theory. While these theories have differences between them, some of them generally imply that the six days described in Genesis 1 are not actually six consecutive 24-hour periods. Rather, they claim that each "day" could be a period of time approximating one or more billions of years. **So let's begin our discussion with this question: according to Genesis, was the universe created in six days or billions of years?**

To answer this question, take a few minutes to read all 31 verses of Genesis 1. As you do, be the judge as to whether the text is as vague as these theories proclaim. The summary of what God created on each of the days of the first week is as follows:

Day 1: Time, heavens, earth, water, light, day, night
Day 2: Separation of waters between land and sky
Day 3: Dry land, vegetation
Day 4: Sun, moon, stars
Day 5: Sea creatures, birds
Day 6: Land animals, humans
Day 7: God rested

The first thing God created in Genesis is implied in the first three words: "In the beginning." It is fairly clear that God is saying "In the beginning . . . (of time)." The first three words of the Bible mention the creation of time itself. Before time existed, there was eternity. Time is a temporary creation that was meant to govern the creation—not the Creator, God. God exists primarily in eternity and interacts with us in time. Time had a beginning, and time as we know it will have an end. It is from this background that Christians must approach this issue. The nature of "time" in Genesis 1 is central to the biblical answer of the earth's age. We also see in the rest of the chapter how God explicitly describes the nature of the "time" that He created. But here is where the distortion begins. God did not create time and then teach us about time in time-confused terms. Genesis 1 is not poetry or prophecy. It is historical narrative. In this context, God is being literal not figurative.

The critic might ignore this logic and press on with the question, "Why couldn't 'day' mean billions of years?" The word "day" in Genesis 1 is the Hebrew word *yom*, which means a 24-hour period in all such contexts. This was the first time *yom* is used in the Bible. Therefore, God went to great lengths to explicitly describe what a *yom* is in this very chapter. So, let's examine from the chapter the characteristics of a *yom*. The *yoms* in Genesis 1 were numbered one through seven, which resulted in the creation of the universal "week." Therefore, there are seven of the Genesis 1 *yoms* in an earthly week. Each of the *yoms* in Genesis 1 had a morning and an evening. And God proceeded to call morning "day" and evening "night." So, each *yom* is comprised of a day and a night. The *yoms* of Genesis 1 also had the sun to "rule the day" and the moon to "rule the night." There should be absolutely zero doubt about what kind of *yom* God is describing. He is describing a literal 24-hour day.

Now for those who wish to say that this characterization of a *yom* was unique to Genesis, God repeated this in the very next book: Exodus, a book of law. Exodus 20:8-11 says, "Remember the Sabbath day [*yom*] to keep it holy. Six days [*yoms*] you shall labor, and do all your work, but the seventh day [*yom*] is a Sabbath to the LORD your God . . . For in six days [*yoms*] the LORD made heaven and the earth, the sea, and all that is in them, and rested on the seventh day [*yom*]. Therefore the LORD blessed the Sabbath [*yom*] and made it holy." Notice also that God characterized *yom* in the same way again in Exodus 31:15-17. In the Scriptures, God has gone out of His way to make sure we know exactly what a Genesis 1 *yom* is. He was not vague; He was explicit.

Further ponder if the *yoms* in Genesis and Exodus are billions of years, and God rested on the seventh *yom*, then that would mean that God is still sleeping right now and will be for a very long time. But notice that "rested" is in the past tense, not present tense. Another problem to consider is how God created vegetation on Day 3 but the sun on Day 4. Using false theories about the days of creation, the vegetation would have to survive without photosynthesis from the sun for more than one billion years. From what we know about vegetation, that is impossible even for one year, much less billions.

Also consider that evolution theoretically requires a constant cycle of mutation and death, which begs the question of **when did mutation (imperfection) and death enter the creation?** A clear reading of Scripture concludes that imperfection and death entered creation *after* the Fall of Man, which was *after* Day 7. These false theories would have us believe that imperfection and death happened repeatedly *before* Day 7. These non-biblical theories do not stand up to legitimate, interpretive questions.

Proponents of these theories also like to quote 2 Peter 3:8, which says, ". . . With the Lord one day is as a thousand years, and a thousand years as one day." However, a thousand years is a far cry from billions of years. Further, this verse cuts both ways since it also teaches the inverse in the same verse. The point of this verse was not to redefine time, but to show how God's eternal reality is so different from earthly time. But in Genesis and Exodus, God spoke in terms of earthly time, not eternity.

If all of this logic does not expose a long enough list of irreconcilable differences between the two views, consider the contradictions between the order of the Bible's creation and the assumed order of evolution:

Bible: Earth before the sun
Evolution: Sun before the earth

Bible: Earth covered in water first
Evolution: Earth was a molten blob first

Bible: Oceans before dry land
Evolution: Dry land before oceans

Bible: Life on land first
Evolution: Life in oceans first

Bible: Plants before sun
Evolution: Sun before plants

Bible: Birds before animals
Evolution: Animals before birds

Bible: Whales before animals
Evolution: Animals before whales

The most important argument of all on this subject was made by Jesus Himself, the author of creation. Jesus also characterized the creation week as a period of time. In Mark 10:6, Jesus said of the timing of human creation, "But from the beginning of creation, 'God made them male and female.'" Here Jesus directly quoted Himself from Genesis 1:1 by saying, "(in) the beginning" and then followed by quoting Genesis 1:27. In doing so, Jesus merged verses 1 and 27. **What do you think Jesus meant by "the beginning"—Day 6 or billions of years later?** Clearly, Jesus is telling us that He created man on Day 6 and not Day 6 billion.

Satan's tactics remain unchanged. He always attacks our identity in God as it is stated in the Bible. Our identity has its foundation in our origin or "in the beginning." In John 5:46-47,

Jesus said, "For if you believed Moses, you would believe me; for he wrote of me. But if you do not believe his writings, how will you believe my words?" That is a cold warning since Moses wrote Genesis and Exodus. Some may ask, "When did Moses write about Jesus?" Moses began writing about Jesus in Genesis 1 (see also John 1).

The desire to make the Bible conform to man's thinking is a poor intention in the wrong direction. The result is a lie introduced through the church that would have us submit God's Word to man's lesser intellect. In Genesis 3:1, Lucifer asked Eve, "Did God actually say . . . ?" Today Lucifer asks us if God actually said six days. The answer is "yes." God most certainly did.

Chapter 44

The Meaning of Life

During the 1990s, there was a popular children's show on PBS called *Bill Nye the Science Guy*, which was famous for teaching children inspirationally about science. Unfortunately, in 2012, Nye released a controversial web video in which he accused people who deny evolution of hurting children. The title of the video was "Creationism Is Not Appropriate for Children." In the video, he also said, "You can believe what you want religiously. Religion is one thing, but science, provable science is something else."

In this chapter, we will discuss "provable science" and explore the scientific evidence regarding the origin of the universe. It is important to keep in mind that all sides of this discussion are looking at the same incomplete body of evidence and coming to very different conclusions. Reasonable Christians accept "provable science," but it is un-provable philosophy wearing the disguise of science with which we and everyone else should take issue. To that end, in this discussion we must distinguish between what is fact, fiction, and opinion. There are assertions on every side that fit into these categories; provable science, however, must emphasize facts.

Every philosophy and belief system seeks to answer the age-old question, "**What is the meaning of life?**" Asking and answering this question is actually where my response to Nye begins. In order to understand the meaning of anything, we have to understand its origin or cause. Like art, the "meaning" of something can best be derived by what ultimately caused that something. For example, if you find the bag of dog food torn into and emptied, the meaning of this mess is determined by the bloated dog painfully sitting in the corner. If you try to determine the meaning while ignoring the cause, you will likely make a wrong determination. Likewise, in order to understand the meaning of life, we must understand its origin.

In this discussion, the majority of people take one of two sides. One side holds that life (and the universe) was ultimately caused by nothing (primarily atheistic evolution). The other side holds that life (and the universe) was ultimately caused by something (primarily theistic creation and intelligent design theory). We will examine the evidence to determine which of these sides is supported best.

For evolution, the argument generally begins with abiogenesis, which means the study of how living things could arise, or evolve, from nonliving matter. The fatal flaw in abiogenesis is that it lacks a single shred of scientific or philosophical evidence. Abiogenesis is a resurrection of a dead relic called the theory of spontaneous generation. Spontaneous generation was first generally credited to Aristotle as the thinking that the formation of living things could happen without coming from similar living things. The main idea was that certain living things such as fleas could arise from nonliving matter such as dust or that maggots could arise from dead flesh. This thinking reigned for approximately 2,000 years.

Then in 1668, an Italian physician named Francesco Redi proved spontaneous generation scientifically false. Cleverly, Redi placed in two sets of jars dead fish and raw chunks of veal. Redi covered the first group of jars with fine gauze so that only air could get in. He left the other group of jars completely open. After several days, he observed maggots appearing on the objects in the open jars, on which flies had been able to land, but not in the gauze-covered jars. He then conducted several other experiments with consistent results.

Redi easily proved that living things arise from living things. Maggots do not arise from dead flesh. Maggots arise from eggs left on dead flesh by flies. This is an example of "provable science," and the theory of spontaneous generation died a slow death. Centuries later, however, it was resurrected under a new name, abiogenesis. The name and the wording of the theory have been tweaked, but the conclusions are the same and still lack any relevant evidence.

It was 1871 when Darwin suggested in a famous letter that the original "spark" of life might have begun in a "warm little pond." By the way, **does that sound like fact, fiction, or opinion?** This "warm little pond" theory ultimately led to experiments conducted by Stanley Miller at the University of Chicago in 1952. Miller designed a chamber to simulate the supposed "warm little pond" assuming a hydrogen-rich mixture of methane, ammonia, and water vapor. He selected these elements assuming/believing they were present in earth's prehistoric atmosphere. However, assumptions and belief about unobserved ponds and its components are not based upon any scientific observations.

When the chamber was electrified to simulate the "spark," the result was the formation of . . . amino acids. This result should not have been a surprise since it was well known at the time that these elements are also the building blocks of amino acids. Miller's experiment was heralded as proving Darwin's "warm little pond" theory. The mixture of elements used by Miller became famously known as the "primordial soup." Based upon this loose string of opinions and deficient experiments, spontaneous generation was deceptively resurrected. But the name had to change to "abiogenesis" in order to seem as not refuting Redi's "provable science."

What really did the Miller experiment prove? Upon what ancient evidence did Miller determine the contents of the hypothetical, primordial "soup?" Do we have any evidence that such a primordial soup ever existed? Would the conditions in the chamber even be suitable for life? The truth is that the only thing Miller's experiment proved was that if you put the building blocks of amino acids deliberately in a chamber and carefully electrify it, certain amino acids may form. Miller's experiment did not prove that the "soup" existed millions of years ago. There is zero evidence for that conclusion. In fact, evolutionists today no longer believe the elements Miller used were even present in the earth's prehistoric atmosphere.

Furthermore, amino acids do not equal life and are in fact immeasurably far removed from life. We can build amino acids without hesitation. But we have never built life from nonliving amino acids. Amino acids are the building blocks of proteins. And you would need the right number of the right kinds of amino acids to link up in the right structure to create a single protein molecule. A single protein molecule, however, is not life. In fact, it is immeasurably far from being a living cell.

To form a single living cell, you would need many protein molecules in the right sequence and structure, plus enzymes. Then the cell would require DNA or genetic information. Lastly, life needs the initial "spark" that has never been repeated since creation. In fact, lightening (which is what Miller was simulating) has never been known to create life but to kill it. Miller's experiment did not prove abiogenesis. In fact, nothing in the entire realm of scientific history ever has proven abiogenesis to be true. In this sense, abiogenesis is ironically familiar to another concept that also can't be proven and is credited by others for the origin of life . . . God.

Interestingly, the chamber in which Miller's experiment was conducted was actually toxic to life. When proteins or even embryos are placed in such a chamber, they are burned beyond recognition. This pseudoscience is the worst of hoaxes embraced by a willing scientific community and its unquestioning subjects, which includes Bill Nye. This is not "provable science" as Nye suggests; it is instead naturalistic philosophy masquerading as science. Primordial soup is not historical fact; it is at best opinion, but most likely fiction.

Since the dawn of man, in every millisecond of time, the earth has had perfect conditions for life and abiogenesis has never been observed. That is a fact. Life has never been observed arising from nonliving things. Life only arises from life. And for the most part, life feeds upon life. Most everything that living things eat was once alive. **Imagine if the first living thing did in fact arise from nonliving matter (in deadly conditions); what did it eat to survive?**

In contrast, creation asserts that life was created by an eternal and living Creator. While this statement of reality cannot be observed either, it is at least an opinion that is logical and does not masquerade as science. An argument that the universe (including life) was caused by nothing is neither logical nor "provable." Evolution has never adequately explained life, much less its origin. If life had no deliberate cause, then life is not a deliberate effect.

First John 5:12a says, "Whoever has the Son has life." The meaning of life is in its origin. God is the origin and meaning of life (John 14:6). Life never comes from non-life. Life, ultimately, is always caused by God. An awesome Cause is why life has such an awesome meaning.

If you remove the Creator and claim that the cause of life is a cosmic burp, then life's meaning is reduced to that burp. And this is far more dangerous to children, which Nye fails to admit.

Chapter 45

Scientists Versus Science

I heard a story of an elementary teacher's attempt to introduce evolution in her class. As part of the lesson, she selected a boy to walk over to the window and look outside. She asked him, "Do you see the trees and the grass?" "Yes," the boy replied. She then asked, "Do you see the sky?" "Yes," he replied. She pressed further, "Do you see God up there?" "No," replied the boy. The teacher concluded, "We can't see God because he isn't there. It is possible that he just doesn't exist." At this point, a girl in the class raised her hand and requested to continue asking the boy questions. The teacher agreed. The girl first asked the boy, "Do you see the teacher at the front of the room?" "Yes," the boy replied. She continued, "Do you see her brain?" "No," the boy replied. Immediately the girl concluded, "Then according to what we were taught today in school, she possibly may not even have one."

Now yes, that was pretty rude of the girl, but children can say the most shocking things at times. And on the subject of evolution, so can adults who claim to be "scientists." **As "scientists" make their arguments for the origin of all things, are they likewise rudely ignoring *science*? Do modern scientists**

violate established scientific methods and laws? If they do, are they still practicing science?

In the prior chapter, we have already learned how many modern scientists ignore scientific laws governing the origins of life. In this chapter, we will examine other scientific methods and laws that are frequently ignored and even violated without conviction. The first one involves the scientific method itself.

The cornerstone of all science is the scientific method, which generally follows these steps:

- From specific observations, form a question. For example, "Why is grass green?"
- Develop a hypothesis (or an educated guess) as to the explanation that you expect might answer the question.
- By using logic, make predictions of how to prove the explanation. Use these predictions to design unbiased experiments that will adequately test the hypothesis.
- Test the hypothesis by conducting well-designed and unbiased experiments that are relevant to your predictions.
- Analyze the data from the experiments including confirming their statistical reliability.
- Repeat any of the above steps as necessary in order to conclude that the resulting data either supports or does not support the revised hypothesis.

Note how the scientific method begins—with observation. This step is precisely what the elementary teacher was attempting to do in the opening story. She was influencing her students to make observations. That said, an observation is not enough to reach any substantial conclusion, much less a scientific one. An observation must be followed by adequate and unbiased experiments in order to ultimately form data-driven conclusions. Far too many scientists have, in the name of science, claimed that God does not exist without employing a single experiment. The hypothesis of God's existence is impossible for them to test, making the scientific method unavailable to them. Being unable to employ the scientific method puts scientists at a disadvantage, which is precisely why they should avoid this and other philosophical hypotheses and stick with science. By attempting to form a conclusion on the matter without experiments and then disguising the conclusions as science, they have almost entirely disregarded the scientific method. Disregarding the scientific method is scientific malpractice. Drawing conclusions without the scientific method is not science but philosophy.

Let's examine the boy's initial observations in the opening story. The teacher asked him to observe the trees, grass, and sky. With these observations, she was pointing to things that can actually be observed. But, these observations result in a very powerful question. **What is the origin of these and all other physical things or "stuff" that we observe daily?** In prior chapters, we discussed the origin of life. Even though that issue alone condemns atheistic evolution, there is a question that follows that is likewise deadly: **Where did all this "stuff" come from?** If someone concludes that the universe began in a "massive ball of matter" that exploded, resulting in the Big Bang, some daunting questions must be answered. **First, was this ball and its explosion ever observed or adequately tested? Second, where did all that matter come from? Third, what caused the explosion?**

Of course, the answer to the first question is obvious. The self-caused Big Bang has never been observed by man or adequately tested. Therefore, it is not an example of properly using the scientific method; instead it is merely a philosophical guess for the most part. Because it was not observed or adequately tested, a self-exploding ball of matter is not fact, but at best an *opinion*. Given that nothing can logically cause itself to exist, this opinion is probably fiction.

Scientists have produced some interesting answers in their efforts to respond to the second question raised by the Big Bang theory regarding the origins of matter. Realizing obvious problems with the theory, some have resorted to suggesting that the entire quantity of matter and energy in the universe existed in a single, lonely, and incredibly dense microscopic atom (instead of the "massive ball of matter"), which always existed and then self-exploded to form the universe. First, this has never been observed or tested either. As an example of arguing with futility, reducing the size of the "ball" of all matter and energy into a microscopic form does not remove the scientific and logical problems with this revised conclusion. They must still answer the question of **where that one atom came from?** The revised conclusion is a failed attempt to avoid answering the central question.

In order to answer the central question more scientifically, we must employ the First Law of Thermodynamics. In its simplest form, this law of science states that the quantity of energy in an isolated system is constant. Energy (and matter) are not decreasing or increasing, just changing forms. A good example is evaporating water. As water evaporates, does the quantity of matter or energy decrease? No, because the water has changed forms from a liquid into a gas. You cannot destroy energy or matter. You can only change its form. This is why we have to ask **where all this matter came from?** Scientists have resorted to the illogical conclusion that matter (a natural thing) has the *supernatural* quality of having always existed. That is not science. That is incredibly bad philosophy and/or religion.

We now arrive at a third question. **What caused the collection of matter to explode?** Unbelieving scientists continue to offer bizarre answers. They nonsensically concluded earlier that matter always was and to answer the third question they say it caused its own explosion. Not only are there zero observations and zero data supporting such claims, neither is there any shred of logic or credible philosophy supporting them either. Again, these conclusions are not scientific—they are nonsensical opinions wearing the disguise of science.

Matter (a natural thing) with a finite nature cannot logically be eternal (having no beginning). However, it is logical for a *super*natural Creator to possess such supernatural qualities. In Ecclesiastes 3:14, Solomon wisely wrote, "I perceived that whatever God does endures forever; nothing can be added to it, nor anything taken from it. God has done it, so that people fear before him."

Unlike God, natural things and their unobserved self-explosions must comply with the scientific laws of cause and effect, among others. Matter is not supernatural nor does it will itself to randomly explode into an amazing and well-designed universe. But a supernatural God has no such limitations. Yes, I admit that this conclusion is an opinion, but at least it is a logical opinion that is totally unopposed by scientific data. All of the scientific laws that I am referencing do not oppose this conclusion, but they do oppose the conclusions of so-called "scientists."

At the onset of this section of the book, I challenged you to put all conclusions in one of three categories: fact, fiction, or opinion. But this challenge is best applied when we are analyzing actual scientific observations, data, and conclusions. Where no observations can be made and no adequate data exists, these conclusions are no longer science but philosophy. With philosophy, logic is the primary governor. In order to test philosophy for truth or falsity, the primary test is logic. If a given philosophy lacks logical consistency, it is false. We as Christians do not deny the possibility of a "Big Bang." We recognize that what God did in the early days of creation likely caused a "bang" like the universe has not seen since. We also admit freely that our faith is an opinion, but one that at least is consistent with logic and available data. When scientists put forth science-defying beliefs that have never been subjected to the scientific method and label them as science, nonsense and deception are the results. Considering the ramifications of their atheistic and evolutionary claims, what could be ruder?

Chapter 46

Are Fossils Really That Old?

I n 1973, the racehorse Secretariat won the Triple Crown and broke several records that have stood for decades. What many people do not know is that it wasn't until June of 2012 that it was finally decided that he also set a new record in the Preakness Stakes, the second of the Triple Crown races. It took 39 years for this to be recognized. The historically recorded race time was 1:55. However, after extensive review of the film and reference to independent clockers, it was determined that his actual race time was 1:53 2/5. With this shorter time, he set another record that has not been beaten since. It is amazing how in modern times with modern clocks, "experts" can get a race time wrong enough to deny a legendary racehorse of a record for 39 years. How could they have gotten such a simple time measurement wrong?

Regarding time measurement, there has been an even more controversial debate raging for centuries over the age of the earth. On one end of the spectrum are "experts" who claim the earth is billions of years old. On the other end are those who claim the earth is several thousand years old. **Where does your opinion fall in this spectrum?** The more important question is this one: **where does reliable evidence point in this discussion? Are the "experts" getting this one wrong as well?**

Fossils and rocks make up the bulk of material that scholars examine to make these time measurements. With these materials, there are three primary methods they use for dating: geologic strata dating, radiocarbon dating, and radiometric dating.

Geologic strata dating is the most common method used and the most simple. Using this method, the experts date the fossils based upon the presumed ages of the geologic strata (the layer of sedimentary rock or soil) in which the fossils are found. **But how do they determine the ages of the geologic strata?** The primary method of determining the age of the geologic strata is to use the ages of the fossils that are found in them. **Did you catch the logical fallacy here?** It is circular reasoning. If the ages of the fossils are used to date the strata, then we cannot reliably use the strata to date the fossils. Circular methods are unreliable and should be rejected.

The second (and most famous) dating method is radiocarbon dating (also known as carbon dating). Radioactive carbon is absorbed by living organisms throughout their lives. When the organism dies, this absorption stops and the radioactive carbon begins to break down into another form of carbon. Because this breakdown occurs at a presumed constant rate, it is theoretically possible to compare the amount of broken-down carbon to the amount of remaining radioactive carbon and then estimate just how long an organism has been dead.

A major problem with this theory is that this radioactive carbon has an expected life of less than 62,000 years. Therefore, using this method to arrive at ages of millions of years is not even scientifically possible, much less available. If anyone suggests that anything is millions of years old citing carbon dating, they are either lying or ignorant of scientific reality.

That is not the only problem with this dating method. First, the original ratio of carbon and radioactive carbon is not known because there were no *observations* of it at the death of the organism. Second, the rate of decay can be altered over time by events. Both of these carbons are formed at rates that can change dramatically over time and over varied conditions. Their rate of formation and breakdown could have changed substantially from ancient times to today. Third, the possibility of contamination of the samples over time is also high. The older the sample, the higher the probability of contamination and unreliability.

The best way to illustrate these problems is with another race analogy. Take for example a swimmer who is competing in a 1,500-meter race. At the instant the swimmer touches the edge of the pool at the end of the race, your wristwatch reads 9:25 a.m. and 14 seconds. How long has the swimmer taken to swim the 1,500-meter race? You cannot know the answer unless you at least know the time on the wristwatch when the race started. Without the starting time, it is impossible to establish the duration of the race. Similarly, accurately dating fossils by using methods like carbon dating is likewise impossible.

This example of the swimmer gets even worse. Actually, knowing the starting time of the race is still not enough. What about these factors?

- Was the wristwatch properly calibrated?
- Did you observe the swimmer during the race to make sure he completed 1,500 meters?
- Did you also observe if the swimmer touched the edge of the pool at the end of every lap?

Without these observations, you cannot be sure that the time is valid. That is why you need two or three observers throughout the entire race to measure the time of the race to the standards needed to enter the record books. The Secretariat example proved the importance of observing variables throughout the race to get the time measurements correct.

Why would we believe that dating ancient fossils or the earth is not also in need of similar observations over time to enter record books of substantially greater importance? Information gleaned from a technique that is limited to 62,000 years and depends on unobserved carbon ratios over time is totally unreliable for aging fossils, much less the earth.

The third method is radiometric dating, a technique used to age materials such as rocks. It is usually based on a comparison of the original amounts of radioactive isotopes assumed to be in a rock (a.k.a. parent atoms) to the amount of the final byproduct that is produced when the isotope decays (a.k.a. daughter atoms). This method suffers from similar problems as carbon dating with a few more of its own. First, we do not know the quantity of daughter atoms when the rock was first formed. We also do not know whether radioactive decay is the only variable that altered the parent and daughter atoms over time. And we do not know whether the decay rate has always been constant. This method is unreliable as well.

A review of the process for radiometric dating by using the isotope potassium argon reveals the shortcomings of this method. Several areas of our planet have been measured by using potassium argon arriving at measurements that are dramatically longer than what we know to be true. For example, potassium argon has been used to date Mount Ngaurhoe lava flows at 275,000 years. But we observed those lava flows less than 100 years ago. It has also been used to date the Sunset Crater near Flagstaff, Arizona at 200,000 years (we *know* it is less than 1,000 years old), Hawaii lava flows at up to 22 million years (we *know* they are less than 300 years old), Mt. Etna's eruption at up to 350,000 years (*actually* occurred in 1971), and the Mount St. Helens' eruption at 300,000 years (*actually* occurred in 1980), just to name a few. There are even more examples of flawed conclusions drawn from using other isotopes as well.

In contrast to these unreliable dating methods, the Bible offers some reliable evidence on the subject. In prior chapters, we have already addressed the evidence supporting the fact that the Bible is the most tested and supported book of history. On the issue of age, the Bible contains confirmed genealogies in both the Old Testament and the New Testament. When you combine them, we actually have a historical record of the genealogies from Adam to Noah to Jesus Christ. In addition, for many of the people in these genealogies, we also have a record of their ages. When aggregated, this places the age of the earth at several thousand years. As we continue to look at evidence here and in the following chapters, we have to keep asking ourselves, **what end of the spectrum for dating the age of the earth is more supported by reliable evidence?**

What does it suggest when we cannot even get a modern, two-minute horse race recorded properly for 39 years, but we believe we can accurately determine the earth to be billions of years old when we have no beginning measurements and we are using dating methods that are known to be significantly flawed due to lacking logic, adequate observations, and reliability? Unlike the Bible, it suggests that the bloated measurements of billions of years are probably wrong.

Chapter 47

Does the Bible Have a Distant Starlight Problem?

I love Christmas more than any other time of the year. From a scientific angle, a fascinating part of the Christmas story is the prophesied star that led the pagan Magi to Jesus. As I ponder this aspect of the story and all of the possible science behind it, I am reminded of the famous poem turned song that was written by Jane Taylor in 1806 entitled "Twinkle, Twinkle, Little Star." Here is the opening stanza:

Twinkle, twinkle, little star,
How I wonder what you are.
Up above the world so high,
Like a diamond in the sky.
Twinkle, twinkle, little star,
How I wonder what you are!

This poem was written from the perspective of a child and accordingly reflects a child's limited knowledge about stars. But apparently 19th-century children at least recognized that stars twinkle. This is scientifically accurate because a star is a burning sphere like our sun. Fire from a distance twinkles

245

because the light source (burning flames) constantly moves. Planets, on the other hand, generally do not twinkle because their light source is a reflection, and not flames. The nature of such twinkling starlight and our limited knowledge of stars have a significant impact on our reasoning regarding the age of the universe. For example, how old was the light from the star that led the Magi? If we see light today from a star burning one million light-years away, what does that suggest about the age of the universe? For the purpose of this chapter, does the Bible have a distant starlight problem?

The speed of light is generally measured at 186,282 miles per second. A light-year is a unit of measurement equaling the distance light will travel at this constant speed in one year. One light-year therefore is actually almost 6 trillion miles. But keep in mind that a light-year is a measure of distance, not time. By using several different methods, astronomers have measured the distance to many stars, resulting in calculations of millions of light-years. Modern scientists then assume that the light we see today must have traveled millions of years to reach us. If this is true, then the Bible's age for the universe (several thousand years) must be wrong and the "old universe" reasoning must be right. This level of reasoning, however, barely scratches the surface of available evidence. **What conclusion does the full breadth of evidence support?**

Given how little we know about the universe, there are a few possible ways to address this issue. The first is to realize that the Bible's creation account is clearly describing a *supernatural* event that will not be fully explained through using arguments confined to *natural* laws (naturalistic arguments). The second approach is to ignore the first approach and proceed to answer these questions strictly through naturalistic arguments that inappropriately ignore supernatural factors. A third approach properly recognizes supernatural factors and scientific laws working in harmony with each other. It is through this third approach that we will address the evidence with proper respect to both the Creator and the scientific laws that He created.

The unit of measurement of a light-year is based upon a constant speed of light. Assuming the speed of light is constant works for distance measurement, but not for time measurement or much else for that matter. In fact, we now have evidence that the speed of light is not constant. Separate experiments have been conducted where the speed of light was slowed down, brought to a complete stop, and then allowed to resume its course. In addition, light pulses have been observed that actually exceeded the speed of light by a factor of 300 times (L.J. Wang, et al, "Laser Smashes Light Speed Record," *Nature*, Volume 406:2000, pg. 277). We can no longer say with any reasonable degree of certainty that the speed of light is constant through either space or time.

Regarding time, in 1916, Einstein published his famous theory of general relativity, which stands largely unopposed. Based on the actual evidence that time moves at different rates in response to gravity, this theory suggests that different timeframes exist at various locations depending upon such factors. Most relevantly, gravity distorts time. For example, the atomic clock in Boulder, Colorado, is five microseconds faster than its twin clock in Greenwich, England (one-mile difference in altitude and in force of gravity). Time is then somewhat relative to the gravitational factors in which it is observed (referred to as time dilation).

In locations of highest gravity, time is distorted to move more slowly. Logically, in locations of lowest gravity, time moves much more rapidly. Therefore, during the universe's extremely rapid expansion in the Bible's creation week, when only a short amount of time has passed on the earth, there could still be adequate time in space for starlight to reach the earth. We can't assume that gravity throughout the early days of the universe was identical to what we calculate today. With supernaturally-induced, unrivaled levels of gravity through rapid expansion of the universe, distant starlight can cross a universe of distance in very little time. This realization coupled with light's varying speed offers the plausibility of no conflict between our present knowledge of the universe, starlight, and the "young universe" reasoning.

In contrast, the models used for the "old universe" reasoning actually have distant starlight problems of their own, if not worse ones. For example, "old universe" reasoning is refuted by a logical error referred to as the "Horizon Problem." The Horizon Problem in summary points out that different regions of the universe have not come into contact with each other because of the great distances between them. Nevertheless, these estranged regions of the universe share identical temperatures and other identical characteristics. The only way this could be possible is if these estranged regions of the universe exchanged energy with each other. But energy cannot travel across the universe any faster than the speed of light. **How then can estranged regions on opposite ends of the universe share identical temperatures and other characteristics if separated by billions of light-years?** The Horizon Problem clearly illustrates a factual flaw in "old universe" reasoning.

In addition, certain galaxies observed by the Hubble Space Telescope have calculated ages (using the same methods in "old universe" reasoning) that are older than the alleged age of the universe itself. But it is impossible for a galaxy to be older than the universe. Clearly one or both measurements are wrong.

According to "old universe" reasoning, it also takes billions of years for the spiral arms of galaxies to wind up tightly. However, the youngest galaxies at the edge of the universe have been found with spiral arms already wound tight. These spiral arms should not have even begun winding tightly because they are still in their infancy. Furthermore, the light of these infant galaxies at the edge of the universe should not be observable given how young they are and how long it should take for their starlight to travel across the universe to where we can observe it. While such realities illustrate significant flaws in the "old universe" reasoning, they present no problem for models that appropriately recognize supernatural factors.

Another example from astronomy that opposes "old universe" reasoning is the existence of comets. A comet is an object made primarily of ice traveling through space. The "tail" of a comet is actually the result of radiation caused by the sun burning off the ice as it travels. To this day, we have no factual idea of where comets actually come from or what produces them. Interestingly, comets we have observed have an average estimated remaining life of less than 10,000 years based upon their current rate of burn. Their existence clearly supports a "young universe." Modern scientists, recognizing the need to account for these "young" comets, have offered strange alternative stories for these comets' origins like the infamous "Oort cloud."

The Oort "cloud" is alleged to spit comets into space mysteriously. One of many problems with this theory is that such a cloud has never been observed. **This theory sounds more like science fiction than science.** Unobserved clouds theoretically spitting ice balls into space without supporting evidence is certainly not science.

Keep in mind that the examples included in this chapter favoring a "young universe" while undermining the possibility of an "old universe" are just a few from a much longer list. In short, our limited understanding of space, time, and light do not allow us to know with 100% certainty exactly how starlight reaches our planet in a relatively short period of time. We can know with certainty, however, that it is a distinct possibility. The so-called "distant starlight problem" does not create problems for young earth creationists as much as it does their opponents.

History has shown repeatedly that claims made in the Bible that are challenged initially by scientific theory are found to be true and the scientific theory lacking. This typically happens once enough data has been collected and once technology has advanced to the place to allow us to make better observations. In fact, a "young universe" conclusion is not conclusively opposed by totality of the evidence.

Sadly, most people today subscribe to belief in an "old universe." Many are intimidated by the opinions of a biased majority of scientists, rather than observable scientific facts. Christians, however, should never place their trust in the fallible opinions of men over God's revealed Word. In short, those who adopt such thinking have opted to believe in a theory that has never been proven right, instead of the Word of God that has never been proven wrong.

Chapter 48

No "Transitional Fossils" Exist

D r. Charles Darwin is widely recognized as the father of evolution because of the influence of his book *The Origin of Species* in 1859. Among many related theories, it was Darwin who is largely credited with claiming that all modern species ultimately evolved from a single-cell, microscopic organism (prokaryote) over millions of years. During the time of his book's publishing, there were not near as many fossils discovered as we have today. Darwin actually expressed doubt regarding his theories if the fossil record did not ultimately support them. In Chapter 10 of his book, he wrote, **"Why then is not every geological formation and every stratum full of such intermediate links?** Geology assuredly does not reveal any such finely-graduated organic chain; and this perhaps, is the most obvious and serious objection which can be urged against my theory."

In spite of the "obvious" problems with his theory, Darwin had faith that future fossil discoveries would support them. **After more than 150 years of archaeology and paleontology since his work was published, does the fossil record in fact**

support his theories? Based on what we know today, in Darwin's own words, would he still support them?

The types of fossils (or "intermediate links") that Darwin was expecting us to find are called transitional fossils. These fossils would be fossilized remains of life forms that would have dominant traits of both an "ancestral" group of animals and a "descendant" group of unlike animals (like whales with feet, for example, which don't actually exist). Today, in the Smithsonian Institute alone, there are more than four million fossils, none of which meet this definition. There are also millions of more fossils in museums around the world with the "obvious" absence of "transitional fossils." After more than 150 years of digging, there are no fossils of whales with feet or even giraffes with short necks.

What does it suggest when the earth is not littered with "transitional fossils" as Darwin reasonably expected? When resulting data opposes your theoretical hypothesis, the scientific method demands that your hypothesis be dismissed. According to Darwin's own words, the data suggests the "obvious" that his theories should be dismissed (referred to herein as Darwin's "obvious" test).

This failure to locate transitional fossils is not due to a lack of effort, however. In 1861, merely two years after the publishing of Darwin's work, the evolution-biased communities joyously announced the discovery of the fossil archaeopteryx and claimed it to be transitional. From just the outline of its fossilized bones, teeth, long tail, and feathers, they claimed it was part bird and part reptile. Many artist renditions were quickly commissioned painting hypothetical pictures of this "bird-reptile." Once more time was devoted to further study, however, it was realized that the archaeopteryx was not part bird and part reptile. Rather, it was 100% bird and 0% reptile. In fact, its teeth, extra claws, and long tail were features that it shared with modern birds. Although today's textbooks ignore these "obvious" facts, the disappointing search for adequate transitional fossils continues desperately to this day.

On a similar note, there has been much discussion over the years about the search for the "missing link." This is referring to the missing link between humans and animals. The truth is that the missing links across *all* animal groups are numerous *and* missing. Even if the archaeopteryx had been a true transitional fossil, one or even a couple transitional fossils are not enough to rescue Darwin's theory from Darwin's own criticism.

There is no better picture of these failures than in Darwin's famous "Tree of Life." In order to illustrate the presumed evolutionary relatedness of all the many species through time, Darwin drew a tree, the base of which was a single-cell organism (prokaryote). Moving up the tree, Darwin drew branches for different animal types and species consistent with the evolutionary beliefs about ancestral interrelationships between unrelated species groups. The resulting picture has all of the many fully "evolved" animal species toward the top, including humans, reptiles, birds, and dinosaurs. However, there is a huge flaw that even a child can observe from Darwin's "Tree of Life." None of the animals in Darwin's tree are "transitional." There are no modern animals or fossils that have dominant traits from two unrelated groups of species before and after them. And modern versions of this tree still lack transitional species.

Even the late Stephen J. Gould, famous and outspoken evolutionary biologist, admitted the following, "The extreme rarity of transitional forms in the fossil record persists as the trade secret of paleontology. The evolutionary trees that adorn our textbooks have data only at the tips and nodes of their branches; the rest is inference, however, reasonable, not the evidence of fossils . . . In any local area a species does not arise gradually by the steady transformation of its ancestors; it appears all at once and fully formed" ("Evolution's Erratic Pace," *Natural History*, Volume 86 (May 1987), pg. 14). In other words, Gould exposed Darwin's tree of being grossly flawed for lack of evidence.

On a secondary note, what Gould is referring to when he says, "It appears all at once," is a reference to the abundance of diversified species appearing in the fossil record at roughly the same time. One of the more famous of such appearances is referred to as the "Cambrian Explosion." The Cambrian Explosion in short is the appearance of most major animals in the fossil record in wide diversification at roughly the same time. One wonders what **would Darwin have thought about the Cambrian Explosion?**

His own words reveal what he would have thought. Darwin wrote in *The Origin of Species*, "If numerous species, belonging to the same genera or families, have really started into life all at once, the fact would be fatal to the theory to descent with slow modification though natural selection." In his own words, if Darwin knew then what we know now, he would be the first to declare evolution dead (referred to herein as Darwin's "fatal" test). At this point his theory is 0-2. Darwin's theory had failed his own two tests—the "obvious" test and the "fatal" test.

For another related argument against Darwin's work, we now have evidence that man actually walked with dinosaurs. In fact, I personally saw one alive just the other day. Walking among us today are the likes of crocodiles, alligators, and komodo dragons. Add to this the facts that we have found human footprints near both extinct dinosaur fossils and their footprints. According to neo-Darwinian evolution, humans and dinosaurs are supposed to be separated by more than 65 million years of evolution. This evidence is just another example of a theory at odds with the facts.

The Bible gives even more evidence of man walking with dinosaurs. In Job 40:15-24, God describes to Job the following animal...

"Behold, Behemoth, which I made as I made you; he eats grass like an ox. Behold, his strength in his loins, and his power in the muscles of his belly. He makes his tail stiff like a cedar; the sinews of his thighs are knit together. His bones are tubes of bronze, his limbs like bars of iron. He is the first of the works of God; let him who made him bring near his sword! For the mountains yield food for him where all the wild beasts play. Under the lotus plants he lies, in the shelter of the reeds and in the marsh. For his shade the lotus trees cover him; the willows of the brook surround him. Behold, if the river is turbulent he is not frightened; he is confident though Jordan rushes against his mouth. Can one take him by his eyes, or pierce his nose with a snare?"

What animal was the "first" (the largest) of animals, had a "tail" like a "cedar" tree, ate "grass," lived under "lotus trees," had an un-snarable nose, and a mouth large enough to confidently withstand a rushing river? This is a near flawless description of something like a brachiosaurus, and it is a description that only matches dinosaurs, not animals that are alive today. The evidence suggests that Job is describing a living dinosaur that he observed in his day.

The fossil record is fact. The lack of adequate transitional fossils is an "obvious" fact. The appearance of a wide diversity of species at roughly the same time in the fossil record is a "fatal" fact. These facts clearly demand the dismissal of Darwinian evolution as a viable theory of origins. In fact, it was Darwin who declared such facts to be obvious and fatal. Ignoring obvious and fatal facts is not science.

Chapter 49

X-Men and the Missing Link

The X-Men is a superhero team in the Marvel Comics universe that was first dreamed up by Stan Lee in 1963. This team derives its superpowers from significant mutations in the human genetic code. They are therefore referred to as "mutants." Throughout the series, there are protagonist mutants (X-Men) who help defend mankind, but they are in constant struggle against the antagonistic mutants who are at war with humans because of humanity's threatening phobia toward mutants.

Take for example the character Beast, who is one of the X-Men. Beast is a mutant who possesses apelike superhuman physical strength and agility, oversized hands and feet, blue fur, fangs, and claws. While the idea of X-Men like Beast was partially inspired by science, **does this notion truly reconcile with science? Does science support or oppose this type of fiction? Or did "science" create this fiction?** Could mutants explain the "missing link" between humans and animals?

The X-Men make for great comic books and movies but the notion is nowhere near being an observable scientific reality. Mutations are accidental changes in a genomic sequence of DNA. However, such changes are fatal because human mutations generally result in relative weakness and/or premature death. But in spite of this logical flaw, mutations are absolutely essential to modern evolutionary theory. In short, neo-Darwinian evolution holds the following assertions:

Defying logic and scientific laws, a single-cell organism (prokaryote) was caused to exist by nothing.

It then proceeded to multiply on its own by cell division and began evolving.

The primary engines of this "evolving" were gradual and dramatic mutations.

These mutations theoretically created new species—both weak and strong.

Via natural selection, the weakest species died off and the fittest survived (survival of the fittest).

This process continued over millions of years and ultimately resulted in humans and all of the other species.

Is there any scientific data supporting this view of mutations? Are mutations ever observed to be beneficial? Do mutations result in newly established species?

Along with the well-known opinions of Darwin, this idea also gained popularity because of the work of Ernst Haeckel, a famous German biologist, physician, professor, and artist who discovered and named thousands of new species, among many other scientific achievements. He was most famous for a conclusion that is often referred to as "Haeckel's embryos."

In 1874, Haeckel published an embryology textbook entitled *Anthropogenie*. In that textbook, he personally sketched side-by-side drawings of the embryos of a fish, salamander, turtle, chicken, pig, cow, rabbit, and human. These sketches can be found today in virtually every basic biology textbook. Eerily, the embryo sketches of these varied organisms look strangely similar. This drawing helped bolster the notion of mutation as the engine of evolution across these varied species.

What has been learned since then is that there are major flaws with Haeckel's sketches. First, Haeckel cherry-picked his examples to include those that came closest to fitting his bias. Second, he doctored the sketches to make them look more similar than they truly are. Even though these and other problems were exposed within a couple of years of his work being published, Haeckel's embryos still grace the pages of textbooks today. Even Gould referred to this as "the academic equivalent of murder."

As further support for the notion of transitional mutations over long periods of time, "science" also looks to the examples of adaptation within species. A certain strain of bacteria (MRSA or Methicillin-resistant Staphylococcus aureus, for example) might adapt to resist antibacterial medication. But keep in mind that *adaptation* is not *mutation*. Adaptation does not accidentally alter the bacteria's DNA. The adapted MRSA is still bacteria—not mutant bacteria. Likewise, certain humans who have developed immunities to certain viruses or resistance to certain drugs are not mutants either.

This misunderstanding of adaptation being equivalent over time to mutation across broadly different species is also aided by a misapplication of the definition of "species." A species is a group of organisms capable of interbreeding and producing fertile offspring. For example, if we breed a unique squirrel that is unable to breed with other squirrels, we have a new species of squirrel. But, it is still a squirrel. What we do not observe in fossils and in modern reality are "transitional" mutants like whales with feet or blue ape-men. What we do observe are examples of microevolution, not macroevolution. Microevolution includes resistant strains of bacteria or a new breed of squirrel. Macroevolution is when organisms cross over from being a squirrel to being part squirrel and part something totally different. To put it simply, we have not observed any examples of X-squirrels, X-bacteria, or X-whales. More to the point, there are zero examples of X-men.

Beneficial adaptation (microevolution) does not equal beneficial mutation (macroevolution). In fact, in humans, "beneficial mutation" is an oxymoron. Adaptations can be beneficial, but human mutations are not. There are several thousand known mutations of human DNA, and not one is truly beneficial. Every known human mutation is ultimately weakening and/or deadly to man. There are some who claim this is not true and solely cite people who have sickle-cell anemia (a mutation) because they are immune from malaria. What they cleverly ignore is that sufferers of this mutation would rather have malaria if it meant that they did not die prematurely from sickle-cell anemia. Malaria is much more easily treated and/or remedied. This example actually proves a flaw in the argument for macroevolution.

Unfortunately, these scientific obstacles have not slowed academia or their textbook printing presses. In addition to these examples, they continue to cite examples from the fossil record of what they distort to be transitional humans, which have also since been proven to be frauds. For example, "Nebraska Man" was actually a pig's tooth, "Java Man" was actually the bones of a gibbon, "Taung African Man" and "Nutcracker Man" were actually the skulls of apes, Australopithecus ("Lucy") was actually the bones of apes, "Rhodesian Man" was actually a man, "Piltdown Man" was actually a complete fraud, and "Peking Man" (only plaster casts) was found in a garbage dump with thousands of other animals.

This brings us to the infamous "Neanderthal Man." Neanderthals have long been heralded as an extinct "species" or "subspecies" of humans. They are still not heralded as the elusive "missing link," but their example is distorted toward that agenda. The scientific positions on Neanderthals were largely unchallenged until 1998. In that year, Jack Cuozzo published his book entitled *Buried Alive*. Cuozzo, an orthodontist, described his lifelong achievement of being one of only a handful of scientists who have actually physically examined and studied all of the known original Neanderthal skulls in the world. He is probably the only dental physician who has done so. His dental expertise is actually significant because the dental condition and dental observations are central to the claims about these skulls being "subhuman."

Cuozzo's work, however, drew an opposing conclusion. He found the skulls to be 100% human in their dental framework. He examined their enamel, photographed it, and established it to be consistent with what we would expect for human skulls of more modest age. He even discovered where a certain skull had a tooth that was apparently sharpened by tools, which is inconsistent of the profile of unintelligent Neanderthals that we are led to believe. Cuozzo also made this repeated observation: "I picked up the . . . skull in my hands and carefully placed the lower teeth against the upper teeth in what we orthodontists call the centric occlusion . . . the jaw condyles (ends) fit perfectly together in the sockets (on the skull) when the teeth were in this maximum centric occlusion position. It didn't look like the drawing at all." What Cuozzo observed was that the Neanderthal jawbones are wrongly manipulated forward in the drawing—even outside of the natural socket in the skull to falsely portray a significant underbite. When the jawbones are properly positioned in their natural sockets, the skulls look more consistently human. The manipulation of these skulls to support a biased agenda is not science, but fraud.

In a paper published in August 2013, by the Proceedings of the National Academy of Sciences, researchers outlined their discovery of four fragments of bone made by Neanderthals in southwestern France that were apparently used as lissoirs, or smoothers, for making animal hides tougher and more water resistant. Leather workers use similar tools today. Contrary to widely held beliefs, this discovery provides "evidence that Neanderthals may have independently made specialized bone tools."

The paper went on to admit that the find "confirms that there is still much we don't know about them." Rachel Wood, an archaeologist and researcher in radiocarbon dating at the

Australian National University, added, "It's adding to a growing body of research, that's growing quite rapidly at the moment, that's showing that Neanderthals are capable and did produce tools . . . in a way that is much more similar to modern humans."

In conclusion, by science's own admission, the "missing link" in the fossil records is still missing. The oldest dated animal fossil we are told died "3.4 billion years ago." Therefore, we allegedly have "3.4 billion years" of fossils and cannot find one example of a transitional human. **What does such evidence suggest?** If it were any other "theory," it would be rejected because of the scientific method.

The fact that this link is still missing suggests that it never existed. It is a sad and comical irony that many in the scientific community, who abuse the scientific method in attempts to dismiss faith, openly admit having a "missing link." In other words, they oppose the notion of faith while practicing faith. They embrace a belief in something that they are unable to prove, yet deceptively disguise it as science. Christianity clearly admits faith and heralds true scientific evidence that supports it.

Chapter 50

What If I Cut Myself in Half?

As Darwin's continuously revised theory goes, approximately 3.5 billion years ago, with nobody observing, "nothing" caused a microscopic, single-cell organism (prokaryote) to emerge into existence from nonliving matter in a toxic pond for the first time ever and never again since. This prokaryote was lonely, so it thought to itself, **"What if I cut myself in half?"** And without any tools or any prior experience, it did just that with perfect precision and success. Then there were two living prokaryotes. Within a matter of years (billions), greater, unguided feats continued until humans and all the other species we currently know evolved, none of which resemble microscopic prokaryotes at all. **Does such a hypothesis sound reasonable?**

Forgive the sarcasm, but this contrived fiction lacks sufficient evidence. It is beyond farfetched. Ironically, those who blindly preach macroevolution are usually very quick to accuse the Bible of telling tall tales. In response, we may submit the following questions: **How did the complex arise from the noncomplex? Does it seem like a natural and intuitive thought for any organism to contemplate cutting itself** in half? Where would an organism get such an idea? Have we ever observed simple organisms creating more complex organisms than themselves?

A prokaryote is a single-cell organism. Two good examples of prokaryotes are bacteria and blue-green algae. A prokaryote is supposedly the "simplest" of all living organisms, but it is far from simple. In fact, it is one of the few organisms that can self-replicate by cell division (asexual). Its "idea" of dividing itself is the function of instinct and not its own original thought. It doesn't even have a brain. Organisms with or without brains do not instinctively self-replicate without the necessary information and instructions in its DNA to carry out such a complex feat. In fact, the DNA of a prokaryote contains millions of characters of genetic information. The sudden existence of genetic information in the presumed first life form leads us to some new questions. **Where would the first living organism get instinct? Who put the millions of characters of genetic information and instructions in its DNA?**

The first problem with all of these concepts is that it is impossible for natural environments with zero complexity to cause complex life forms. The second problem is that organisms of lesser complexity cannot perform tasks of greater complexity without experience and/or instructions. For example, in order to get your computer to perform a more complex function than its operating system allows, you have to install a new software code in its operating system. Likewise, if you want the simplest living organism to perform a function of higher complexity, you have to provide information somewhere in its operating system, which is its DNA. Even Bill Gates, Microsoft founder and professed agnostic, said, "DNA is like a software program, only much more complex than anything we've ever devised."

George Sim Johnston, author of *Did Darwin Get It Right?: Catholics and the Theory of Evolution*, ironically added, "Human DNA contains more organized information than the Encyclopedia Britannica. If the full text of the encyclopedia were to arrive in computer code from outer space, most people would regard this as proof of the existence of extraterrestrial intelligence. But when seen in nature, it is explained as the workings of random forces."

Even if toxic ponds had the right chemical components of a living cell, information is still needed for how to arrange them in very specific configurations in order to perform vastly complex biological functions. Most humans transfer information with a 26-letter alphabet or even with just a few characters (zeroes and ones as in the binary code).

One of the most extraordinary discoveries of the 20th century was that DNA actually stores information, including the detailed instructions for its functions, in the form of a four-character genetic code. The characters are chemicals named adenine, guanine, cytosine, and thymine (represented with the characters A, G, C, and T in the genetic code). Properly arranging these genetic characters will instruct the cell on how to build different sequences of amino acids, which are the building blocks of proteins. Proteins are the key functional molecules in the cell. In other words, you cannot have life without them.

To build one protein, you typically need 1,200 to 2,000 genetic characters and that would only be one protein. A minimally complex cell would need between 300 and 500 proteins. Given that prokaryote DNA contains millions of genetic characters of information, this continues to demand an answer to the question of the origin of that information and how complex and organized information suddenly arose from toxic non-complexity.

Michael Behe is a professor of biochemistry at Lehigh University. In 1996, he published his famous book, *Darwin's Black Box*. "Black box" is a term used when describing a system or machine that is interesting but we don't know how it works. When Darwin wrote his book in the 1800s, the cell was a "black box" because microscopes of his era did not allow him to see the cell details that we see today.

In his book *The Origin of Species*, Darwin said, "If it could be demonstrated that any complex organ existed which could not possibly have been formed by numerous, successive, slight modifications, my theory would absolutely break down." This is Darwin's test of "irreducible complexity." A system or device is irreducibly complex if it has a number of different components that all work together to accomplish the task of the system, and if you were to remove one of the components, the system would no longer function in any reasonable way.

We probably have no more perfect example of irreducible complexity than the prokaryote. It was allegedly the first and simplest living organism. Therefore, there were none simpler before it. But the prokaryote by definition is irreducibly complex in its structure, its DNA, and its alleged origin. Everything before it was nonliving, had zero complexity, and zero DNA. Using Darwin's own words, the emergence of the prokaryote makes his theory "absolutely break down" because it is a complex organism that evolution alleges emerged in one step.

By admission, evolution claims that it "could not possibly have been formed by numerous, successive, slight modifications." The sudden, one-step emergence of the complex prokaryote represents a third Darwinian test that evolution has failed. (The prior chapter on evolution described how Darwin's "obvious test" and his "fatal test" were failed.)

Another helpful example of an organism that is irreducibly complex is the bombardier beetle, which is most notable for its defense mechanism. When disturbed, these beetles eject a deadly chemical spray in a rapid burst of about 70 pulses from special glands in their abdomen. They produce and store two reactant chemical compounds—hydroquinone and hydrogen peroxide—in separate chambers. They instinctively force the two reactants into a mixing chamber containing water and catalytic enzymes. When combined, a violent exothermic chemical reaction occurs, raising the temperature to near the boiling point of water. The pressure buildup forces the entrance from the storage chambers to close, protecting the beetle's internal organs. What follows is a projection of its deadly spray upon its unsuspecting attacker.

This extraordinary spray that the beetle produces is sometimes deadly to small creatures. This defense mechanism is not only amazingly complex in an otherwise simple beetle, but it also defies the suggestions of evolution. Scientists have been unable to illustrate how the bombardier beetle and its dangerous abilities could have evolved "by numerous, successive, slight modifications." Further, **how did a bombardier beetle evolve from a single prokaryote? Who added genetic information to the DNA to accomplish such an evolutionary change?** The answers to these questions remain so elusive that attempts to answer them have been all but abandoned.

Darwin also submitted his own example of irreducible complexity by using the example of an eye in *The Origin of Species*: "To suppose that the eye, with all its inimitable contrivances for adjusting the focus to different distances, for admitting different amounts of light, and for the correction of spherical and chromatic aberration, could have been formed by natural selection seems, I freely confess, absurd in the highest possible degree." I agree with him. The eye is irreducibly complex. **How did a prokaryote that has no eyes evolve to become many different organisms with eyes? How did a "simple" prokaryote with no genetic information for assembling a complex machine like an eye through successive evolution obtain information to construct eyes?** Evolutionists will never adequately answer these questions because adequate answers don't exist apart from a creator and special creation.

If you can't explain where the original genetic information (and subsequently added information) comes from, you cannot even begin to explain life or its origin. It is the information that makes the molecules into something that actually functions. It is just simply impossible that all this vast complexity fell into place by itself from non-complexity. Francis Crick, a molecular biologist and co-discoverer of the structure of the DNA molecule, said, "An honest man, armed with all the knowledge available to us now, could only state that in some sense, the origin of life appears at the moment to be almost a miracle, so many are the conditions which would have had to have been satisfied to get it going."

Crick almost got it right. Life is not "almost" a miracle, it *is* a miracle. The thing about miracles is that they don't happen naturally. Someone would have had to give the prokaryote genetic instructions on how to cut itself in half in order to reproduce itself supernaturally. That "Someone" would be God. **Who else could it be?** Rather than jumping through hoops to explain how God could have been involved in an evolutionary process, it makes more sense to just accept what the Bible teaches about creation.

Chapter 51

The "Simplest" Life-Form Is Not Simple

Imagine the first hypothetical manned visit to Mars happening sometime in the distant future. After days of exploration, the astronaut team stumbles upon the most amazing discovery. Buried just under the surface of the Martian soil, they find a mechanical device that is clearly of nonhuman origin. It has the look of a small weapon that could be worn on the arm. The device is brought back to earth for further examination. There it is determined that it is an instrument for measuring and tracking planetary orbits. It is apparently an alien version of a solar wristwatch. **What would such a discovery suggest?**

There are generally two approaches to answering that question. The first approach is to argue that this Martian wristwatch was the result of undirected forces that randomly assembled the device without any intelligence applied. The other approach is to argue that it was designed, made, and left by an intelligent being. Having to choose between these two approaches may seem ridiculous. In this context, we probably all agree. When we stumble upon much more complex "machines" in nature on our planet, however, the first approach is taken seriously by many. This conclusion is drawn because intelligent life hypothetically evolving on other planets fits an evolution-biased agenda, while evidence pointing to more complex natural design on our planet does not. This inconsistency, however, displays a lack of intellectual integrity.

The evidence of design in something is the presence of a coherent or purposeful pattern. Finding such evidence in natural machines raises deserving questions. **Can complex and coherent design in nature be caused by random undirected forces? Have we ever observed any examples of purely random and undirected forces causing complex and coherent design? Does coherent and complex design require a coherent and complex cause?**

Prior chapters introduced us to the single-cell organism (prokaryote) and how "science" preaches that it was (illogically) caused by "nothing." The flaws of abiogenesis also were exposed in that it is scientifically and logically impossible for life to emerge from nonliving matter on its own. Lastly, we studied how embedded in the genetic information of the DNA of a prokaryote are the instinctual instructions of how to reproduce itself by asexual cell division (contrary to reasonable expectations of intuition). In spite of all this evidence to the contrary, the prokaryote is still the champion of evolution because it is the "simplest form of life." Evolution assumes that the simpler the organism, the easier for it to have emerged from nonliving matter (without evidence).

This logic is false and inconsistent with accepted, scientific laws. Additionally, a prokaryote, although simpler than us, is an organism that is far from simple. Its DNA contains millions of genetic characters of information that direct thousands of self-contained chemical reactions simultaneously and on a microscopic scale.

If that were not enough, in 1973 scientists discovered the flagellum of prokaryotes. Flagellum are long tails that perform like rotary submarine propellers. Flagellum spin at 10,000

RPM, can stop spinning within a quarter turn, and instantly start spinning in the opposite direction at 10,000 RPM. By comparison, consider the Honda S2000, with a state-of-the-art, four-cylinder, two-liter, dual-overhead-cam aluminum block engine, featuring four valves per cylinder and variable intake and exhaust valve timing. The S2000 has a "redline" of only 9,000 RPM and is totally unable to stop and reverse direction like a prokaryote's flagellum. For this reason, Howard Berg, a professor of physics, molecular biology, and cellular biology at Harvard University, called bacterial flagellum "the most efficient motors in the universe." Under the microscope, the structure of flagellum looks uncannily like "motors" that intelligent beings would build, but they are way beyond anything we can make—especially when you consider their microscopic size (flagellum are on the order of 1/20,000 of an inch).

Flagellum are just the beginning of the Darwin-defying complexity in the microscopic world of the living cell. Another example is the intracellular transport system within cells. Cells typically contain more than 20 internal compartments. For those compartments, cells constantly discard old components and manufacture new ones. These components are custom-designed to work in certain compartments and not in others. Most new components are made at a central location in the cell by ribosomes. Ribosomes are factories of sorts (within the cell) that can manufacture any protein, following instructions given by DNA. They can also construct any protein-based biological machine (including another ribosome) regardless of complexity. Michael Denton is a biochemist and famous author of *Evolution: A Theory in Crisis*. According to this scientist, the ribosome is more remarkable than our own intelligent abilities as humans.

"It is astonishing to think that this remarkable piece of machinery, which possesses the ultimate capacity to construct every living thing that has ever existed on earth, from a giant redwood to the human brain, can construct all its own components in a matter of minutes and . . . is of the order of several thousand million times smaller than the smallest piece of functional machinery ever constructed by man."

Evolutionists would like us to believe that the single-cell prokaryote is quite simple. However, in truth, the prokaryote is a far more complex "machine" than a NASA space shuttle. In reference to the illustration shared at the beginning of this chapter, the prokaryote is an immeasurably more complex machine than a solar wristwatch. The flagellum alone puts manmade devices to mechanical shame comparably speaking. Today, with all of our intelligence and technology, man is unable to mimic a prokaryote's one-step emergence from nonliving matter. **Therefore, what evidence would lead us to conclude that it can happen on its own with zero intelligence and/or technology applied?** No such evidence exists.

The core claim of modern evolutionary theory on this subject is that the apparent design of living systems is an illusion. **Isn't it more reasonable to suggest that an irreducibly complex, functional, and interdependent microscopic machine was deliberately designed?** A watch suggests a watchmaker. It is reasonable to suggest that far more complex "biological machines" that show similar, yet more complex characteristics were also designed.

I will close with a poem by Dave Hawkins that eloquently reinforces this conclusion, entitled "The Watchmaker":

A long time ago on a planet so bare,
Some water and dirt got mixed up with the air.
Some sand and some rocks to make it just right,
The stage was all set in the deep of the night.
A bolt of white lightning, a great peal of thunder,
And suddenly there was a marvelous wonder.
The rocks yielded metal, the sand turned to glass,
And as the years flew, a new thing came to pass.
The metal formed gears, the glass a watch face,
And little by little, things fell into place.

The parts came together, just like a good rhyme,
With ticks and with tocks and with hands that tell time.
A beautiful watch began ticking one day,
Formed all by itself in a wonderful way.
"Ridiculous story!" you say with a grin.
"Impossible, laughable . . . surely a sin!
A watch needs a watchmaker, that's plain to see.
A designer and builder that makes it for me."
Now all life is made of some interesting stuff.
Cells of all shapes like blobs filled with fluff.
But looks are deceiving and what we find there.
Are factories and highways and gadgets to spare.
Assembly lines, robots, electrical cable.
Libraries, software; just look, if you're able.
The marvels we see with a microscope's stare,
Make a watch look so simple, we dare not compare.
Now the doctors from Oxford say cells came by Chance,
From Goo down to You in a beautiful dance.
What's wrong with their thinking to have such odd
notions?
That cells could just happen from dirt and warm oceans!
A cell and its wonders amaze all who see,
And a cell, like a watch, by Chance cannot be.
Those cells can build hummingbirds, agile and free,
Bumble bees, snails, my backyard oak tree.
A woodpecker built with a jackhammer nose?
Lightning bugs, monkeys, a beautiful rose,
And beetles with bombs that give frogs a surprise,
Chameleons with camouflage and some weird eyes.
All nature on Earth is so perfectly fine,
We have to admit that it's all by Design,
And our Maker owns everything both great and small.
He's the masterful "Watchmaker," Lord over all.

Chapter 52

Need Life? Just Add Water

I n 2011, Leslie Grange, a sign-language interpreter for BBC News, was famously terminated after complaints revealed she was sometimes "making things up" as she interpreted the news to deaf viewers. One of the funnier complaints was regarding a story about survivors of a nuclear reactor meltdown in Japan that was interpreted to deaf viewers as "radioactive zombies being sighted." This story humorously shows how a faulty interpreter can mislead many. In this case, the damage was minor.

This example of being misled pales in comparison to how cosmic events that occur throughout our planet and the universe are grossly misinterpreted daily on most news stations. A prime example is how the vast majority in the scientific community continually claim that life is sure to have evolved on other planets wherever water exists. They reason (without evidence) that if life can (illogically) emerge from non-life on a planet like ours then why not throughout the billions of galaxies in the universe? Under this thinking, life is like a soup mix . . . just add water. **But has anything in the universe truly shown this idea to be fact? Have we ever observed life emerging from nonliving matter in water? Since this conclu-**

sion is not factual and not logical, isn't it just fiction? Is the scientific community a faulty interpreter?

In 2004, Guillermo Gonzalez and Jay Wesley Richards published *The Privileged Planet*, and their work documented amazing evidence pointing toward a pattern of life-sustaining design throughout our planet and the universe. They stated that it is true that in order to have life you need water for chemical reactions to take place, but so much more is also required. Setting aside for a moment the supernatural spark of life and genetic information required, not just any planetary body can be the source of all the chemical ingredients in the formulations and balance required to sustain life.

Below is a partial list of facts revealing how the universe is amazingly designed to sustain life on earth:

Only terrestrial planets (like Earth) are capable of sustaining life, and terrestrial planets require an abundance of heavy elements such as carbon, nitrogen, oxygen, phosphorus, and calcium. Earth and its sun have a rarely high and balanced abundance of these elements.

The more massive the galaxy, the more heavy elements it is likely to possess (mass strengthens gravity, attracting more hydrogen and helium, which are processed to build heavy elements). Our galaxy, the Milky Way, is in the top 1% to 2% of massive galaxies. The second tier of galaxies (the vast majority) have relatively low mass (containing thousands of stars without a single terrestrial planet). And the galaxies in the third tier are irregular, which are the deadliest.

Earth is located in a rare, optimal safe zone of the Milky Way, which is between (outside of) the spiral arms named Sagittarius and Perseus. In contrast, inside the spiral arms a high rate of deadly supernovae explosions occur coupled with deadly molecular clouds.

It is widely held that most large galaxies have a black hole at their centers, which is a very dangerous location because of the extremely high radiation levels. If so, a black hole likely resides in the Milky Way's center. Earth is optimally located far from that region. However, it is rare for planets where the earth is located to have an abundance of heavy elements. These are typically located near the deadly center of a galaxy where gravity is strongest.

The Milky Way, if viewed from the side, would resemble a relatively thin disk. Since stars orbit within a galaxy, the Milky Way being thin keeps our sun's orbit optimally circular (which is rare). Most galaxies are more egg-shaped, making noncircular orbits typical. If our sun had a noncircular orbit, it would likely cross spiral arms and visit the dangerous regions of the galaxy, dragging the earth in fatal tow.

Earth has a rare, stable, and circular orbit around the sun, as opposed to deadly noncircular orbits, which is most common throughout the universe. If its orbit was noncircular, it would experience deadly surface temperature swings. In fact, even small variations in Earth's orbit would cause significant, frequent "ice ages."

Fortunate for earth, Jupiter also has a circular orbit. Given Earth's lesser size, its orbit is affected by the gravitational impact of this gas giant, which is 300 times the size of earth. Earth's optimal circular orbit is only possible because Jupiter's orbit is also optimally circular.

Since Jupiter is so massive, its gravitational pull also shields us from deadly comet impacts. It attracts comets, keeping many from entering the inner solar system (For example, Comet Shoemaker-Levy 9 impacted Jupiter in July 1994.) Saturn and Uranus also attract comets away from Earth.

Earth is the perfect distance from our sun to sustain life. If adjusted by 5%, animal life would be impossible.

Terrestrial planets must be of a minimum size to gravitationally retain a protective atmosphere like Earth's. If our planet was smaller, we would have insufficient to no protective atmosphere.

A planet also needs an oxygen-rich atmosphere to support humans. Earth's atmosphere is optimally 20% oxygen.

A planet must be of a minimum size to keep heat from its radioactively decaying interior (9,000 degrees Fahrenheit) from being lost too quickly. If our planet was smaller, it would cool quicker and "die" like Mars.

If the earth were larger, its surface gravity would increase. This increase would result in a greater pull on mountains and all exposed land masses, ultimately creating a smooth sphere. A smooth sphere would mean no exposed landmasses or a deadly water world. The life essential elements would sink to the bottom, and the salt concentration would be deadly.

Of all the planets and moons we have observed, plate tectonics is found only on Earth. Plate tectonics help develop continents and mountains, which prevents a deadly water world.

Earth's unique plate tectonics also drive the planet's carbon dioxide–rock cycle by cycling fragments of Earth's crust down into the mantle. There, the planet's internal heat releases the carbon dioxide, which continually vents into the atmosphere through volcanoes. These gases absorb infrared energy and help warm the planet optimally. The end result is that the earth operates like an elaborate thermostat that keeps gases in balance and our surface temperature optimal for life.

The radioactive decay of Earth's core also generates our amazingly unique magnetic field. This is crucial to life by shielding our atmosphere (and us) from low-energy cosmic rays, dangerous radiation, and solar wind particles.

Albedo is the proportion of sunlight a planet reflects. If light is not reflected, it is absorbed. The more a planet absorbs light, the higher its surface temperature is increased. But the earth has a uniquely rich variety of albedo sources (oceans, polar ice caps, continental interiors, deserts, etc.), which is critical to regulating the climate in a delicate balance.

Our sun is a yellow dwarf (a term that refers to color and size), which is optimal for sustaining life. In contrast, red dwarfs, that make up about 80% of stars, have frequent and deadly flares. These flares increase orbiting planetary surface temperature spikes and particle radiation (destroying protective ozone layers). Red dwarfs also do not produce much ultraviolet light, which is needed to build up required oxygen to sustain life.

Fortunately, our sun not only has an optimal size, but it also emits an array of colors of light that are optimal for sustaining life. The sun is also highly stable compared with most stars. Its light output only varies by one-tenth of 1%, which prevents deadly climate swings on Earth.

The moon actually does support life—ours. Our moon, due to its rare size relationship to Earth, stabilizes the tilt of Earth's axis (23.5 degrees). This tilt is required for our optimally mild seasons. This particular relationship between a planet and a moon is rare both inside and outside of our solar system. The stability of our climate is in large part attributable to the moon. If the moon was smaller or larger, it would have a deadly impact on the tilt of Earth's axis.

The moon also contributes 60% to our tides (the sun contributes 40%). Lunar tides keep large-scale ocean circulation moving. A larger moon would slow Earth, making tides deadly strong and temperature swings fatal.

The universe, our galaxy, our solar system, and our planet reveal and declare that they are amazingly designed systems that actively work together to sustain life on Earth. The universe is so glorious in structure and magnitude that it is the single greatest inspiration for wonder. Many in the scientific community attempt to reduce this grand display of design down to random coincidence. Like the BBC's deaf viewers, I refuse to stand for gross misinterpretations of what is actually being said. Instead I will cry out with the psalmist, "The heavens declare the glory of God!" (Psalm 19:1)

Chapter 53

What Does a Finely Tuned Universe Suggest?

I f I bet you $1,000 that I could flip a coin and get heads 22 times in a row and then I proceeded to do it, you probably wouldn't accept the result. You would know that the odds against this happening are so high that it is virtually impossible. The fact that I was able to do it against such enormous odds would be strong evidence that my wager was rigged. **What would you think about someone who accepted my wager and accepted the result because he refused to believe rigging ever happens? Isn't that a foolish bias?**

However, this same depth of bias is displayed, if not to a higher degree, regarding attempts to ignore the numerous ways in which our universe is so finely tuned. By finely tuned, I mean the extraordinary balancing of the fundamental laws, parameters, and constants of physics across the universe even down to its microscopic framework. Our minds cannot even comprehend the precision of some of these many constants, and the coincidences are simply too amazing to have been the result of chance. And before concluding that mindless chance caused such fine-tuning, we would conclude that the evidence suggests the universe was favorably "rigged" . . . that is, designed.

Many attributes about the basic structure of the universe are optimally balanced on a razor's edge in order for life, and everything, else to exist. As *Discover* magazine marveled in 2002, "The universe is unlikely. Very unlikely. Deeply, shockingly unlikely." Similarly, even Stephen Hawking, who has publicly denounced the "need for God," ironically noted, "The laws of science, as we know them at present, contain many fundamental numbers . . . The remarkable fact is that the values of these numbers seem to have been very finely adjusted to make possible the development of life."

Some critics, however, have attacked positions that recognize the universe's fine-tuning, arguing that if the universe were not fine-tuned for life, then human beings would not be around to observe it. In other words, if the universe was not finely tuned, we would not know because we would not be here to observe it. This argument proves nothing. For example, suppose you were standing before a firing squad of 22 highly trained marksmen who were all aiming directly at your chest from a short distance away. You heard the order, "Ready! Aim! Fire!" But after you hear the gunshots, you don't feel anything. You remove your blindfold and realize that not one bullet has hit you. In this case, you would not allow a critic to dismiss these amazing odds by claiming that if they had shot you, you wouldn't be there to comment on the odds. The circumstances of even the possibility of a finely tuned universe are amazing, regardless of contrived criticism.

Another related criticism is that there could be millions and millions of different universes, each created with different settings of the fundamental laws and constants, so many in fact that the right set was bound to turn up by sheer chance. We just happened to be the lucky universe. Again, there is zero evidence that a single parallel universe exists. The very fact that critics have to use such an outlandish and unsupported fiction is because the fine-tuning of the universe is such a powerful piece of evidence that points to an intelligent designer—God. Further, our universe's fine-tuning is what allows it to exist. If these constants were off by the slightest of margins, our universe would not exist. **How could these other "millions and millions" of universes exist, if they were tuned in a way that they are incapable of existing?**

In 1989, John Gribbin and Martin Rees wrote an exhaustive treatise on the fine-tuning argument in their book, *Cosmic Coincidences*. According to Gribbin and Rees, carbon-based life did not develop haphazardly but deliberately in a manner "tailor-made for man." Similarly, in 1998, Hugh Ross published *Big Bang Refined by Fire*, in which he shared a partial list of the fine-tuning parameters and constants that the universe reveals.

Below is a partial list of 22 parameters that point to an intelligent designer. Each of these parameters must be in place for life, even the universe, to exist. The consequences of a lack of fine tuning are highlighted by (+) and (-).

1. "Strong Nuclear Force Constant" in particle physics

(+): No hydrogen would form and atomic nuclei for most life-essential elements would be unstable; therefore, there would be no life chemistry.

(-): No elements heavier than hydrogen would form; therefore, there would be no life chemistry.

2. "Weak Nuclear Force Constant" in particle physics

(+): Stars would convert too much matter into heavy elements; therefore, there would be no livable environments.

(-): Stars would convert too little matter into heavy elements; therefore, there would be no livable environments.

3. "Gravitational Force Constant" throughout the universe

(+): Stars would be too hot and would burn too rapidly and too unevenly for life-sustaining conditions.

(-): Stars would be too cool to ignite nuclear fusion; many of the elements needed for life would never form.

4. "Electromagnetic Force Constant" between particles

(+): Chemical bonding would be disrupted; elements more massive than boron would be unstable in reaction to fission.

(-): Chemical bonding would be insufficient for life chemistry.

5. Ratio of Electromagnetic Force Constant to Gravitational Force Constant

(+): Stars would be at least 40% more massive than the sun; stellar burning would be too brief and too uneven for life support.

(-): Stars would be at least 20% less massive than the sun; therefore, they would be incapable of producing sufficient heavy elements.

6. Ratio of electron to proton mass inside the atom

(+)/(-): Chemical bonding would be insufficient for life chemistry.

7. Ratio of number of protons to number of electrons inside the atom

(+)/(-): Electromagnetism would dominate gravity, preventing galaxy, star, and planet formation.

8. Expansion rate of the universe

(+): No galaxies would form.

(-): The universe would collapse even before stars could form.

9. Entropy level of the universe

(+): Stars would not form within protogalaxies.

(-): No protogalaxies would form.

10. Mass density of the universe

(+): Stars would burn too rapidly for life.

(-): A deadly shortage of heavy elements would result.

11. Average distance between galaxies

(+): Star formation would be hampered by lack of material.

(-): Intergalaxy gravity would destabilize the sun's orbit.

12. Density of galaxy clusters

(+): Galaxy collisions and mergers would disrupt the sun's orbit.

(-): Star formation would be hampered by lack of material.

13. Average distance between stars

(+): Heavy element density would be too sparse for terrestrial planets to form.

(-): Planetary orbits would be too unstable for life.

14. Decay rate of protons inside the atom

(+): Life would be exterminated by the release of radiation.

(-): The universe would contain insufficient matter for life.

15. ^{12}C to ^{16}O nuclear energy level ratio

(+): The universe would contain insufficient oxygen for life.

(-): The universe would contain insufficient carbon for life.

16. Ground state energy level for ^{4}He

(+)/(-): The universe would contain insufficient carbon and oxygen for life.

17. Decay rate of ^{8}Be

(+): No element heavier than beryllium would form; therefore, there would be no life chemistry.

(-): Heavy element fusion would generate catastrophic explosions in stars.

18. Ratio of neutron mass to proton mass inside the atom

(+): Neutron decay would yield too few neutrons for the formation of many life-essential elements.

(-): Neutron decay would produce so many neutrons as to collapse stars.

19. Polarity of the water molecule

(+): Heat of fusion and vaporization would be too high for life.

(-): Heat of fusion and vaporization would be too low for life; liquid water would not work as a solvent for life chemistry.

20. Number of effective dimensions in the universe

(+)/(-): Quantum mechanics, gravity, and relativity could not coexist; therefore, life would be impossible.

21. Mass of the neutrino

(+): Galaxy clusters and galaxies would be too dense.

(-): Galaxy clusters, galaxies, and stars would not form.

22. Size of the relativistic dilation factor

(+)/(-): Certain life-essential chemical reactions would not function properly.

And those are just 22 constants from a much longer list. There is extraordinary beauty, elegance, harmony, and ingenuity in the laws of nature that only God could have designed. The fine-tuning argument is not conclusive in the same sense that mathematics tells us that two plus two equals four. Rather, it is a cumulative argument. The extraordinary fine-tuning of the laws and constants of nature—their beauty, their discoverability, their intelligibility—all combine to make God the most reasonable suggestion for a cause of the universe.

If you see this evidence and refuse to even consider the possibility that God exists, then you have been blinded by your bias. Bias against "fine-tuning" is not only self-refuting, it is not even permitted by the scientific method. That said, all opposing arguments for the origins of the universe are suggested by humanity, not the evidence. Arguments that exclude God, biased or not, still fall far short of Him.

Chapter 54

What Is the God Particle?

From mid-2012 through early 2013, scientists at the Geneva-based European Organization for Nuclear Research (CERN) have been making a series of announcements about the possible finding of a theoretical subatomic particle commonly referred to as the "God particle." This potential discovery supposedly has advanced our knowledge toward explaining the origins of the universe and is the result of work conducted by thousands of scientists over several decades. Key to this discovery was the use of the $10-billion Large Hadron Collider (a 17-mile structure used for colliding subatomic particles and analyzing the results). These announcements and the name "God particle" can invoke a very interesting discussion with regards to whether there is a God, whether there is a God particle, or whether both exist.

The nickname, the "God particle," was coined by the physicist Leon Lederman, a Nobel Prize winner, and Dick Teresi in their 1993 book, *The God Particle: If the Universe Is the Answer, What Is the Question?* The actual name of this particle is the "Higgs boson." The Higgs boson is believed to give mass to particles, which allows them to bind together to form objects like stars and planets. Due to our limited understanding, without this theoretical particle, physicists have little clue about how most particles could have naturally obtained mass.

The related Higgs field is an invisible energy field that theoretically permeates the entire universe. This invisible field is likened to a cosmic broth believed to be composed entirely of Higgs boson particles. As other particles theoretically move through it, they slow down and increase in mass at varying rates as they interact with Higgs boson particles. Without the Higgs boson and the Higgs field, physicists popularly believe that particles would probably have no mass at all. However, the discovery of the Higgs boson or the Higgs field has not yet been confirmed. Therefore, these ideas have not been proven to be true. Lawrence Krauss, author and physicist, said, "Introducing an invisible field to explain stuff is more like religion than science." His point is that until we have scientific data, these announcements look more like declarations of faith or religion.

Speaking of religion, Peter Higgs, the Higgs boson's namesake, is a British theoretical physicist and emeritus professor at the University of Edinburgh. He is best known for predicting these Higgs-named hypotheses. While Higgs does not openly claim a religious faith, he has reasonably argued that faith and science can coexist. He has even accused outspoken atheist, Richard Dawkins, of adopting a "fundamentalist" approach when interacting with people of faith. In fact, Higgs was displeased that the Higgs boson was nicknamed the "God particle" because he believes that the name is unnecessarily offensive to people of faith. I would add that it is foolish as well.

What I described earlier regarding the Higgs boson and the Higgs field are accurate summations of what they are believed to be. These concepts, however, are being distorted into much more grandiose beliefs than the evidence might eventually warrant. For example, many scientists claim that the Higgs boson is "the origin of all things," which is why they favor such an offensive nickname. Not only do the Higgs theories not support such a position, the position itself is illogical. Even if the results of scientific experiments could suggest that the Higgs boson is "the origin of all things" (although they could not), such a result would not explain the origin of the Higgs boson itself. Keep in mind that the Higgs boson is a thing that would be included in "all things." With this reasoning, these scientists have committed the reductive logical fallacy. They are also guilty of circular reasoning. **Did the Higgs boson cause itself to exist? Something had to cause the other subatomic particles to exist before they could interact with the Higgs boson; what caused them?**

These fallacies illustrate the truth that obtaining mass does not define existence. There are many things that exist with no mass at all. Light, for example, has no mass, but light exists. **Who created light? For that matter, who created subatomic particles? Is an almighty, eternal, and supernatural God not capable of creating things with mass with or without the Higgs boson?** Not only is naming Higgs boson the God particle a fanciful stretch, it is being used by prominent scientists as a direct and undisciplined assault on religious faith while they hypocritically display a different kind of faith with their conclusions and pronouncements. Using "God" even in a nickname is a step towards idolatry, the pursuit of a mindless theoretical particle rather than the creator of such a particle.

If the discovery of the Higgs boson is confirmed, the truth is that it would represent yet another amazing layer of complexity to the universe that has escaped the human eye for millennia. That alone is more proof of the amazing subatomic design of the universe and its supernatural Designer. It will have taken millennia of human intellectual advancement, thousands of scientists, a $10-billion atomic collider, and possibly millions of experiments to discover one Higgs boson, if it actually exists. **How can anyone reasonably claim such a thing was caused by chance?**

In conclusion, here is my final question to submit to this discussion: **"If the Higgs boson does exist, then who created it?"** The answer is God!

Chapter 55

More Evolution "Myths" Busted

I n the front of the textbook *Biology* by Peter Raven and George Johnson, the question is asked, "How do scientists establish which general principles are true from among the many that might be true?" According to the textbook, here is the answer: "They do this by systematically testing alternative proposals. If these proposals prove inconsistent with experimental observations, they are rejected as untrue. After making careful observations . . . scientists construct a hypothesis . . . A hypothesis is a proposition that might be true. Those hypotheses that have not yet been disproved are retained . . . but they are always subject to future rejection if, in the light of new information, they are found to be incorrect."

In light of this declaration, I must ask the question: **Is evolution truly "always 'subject to future rejection'"?**

That textbook declaration *sounds* well meaning, but it is far from being intellectually honest. **Have you ever seen an instance where the scientific community at large has either challenged or presented new evidence opposing evolution? Should we really believe that none exists? Or is it truer that bias rampantly exists?** This same community is very quick to aggressively attack any observations and evidence that supports creationism or intelligent design, so they have shown that they are capable of the task.

In this chapter, I have included a few "myths" of evolution that have been challenged with actual facts and observations, and thereby "busted." I use the word "myth" because generally a myth is a story without a determinable basis in fact. Therefore, we will "bust" these "myths" with facts. Each of these myths is typically used to bolster the "old universe" reasoning. In each case, we will discuss observable facts that disprove them. But you won't find these opposing facts in biology textbooks:

Fish fossils with extra fins. Remember the Coelecanth fish that we discussed in Chapter 31 regarding the world flood? Evolutionistic interpretations of fossil remains date the Coelecanth at almost 400 million years and claim it became extinct 65 million years ago. Then in 1938, a living Coelecanth was caught off the coast of South Africa, and it was found that the fish had not evolved in the slightest in almost 400 million years. What is more interesting about this fish is that, in spite of the realization that it was a modern fish that is not a mutant, it is *still* heralded as a potential transitional species in biology textbooks since it has extra fins that were once believed to be the precursors to feet. However, we now know from observation that the Coelecanth is a deep-sea fish found nowhere near land and never approaches land. In addition, scientists have observed the Coelecanth in its natural habitat to find that it uses its extra fins for swimming and not as precursors to feet.

Erosion. Emphasizing selective facts about erosion is a favorite tool of evolutionists when claiming that evolutionary time spans exceed "billions of years." Examples that oppose evolutionist interpretations are never used. For example, the Niagara River causes the cliffs of the Niagara Falls to erode at a historically average rate of approximately three feet per year. The gorge is seven miles (or 36,000 feet) across, meaning the equivalent of 12,000 years of erosion when using the average rate. Even if the erosion rate was different from the average, no method will support evolutionary time spans.

In another example, we know that the world's rivers erode and carry a global total of 28 billion tons of dirt and sediment into the oceans every year. Keep in mind that the combined volume of the oceans far exceeds the combined volume of all of the land above sea level. That means that all exposed continents and mountains can fit underwater leaving no exposed land. If you assume the erosion rate is constant and extrapolate it backwards (coupled with erosion from wind, waves, etc.) over the "billions of years" as evolutionists claim, we probably would not have the landmasses (continents) as we observe them today.

The Grand Canyon is another oft cited example used to support evolutionary ages. The prevailing theory is that the Colorado River cut through the sediments in Arizona to create the Grand Canyon over 17 million years ago (some estimates are as high as two billion years ago). Since this is one of the largest and most unique canyons in the world, the Colorado River should be one of the most powerful rivers in the world if it is the cause of the impressive Grand Canyon. The Colorado River, however is not even close to being one of the largest and most powerful rivers in North America, much less the world. When you rank the top 60 rivers in the world by average discharge or water flow, the Colorado River does not make the list. These larger and more powerful rivers are causing no such canyons. **Could there be another explanation for the erosion that created the Grand Canyon?** When Mount St. Helens erupted in 1980, it created a canyon similar to the Grand Canyon with multiple layers of exposed sediments and a small river running through its basin. This canyon, however, was created in a matter of several days.

Stalactites and stalagmites. A stalactite is a type of dripstone that hangs typically from the ceiling of limestone caves. The corresponding formation on the floor of the cave is known as a stalagmite. The longest stalactite in the world is located in the White Chamber in the Jeita Grotto's upper cavern in Lebanon and is 27 feet long. Evolutionists claim that this sta-lactite took millions of years to form by using current drip and deposit rates. This conclusion, however, ignores the possibility that drip and deposit rates might vary over different times and locations. In 1922, for example, the Lincoln Memorial was con-structed in such a way that a new cavern was formed beneath its foundation. Fifty years later, in that same cavern, stalactites formed and grew over 5 feet tall (or 1 foot every 10 years).

The emergence of modern humans. Evolution holds that modern humans emerged approximately 200,000 years ago. The written history of modern humans, however, began only several thousand years ago. Such written history starts abruptly and broadly. This observed evidence suggests a much younger emergence for modern humans.

Ancient rocks and isotopes. Radioactive isotopes are a favorite of evolutionary aging methods that we exposed in Chapter 46. These methods are unreliable as evidenced by the fact that they cut both ways.

Uranium 236 on the Moon. For example, we know that Uranium 236 has an estimated half-life of 23.9 million years and Thorium 230 has a half-life of 80,000 years. Both of these elements have been observed in abundance on the moon. However, lunar volcanic activity would be the only source of such isotopes. Evolutionists claim that the moon is approxi-mately 4.5 billion years old and that the youngest volcanic activity occurred on the moon over 1.2 billion years ago. Today we know that the moon has no mountains (evidence of volca-nic activity) and lacks any evidence of other similar tectonic events. Therefore, according to evolutionists, there has been no ongoing production of Uranium 236 or Thorium 230 on the moon for the past 1.2 billion years. With the half-lives (23.9 million years and 80,000 years) dramatically shorter than the last age of volcanic activity, we would see very little of these elements on the moon if the evolutionist reasoning was correct. Scientists, however, have instead observed an abundance of those elements—evidence that opposes the evolutionary conclusions about the date and origin of the moon.

Polonium in granite. When compromised, polonium forms "halos," but only for a fraction of a second. These halos have been observed in granite, which according to evolutionary models, is believed to have taken a long period of time to cool and form. Therefore, polonium halos should not exist in granite unless such granite was formed more instantaneously as a creation model suggests.

Helium in the atmosphere. Another example involves helium. The quantity of helium in our atmosphere grows at a net rate that, if constant, suggests the atmosphere is 11,600 years old. If the earth was billions of years old, we should expect approximately 400,000 times more helium than what is present now in the earth's atmosphere.

Meteor crater dating: While we find meteor craters on the surface of the earth and the moon, we do not find any such craters in the geologic column under the earth's surface strata. This lack of craters would suggest that either we had no such meteors on our planet during the "billions of years" that the earth was aging or that the earth is much younger than evolutionists claim.

In fact, by making assumptions about numerous craters over evolutionary time spans, NASA even miscalculated the structure of the lunar landing module. In the first moon landing, NASA expected to find a couple feet of meteor dust on the moon based upon extrapolations from their evolutionary dating models. As a result, they shortened the ladder off the module by 18 inches to compensate for this expectation. When they landed, they found only one-eighth of an inch of dust.

Life on other planets: Evolutionary fiction about abiogenesis and the assumed age of the universe has directly led to presumptions about life existing on other planets. The

SETI (Search for Extra-Terrestrial Intelligence) Project has produced zero evidence of life on any other of the countless planets in the universe. Their efforts have included satellite receivers on Earth, receivers orbiting Earth, receivers on the moon, and even some around Mars. These receivers are constantly searching unsuccessfully for just one intelligent signal from outer space. By using evolutionary models coupled with statistical principles, it is further presumed that other alien civilizations probably formed billions of years before us. Given the speed of light and the abundance of planets within the distance of light travel over that period, receiving zero signals suggests that their evolutionary assumptions are flawed.

These are just a few of the many observations that continually "bust" evolution's myths. **What does it suggest when scientists refuse to acknowledge evidence against their theories, while constantly attacking opposing theories?** It suggests that they have violated their own assertions in their own textbooks—not to mention violating the scientific method itself. This is how politicians behave, not people devoted to the unbiased and constant challenge of hypotheses.

Section 9

Responding to Other Attacks on the Gospel

W hen I used to teach this material in a classroom setting, I spent several weeks examining other religions and exposing their fallacies. While exposing fallacies in
other religions has its place inside a family discussion either at
home or with a spiritual mentor, this book is not that place. As
Christians, we are never called to attack others or attack what
they believe. Rather, we are called to love others and proclaim
the gospel of Jesus Christ as the only means by which we can
be saved.

To the extent that certain religions openly attack the gospel
of Jesus Christ, however, the Christian needs to be prepared to
respond in a manner consistent with Jesus Himself. Therefore,
this section is dedicated to just a few of those religions who
attempt to gut the gospel. There are other lesser religions that
openly do the same, but we will restrict our discussion to
atheism, Satanism, and universalism.

Chapter 56

Atheism Is a Religion

In 2008, atheist and comedian Bill Maher starred in a semi-comedic documentary titled "Religulous." The title says it all, as isn't it a combination of the words "religion" and "ridiculous." Anyone who follows Maher can easily predict the offensive style in which he narrated the movie. In a nutshell, this was an attempt to mock the notion of religion by primarily focusing on bizarre extremists within each religion. There was one major religion that the movie did not mock—atheism. Is atheism a religion? What do you think?

To answer this question, we should start with the definition of "religion." Below are a few definitions from different dictionaries:

"a set of beliefs concerning the cause, nature, and purpose of the universe"

"a specific fundamental set of beliefs and practices generally agreed upon by a number of persons"

"persons adhering to a particular set of beliefs"

In summary, a religion is a system of beliefs (faith) that people follow. **Based upon these definitions of "religion," it is obvious that atheism qualifies as a religion?** Regarding faith, the Bible has a definition of its own recorded in Hebrews 11:1.

"Now faith is the assurance of things hoped for, the conviction of things not seen." Atheism expresses profound faith in things not seen. Many even argue that atheism requires more faith than theism (the belief that there is a God).

A great book on this subject is *I Don't Have Enough Faith to Be an Atheist* by Norman Geisler and Frank Turek. Theism requires and openly admits faith, but atheism requires faith while deceptively refusing to admit it. For example, atheists believe that God does not exists in spite of their inability to prove their conclusion. Regarding believing in "things not seen," atheists believe, without proof that everything ultimately was caused by nothing. I must confess that my personal faith is pretty small compared to that.

Consider too that atheism is defined as "the doctrine of belief that there is no God" and the "disbelief in the existence of a supreme being or beings." By this definition, atheists cannot even escape the words "doctrine" and "belief." Belief always implies that knowledge is lacking. In other words, atheism also is a religion that is, to a large extent, based upon faith.

Earlier this year, at the Cambridge Union Debating Society, a much publicized debate was held between the famous and outspoken atheist, Richard Dawkins, and the former Anglican Archbishop, Rowan Williams. The exact subject of the debate was whether "religion" has a role in the 21st century. Dawkins argued that it did not. Williams responded by proving that atheism was, in fact, also a religion. He argued that even Dawkins believes in something that he does not fully know and/or understand. He further argued that almost everyone is religious to some extent. In the end, the audience awarded Williams a decided victory with two-thirds of the vote.

What was clear to the debate audience was that atheism actually has a functioning "god" that atheists follow (self, science, rationality, etc.). Contrary to the aforementioned second definition above, atheists do share a belief in a supreme being—themselves. This belief influences the way atheists live and interpret life. It also influences their biases, values, morality, and ethics. Their beliefs are used to fill in the gaps of what they do not know or understand. Lastly, atheism also influences its followers' preaching. Just like many Christians, atheists also proclaim a message about life. In fact, I think there is not one religion that invokes the name of God in the public square more often than atheists.

This public, negative fixation is ironic and causes one to question, **"If you truly do not believe in something, wouldn't the logical approach be to not speak of it at all?"** Like Dawkins, however, many atheists seem to preach incessantly that theists cannot prove God exists while failing to confess themselves that they likewise cannot prove that He does not.

It is the saddest of characterizations when a "religion" generally limits its outreach to a constant expression of what it stands against rather than what it stands for. This is why atheism rarely (if ever) invokes a positive image—it instead retains a negative one that is reduced simply to attacking theism and theists alike. In the profound words of atheist-turned-Christian C. S. Lewis, "Atheism turns out to be too simple." For example, like Dawkins and Maher, many seem to spend an unhealthy portion of their efforts narrowly focused on accusing theists of being simple. When atheists employ such a shallow and unnecessary personal attacks, while ignoring their own leaps of faith, they are actually guilty of the same shortcomings of which they claim theists are guilty. They ultimately mock themselves because they, too, have faith in unprovable propositions.

The truth is that everyone needs and has a "god." We are all profoundly religious. It is just a matter of which religion you choose. The Christian God offers His love freely, even to those that do not believe in Him. In fact, He offers His love to unbelievers just as much as He offers it to believers. **When comparing Christianity's Supreme Being with the notion of man as the supreme being (atheism), which notion seems more "ridiculous"?**

Chapter 57

God Loves Satanists Too

M any people when they hear the word "Satan" picture an ugly and monstrous demon with a long tail and a pitchfork. They also think of his followers as hell-bent people seeking to kill whomever they can. **But are these caricatures real? If you were Lucifer and opposed an all-powerful, all-loving God, how would you seek to draw people away from Him? Would you approach people with clear intentions to kill or would you be more subtle in your efforts? Would you confirm God's warnings, or would you distort God's motives? Wouldn't you portray yourself deceptively as a counterfeit substitute for God as subtly as possible?** You certainly would not approach people with blood dripping from your mouth, screaming, "Worship me!"

The late Anton LaVey is largely credited as the founder of the modern Church of Satan. He also authored *The Satanic Bible*, which promotes his synthesized views of human nature and insights of philosophers who advocated teachings on individualism, self-indulgence, and "eye for an eye" morality. If you read his bible, you would be surprised to find subtle yet broadly appealing statements promoting "indulgence instead of abstinence," "vital existence instead of spiritual pipe dreams," "wisdom instead of hypocritical self-deceit," and "kindness to those who deserve it"—not the kind of words you would expect to hear from a blood-spewing demoniac.

There are generally two types of practicing Satanists: atheists and theists. Atheistic Satanism is largely led by LaVey's Church of Satan, and it is the fastest growing sect of Satanism in contemporary society. Atheistic Satanists generally dislike theistic Satanists, referring to them as "Devil-worshippers" (atheists don't believe in a literal "Devil"). These atheists recognize Lucifer as a fictional hero for his rebellious efforts to reveal the knowledge of good and evil to mankind. They also view God as the fictional figure who suppresses knowledge from man, believing further that Lucifer allowed man to be "free" to know all that man could know. In this respect, Satanism views the church as a co-suppressor of knowledge.

These Satanists also credit the church with inflicting much harm and death upon innocent humans in the name of religion. As a result, they believe the church must be opposed. It is this rebellious freedom from the church and the religion it represents that fuels their countercultural behaviors. Since to them there is no God and man is the Supreme Being, they adopted the motto, "Do as thou wilt," but only as long as it does not hurt others. Accordingly, true members of the Church of Satan are actually quite benevolent and giving, abiding generally by a "live and let live" mentality.

In contrast, theistic Satanists believe in a literal "Devil." The main reason atheists oppose theists is because theism is an admission that there is a God. This sect of Satanism, because they are theists, focuses on the supernatural. They believe that demons are beings that humans can manipulate for power and service. While atheistic Satanists practice sexual rituals primarily for self-gratification, theistic Satanists practice them to obtain supernatural power. This group and their practices are the ones who largely intersect with other forms of the occult.

One group that is commonly misunderstood in this regard is the Wiccan religion. The practice of Wicca (or witchcraft) is alive and well today, but its members do not claim to be Satanists. Rather, they claim a theistic belief in other gods who give them supernatural power. For these reasons, it is not effective to approach them with the word "Satan" in your vocabulary. Wiccans are also largely benevolent. For example, consider the Wicca's "Rule of 3's." Wiccans believe that everything you do to others will be visited back to you threefold. Therefore, the vast majority of Wiccans practice blessing others instead of cursing others. This is similar in some respects to biblical teachings of "reaping what you sow" except for its motives. The Wiccans' motive for this form of blessing is largely self-centered.

All Satanists value the pursuit of knowledge and admire Lucifer's heroic efforts to make knowledge "free." It is in this vein that Gnosticism and the counterfeit gnostic gospels find their root (non-contemporaneous books written by gnostic leaders that have been widely discredited as lacking authenticity and factual basis and were rejected from inclusion in the Bible).

Gnosis is the conviction that true freedom comes through knowledge. Satanism holds that the Bible is just religious propaganda that suppresses knowledge. Interestingly, the "goat" they place in the center of the pentagram symbol of the Church of Satan bears the name, Baphomet. This name is an Atbash cipher that in Hebrew spelling is "Sophia," which means wisdom or knowledge.

Since man's identity is spirit housed in flesh, mankind is understandably in pursuit of that which transcends our limited flesh, namely the spiritual. Immortality is the most common spiritual pursuit. Since our current flesh is not immortal and our spirit is, it is in the spirit where we obtain true freedom from mortality. Therefore, Christianity seeks gratification of the eternal and immortal spirit over temporal flesh (Romans 8:5-8). The deception of Satanism is to seek to gratify the flesh over the spirit, which is a mortal dead end. For theistic

Satanists, this deception results in a grave irony as they seek to use the spirits to gratify the flesh. In fact, all forms of selfish and fleshly motives are truly satanic distortions whether carried out by a Satanist or even a Christian.

In response to Satanists' claims against Jesus, there is a clear difference between the teachings and actions of Jesus Christ and the heinous acts performed by the "Christian church" in the name of "religion." Satanists, however, are blinded from seeing that separation. In fact, their spiritual blindness is a large reason why they oppose Jesus and Christianity so harshly. Acts of hatred are impossible to perform in the true name of Jesus. Many fringe zealots use the name of Jesus, but do not actually represent him. In spite of this reality, Satanists still see Jesus as one who places limits on freedom and knowledge.

The truth is that Jesus represents true freedom and love, not suffocating restrictions and hatred. Jesus frees us from the constricting flesh into an eternally free spirit, His own Spirit. For those seeking true rebellion from limitations, dying flesh is a trap and the last place to turn. Alice Cooper, famous rock star and Christian, once said, "Drinking beer is easy. Trashing your hotel room is easy. But being a Christian, that's a tough call. That's rebellion."

Approaching Satanists to reason with them can only be effective through a genuine, sacrificial display of unconditional love. Remember that God died for Satanists because He loves them too. I recently watched a great example of this kind of love in a YouTube video featuring Todd White, a modern-day street evangelist. In the video, he told of his encounters of reaching out in love to Wiccans (witches) and Satanists that he met while shopping with his daughter (www.youtube.com/watch?v=0Jne5iIjRFo). The first words out of his mouth included, "Can I hug you? . . . I just want to tell you I love you and I'm really sorry for what the church has done to you guys." His agenda was not that he was there to convert them first, but to love and bless them first. It is only through such a genuine display of God's love that we can reach those who view the church in such a negative light. Todd White did not express any fear of them, and neither should we.

Ephesians 6:12 says, "For we do not wrestle against flesh and blood, but against the rulers, against the authorities, against the cosmic powers over this present darkness, against the spiritual forces of evil in the heavenly places." We should have no fear because "spiritual forces of evil" have to flee when God's love shows up. Even if Satanists wanted to curse God's children, I believe it is impossible to curse something that God has blessed. In fact, 1 John 4:4 says, "Little children, you are from God and have overcome them, for He who is in you is greater than he who is in the world." No matter how monstrous and evil Lucifer may be, one person in Christ is a powerful majority. And, when Christ was here, He approached those influenced by Satan and prayed for them. Following our leader, so should we.

While apologetics is our *defense*, the gospel of Jesus Christ is our *offense*. And that gospel is the testimony of God's radically freeing love for all. Therefore, God's love is our offense. I'm reminded of the story when Peter declared to Jesus his confession that Jesus is the Christ and Son of the living God. Jesus responded in Matthew 16:18 with these words: "On this rock I will build my church, and the gates of hell shall not prevail against it." When I was young, I misunderstood this verse to be referring to hell attacking Christians. But "gates" are for defense, not offense. Our offense includes literally reaching into hell with God's love and pulling out as many as we can. The gates of hell are no match for God's love.

Chapter 58

Do All Religions Lead to God?

I was on a flight to Belize, leading a high school mission team, when a stranger and his son engaged me in a conversation about God. Our team was wearing team T-shirts, which helped him determine the nature of our mission. He addressed me as one of the leaders in order to share his faith, and he proceeded to tell me that he believed in Jesus like I did—with one exception. He believed that all religions, including faith in Jesus, lead to the same god. He described it to me with the analogy of a wheel. He said that Jesus is a "spoke" in the wheel, like Allah and Buddha, and that all religions share the same hub or god. **Is Jesus a spoke, a hub, or like something other than a wheel?**

I gently responded to the father with a few questions: **"If Jesus (God) knew there were other ways to God when He spoke, why did He say that He is the only way?"** Why does every major religion (their gods, prophets, and "holy" books) openly reject all other religions as false?"** He then changed the subject.

The "faith" that this father was professing is best referred to as universalism. Universalism is the faith that claims the universal fatherhood of god and the ultimate salvation of every soul. In other words, everyone is going to "heaven" (or its equivalent) because all religions share the same god only by different names. **But do the gods of all of these mutually exclusive religions leave that option available (including atheism)?** The answer, without exception, is "no." Every major religion rejects the central beliefs, authority, and conduct of all other religions. **Does anyone who has actually read both the Bible and the Qur'an truly believe that "Jehovah" is the same as "Allah"?** They are dramatically different, and both claim the other to be blasphemy.

All religions cannot be true. Not only do all religions teach this to be the case, but the Three Laws of Logic demonstrate universalism is false as well. It is not logical that separate religions that clearly deny each other are all true. It *is* logical that one of them is true or that none of them are true. But they cannot *all* be true.

For example, John 14:6 records the words of Jesus on the matter, "I am the way, and the truth, and the life. No one comes to the Father except through me." He made this same claim a number of other times in multiple ways and with multiple analogies to varied ethnic and religious groups. If it was possible that other religions could lead to God without Jesus, then Jesus was a liar or deceiver, and by definition, not God, but a divisive cult leader. Jesus proved Himself to be God through His resurrection. Therefore, when He spoke, "I am the way," He clearly meant it. And until another "god" proves Him wrong, Jesus stands uncorrected, unedited, and Lord of all (see also Acts 4:10-12).

That said, outside of the confines of our minds, God did not call for us to attack other religions. We will not find a verse where Jesus commands us to openly prove people wrong or to be fishers of winning arguments. We were never called by God to bash or judge others, including what they believe (James 4:12). I have resolute faith that Jesus is the only way. I am willing to die for this truth. All other religions and cults are false to me. But I am not personally offended when someone claims faith in a different god than mine. I also will not achieve God's goals by attacking others. Verbal (flesh-centered) aggression can never display God's love (spirit-centered). We were never called to argue with others, but we were called to defend the gospel by presenting the love of Jesus in a manner that displays the love of Jesus.

Since universalism attempts to diminish the gospel of Jesus Christ, at least in our minds, we must examine it deeply and expose it. Universalism holds that everyone will be redeemed and saved from eternal judgment. This thinking is the result of choosing human conclusions about the future of humanity rather than God's own revelation of Himself and the way of salvation.

For some, it is more comfortable to believe that "God is love" and nothing else. The fatal flaw with such reasoning is that it is human. It is another example of trying to make God fit into the human brain, but an all-powerful and infinitely eternal God will never fit there. If God is love and nothing else, then His love is weak because it lacks justice and righteousness. **How strong can His love be if it does not save us from something, such as justice?**

To illustrate this problem, universalism would have us believe that—with everything we know today—Judas and Hitler will definitely be in heaven. **Does anyone reasonably believe that Judas and Hitler will be in heaven? What would it say of God if, absent of unknown, near death conversion and repentance, Hitler was in Heaven at this very moment?** Regarding Judas, even Jesus said in Matthew 26:24b, "But woe to that man by whom the Son of Man is betrayed! It would have been better for that man if he had not been born." If Judas is ultimately redeemed to enjoy forgiveness and grace in heaven eternally, Jesus would be flawed to speak what He spoke. But Jesus, being eternal God, spoke prophetically of Judas' destiny.

I am sure that Judas, who now realizes his own destiny, agrees with what Jesus said. I am not able to judge Judas. However, Jesus is able, and He gave us a pretty strong hint.

Universalists are guilty of more than just choosing to elevate human reasoning above God's revelation. They also deny our objective authority, but lack their own. In fact, there is no foundation at all. There is no Bible or other objective book of revelation Universalists can point to for understanding, no source of ultimate authority. Universalism exists only in the finite minds of fallen men. Even worse, there are as many brands of universalism as there are believers in universalism. Since there is no objective source of authority, every Universalist has his or her own unique belief that is different from many other Universalists. Without an objective authority, everyone is right and no one is wrong. **If everyone ultimately is right, what about a religion where followers appease their god through killing other human beings? Will they also be going to heaven?** What exposes universalism as false more than all other faiths is that it lacks logical consistency, evidence, and an objective moral authority. Regarding Christianity, universalism attempts to remove all power and glory from the amazing gospel of Jesus Christ.

Finally, many Universalists also promote the idea that all religions should ignore their doctrinal differences in order to fight today's culture war (the war between competing moral norms) with a united front. I see some virtue in fighting a culture war, but denying Jesus and His gospel in the process is not an option. I would rather be dead before denying anything about Jesus and His gospel. Jesus is not only my God, precious Savior, and the only Way to the Father, He is also my General.

The culture war is a fleshly distraction from the real and spiritual war raging between Jesus and His enemies over the souls of men. The culture war is secondary to the spiritual war of the Great Commission in every respect. I certainly have no desire to fight any war except that which my General has commanded me to fight. He has never commanded me nor any of His children to fight a culture war. Rather, He has commanded us to love God with all our hearts, souls, minds, and strength. He has commanded us to love one another as He loves us. He has commanded us to advance His kingdom on earth by reconciling others to God through the gospel. Those commands should reign supreme in our lives. Until He returns, no other war should distract us from passionate obedience to the King of kings.

David Platt is a pastor and author of the best-selling book *Radical: Taking Back Your Faith from the American Dream*. Take a few minutes to watch this YouTube video of David Platt responding to universalism (www.youtube.com/watch?v=e8vAAcesta4). In this video, Platt shared a summary of the gospel and closed with this beautiful challenge: "The just and gracious Creator of the universe has looked upon hopelessly sinful men and women in their rebellion. And He has sent His Son, God in the flesh, to bear His wrath against sin on the cross, and to show His power over sin in the resurrection, so that everyone who believes in Him, and turns from themselves and trusts in Christ will be reconciled to God forever. Likewise, the converse is true. Everyone who trusts in themselves and turns from God will be condemned by God forever . . . but . . . do we really believe what we're saying? . . . Intellectual universalism is dangerous; thinking that in the end everyone is going to be okay. But 'functional' universalism is worse; *living* like in the end everyone is going to be okay. So, let's fight them both . . . Let's hold fast to the truth of this gospel. And in our lives let's sacrifice everything we have . . . to make this gospel known among all peoples.

Amen!

Made in the USA
Columbia, SC
19 August 2019